Learning Highcharts

Create rich, intuitive, and interactive JavaScript data
visualization for your web and enterprise development
needs using this powerful charting library — Highcharts

Joe Kuan

 open source*
community experience distilled

[PACKT]
PUBLISHING

BIRMINGHAM - MUMBAI

Learning Highcharts

First published: December 2012

Production Reference: 1131212

Published by Packt Publishing Ltd.
Livery Place
35 Livery Street
Birmingham B3 2PB, UK.

ISBN 978-1-84951-908-3

www.packtpub.com

Cover Image by Asher Wishkerman (wishkerman@hotmail.com)

Credits

Author
Joe Kuan

Reviewers
Torstein Hønsi

Tomasz Nurkiewicz

Gert Vaartjes

Acquisition Editor
Kartikey Pandey

Lead Technical Editor
Ankita Shashi

Technical Editors
Devdutt Kulkarni

Ankita Meshram

Pooja Pande

Copy Editors
Aditya Nair

Alfida Paiva

Project Coordinator
Abhishek Kori

Proofreader
Maria Gould

Indexer
Monica Ajmera Mehta

Graphics
Aditi Gajjar

Production Coordinator
Nilesh R. Mohite

Cover Work
Nilesh R. Mohite

Foreword

Back in 2003, when I wanted to implement charts for my home page, Flash-based charting solutions were totally dominating the market. I resented the idea of meeting my nontechnical readers with a prompt to install a browser plugin just to view my content, so I went looking for other solutions. There were server-side libraries that produced a static chart image, but they didn't provide any form of interactivity. So I built a chart based on an image created dynamically on the server, overlaid with tool tips created in JavaScript. This still runs on my website and has survived the coming of the touch age without modification. But I still had an idea of something simpler. By 2006 all major browsers had support for vector graphics through either SVG or VML, so this seemed the way to go. I started working on Highcharts on weekends and vacations, and released it in 2009.

It was an instant success. Today, three years later, it has grown to become the preferred web charting engine by many, perhaps most, developers. Our bootstrapper company has nine persons working full time on developing, marketing, and selling Highcharts, and we have sold more than 22,000 licenses. Our clients include more than half of the 100 greatest companies in the world.

I was thrilled when Packt Publishing contacted me for reviewing this book. I soon realized that the author, Joe Kuan, has a tight grip on Highcharts, jQuery, and general JavaScript. He also does what I love the most to see from Highcharts users—he bends, tweaks, and configures the library, and creates charts that surpass what we even thought possible with our tool. All done step by step in increasingly complex examples.

I can't wait to recommend this book to our users.

Torstein Hønsi

CTO, Founder

Highsoft Solutions

About the Author

Joe Kuan was born in Hong Kong and continued his education in the UK from secondary school to university. He studied Computer Science at University of Southampton for B.Sc. and Ph.D. After his education, he worked with different technologies and industries in the UK for more than a decade. Currently, he is working for iTrinegy – a company specializing in network emulation and performance monitoring. Part of his role is to develop frontend and present complex network data into stylish and interactive charts. He has adopted Highcharts with iTrinegy for nearly three years. Since then, he has been contributing blogs and software on Highcharts and Highstocks.

Apart from his busy family schedule and active outdoor lifestyle, he occasionally writes articles for his own blog site http://joekuan.wordpress.com and puts some demonstrations up at http://joekuan.org. You can contact him at learning.highcharts@gmail.com.

I hope this book has its place in the web publishing market. This book is like all technical books; they are nurtured by two teams of people—technical and personal. For the technical people, I am grateful to Packt Publishing for asking me to write this book—an opportunity that has never come to my mind and a valuable journey I will look back on. To the team of reviewers; Tomasz Nurkiewicz for giving purposeful comments beneficial to the readers, and Torstein Hønsi and Gert Vaartjes for making sure of technical correctness, and Kartikey Pandey and Ankita Shashi for improving the readability. For the people whom I care about the most, I am thankful to my loving parents for showing me the importance of kindness and hard work in life, and my wife, for continual unconditional support and patience in helping me get this book sitting on a shelf. Finally, for my big little boy, Ivan:

"A thousand miles of journey, starts beneath the feet" – Lao Tzu

About the Reviewers

Torstein Hønsi is a programmer and entrepreneur who has a passion for frontend developing and user interface design. He is the creator and lead developer of the Highcharts JavaScript library, and the CTO of Highsoft Solutions, the software company founded to manage Highcharts. Apart from work, he enjoys spending time with his family, preferably in the great outdoors of Norway.

Tomasz Nurkiewicz is a Java developer with six years of experience, typically working on the server side. He is also a Scala enthusiast. Currently, he is developing a track and trace system for Kezzler AS in Oslo, Norway. Tomasz strongly believes in the power of testing and automation. He claims that every functionality not tested automatically is not trustworthy and will eventually break.

Tomasz happily implements monitoring and data visualization solutions, hence his interest in client-side JavaScript charting libraries. He is also a technical blogger and blogs at http://nurkiewicz.blogspot.com.

Gert Vaartjes started as a specialist in geographical information systems. While customizing these programs, he was intrigued by what's actually under the hood. Here started his passion for programming. This programming journey led him through all kinds of programming languages. As a technical consultant, he worked for several governmental and nongovernmental companies. He has been developing software for more than 10 years. Now he's working as a programmer at Highsoft Solutions, focusing on backend integration of the Highcharts product.

When he is not programming, you can find him working on his small-scale farm in Norway, where he grows potatoes, chases sheep, chops wood, and does other basic stuff.

www.PacktPub.com

Support files, eBooks, discount offers and more

You might want to visit www.PacktPub.com for support files and downloads related to your book.

Did you know that Packt offers eBook versions of every book published, with PDF and ePub files available? You can upgrade to the eBook version at www.PacktPub.com and as a print book customer, you are entitled to a discount on the eBook copy. Get in touch with us at service@packtpub.com for more details.

At www.PacktPub.com, you can also read a collection of free technical articles, sign up for a range of free newsletters and receive exclusive discounts and offers on Packt books and eBooks.

http://PacktLib.PacktPub.com

Do you need instant solutions to your IT questions? PacktLib is Packt's online digital book library. Here, you can access, read and search across Packt's entire library of books.

Why Subscribe?

- Fully searchable across every book published by Packt
- Copy and paste, print and bookmark content
- On demand and accessible via web browser

Free Access for Packt account holders

If you have an account with Packt at www.PacktPub.com, you can use this to access PacktLib today and view nine entirely free books. Simply use your login credentials for immediate access.

Table of Contents

Preface

Learning Highcharts aims to be the missing manual for Highcharts from every angle. It is written for web developers who would like to learn about Highcharts using the following features included in the book:

- A step-by-step guide on building presentable charts from basic looking ones
- Plenty of examples with real data covering all the Highcharts series types—line/spline, column, pie, scatter, area range, column range, gauge, and polar
- Subject areas that haven't yet been covered in online reference manuals and demos such as chart layout structure, color shading, series update performance, and so on
- Applications demonstrating how to create dynamic and interactive charts using Highcharts' APIs and events handling
- Applications demonstrating how to integrate Highcharts with a mobile framework such as jQuery Mobile and a Rich Internet Application framework such as Ext JS
- Applications demonstrating how to run Highcharts on the server side for automating charts generation and export their graphical outputs

This book is not a reference manual as the Highcharts team has already done an excellent job in providing a comprehensive online reference, and each configuration is coupled with jsFiddle demos. This book is also not aiming to be a chart design guide or not tutorial for programming design with Highcharts.

In short, this book shows you what you can do with Highcharts.

What this book covers

Chapter 1, Web Charts, describes how web charts have been done since the birth of HTML to the latest HTML 5 standard with SVG and canvas technologies. This chapter also gives a short survey of charting software on the market using the HTML 5 standard and discusses why Highcharts is a better product.

Chapter 2, Highcharts Configurations, covers the common configuration options in chart components with plenty of examples and explains how the chart layout works.

Chapter 3, Line, Area, and Scatter Charts, demonstrates from plotting a simple line, area, and scatter charts to a poster-like chart including all three series types.

Chapter 4, Bar and Column Charts, demonstrates bar and column charts as well as various derived charts such as stacked chart, percentage chart, mirror chart, group chart, overlap chart, mirror stacked chart, and horizontal gauge chart.

Chapter 5, Pie Charts, demonstrates how to build various charts, from a simple pie chart to a multiseries chart, such as multiple pies in a chart and a concentric rings pie chart, that is, a donut chart.

Chapter 6, Gauge, Polar, and Range Charts, gives a step-by-step guide on constructing a twin dial speedometer and demonstrates polar chart characteristics and its similarity to a cartesian chart. It also illustrates the use of range data on area and column range charts.

Chapter 7, Highcharts APIs, explains the usage of Highcharts APIs and illustrates this by using a stock market demo to draw dynamic charts. The chapter discusses the use of different methods to update the series and analyses the performance of each method on various browsers, as well as the scalability of Highcharts.

Chapter 8, Highcharts Events, explains Highcharts events and demonstrates them through various user interactions with the charts from the portfolio application demos.

Chapter 9, Highcharts and jQuery Mobile, gives a short tutorial on the jQuery Mobile framework and demonstrates how to integrate it with Highcharts by creating a mobile web application browsing an Olympic medals table. The chapter also covers the use of touch-based and rotate events with Highcharts.

Chapter 10, Highcharts and Ext JS, gives a short introduction on Sencha's Ext JS and describes the components likely to be used in an application with Highcharts. It also shows how to use a module, Highcharts extension, in order to plot Highcharts graphs within an Ext JS application.

Chapter 11, Running Highcharts on the Server Side, describes different approaches for running Highcharts on the server side for automating chart generation and exporting the charts into SVG or image files.

What you need for this book

Readers are expected to have basic knowledge of web development in the following areas:

- Structure of HTML document and its syntax
- Ajax

As this book is all about Highcharts which is developed in JavaScript, readers should be comfortable with the language at an intermediate level. Highcharts is developed as an adapter plugin to support several popular JavaScript frameworks such as jQuery, Mootools, and Prototype. By default, Highcharts uses jQuery library, which is the most popular amongst them. This book not only follows such choice so that all the examples are implemented in jQuery, but also uses a very moderate way. Hence, a basic knowledge of jQuery should be sufficient and preferably some knowledge of jQuery UI would be an advantage, as it is lightly used in *Chapter 7* and *Chapter 8*.

Who this book is for

This book is written for web developers who:

- Would like to learn how to incorporate graphical charts into their web applications
- Would like to migrate their Adobe Flash charts for an HTML 5 JavaScript solution
- Want to learn more about Highcharts through examples

Conventions

In this book, you will find a number of styles of text that distinguish between different kinds of information. Here are some examples of these styles, and an explanation of their meaning.

Code words in text are shown as follows: "The `renderTo` option instructs Highcharts to display the graph onto the HTML `<div>` element with `'container'` as the ID value, which is defined in the HTML `<body>` section."

A block of code is set as follows:

```
<svg xmlns="http://www.w3.org/2000/svg" version="1.1">
  <path id="curveAB" d="M 100 350 q 150 -300 300 0" stroke="blue"
stroke-width="5" fill="none" />
  <!-- Mark relevant points -->
  <g stroke="black" stroke-width="3" fill="black">
    <circle id="pointA" cx="100" cy="350" r="3" />
    <circle id="pointB" cx="400" cy="350" r="3" />
  </g>
  <!-- Label the points -->
  <g font-size="30" font="sans-serif" fill="black" stroke="none" text-
anchor="middle">
    <text x="100" y="350" dx="-30">A</text>
    <text x="400" y="350" dx="30">B</text>
  </g>
</svg>
```

Any command-line input or output is written as follows:

```
java -jar batik-rasterizer.jar /tmp/chart.svg
```

New terms and **important words** are shown in bold. Words that you see on the screen, in menus or dialog boxes for example, appear in the text like this: "The first four series—**UK**, **Germany**, **S. Korea**, and **Japan** are stacked together as a single column and **US** is displayed as a separate column."

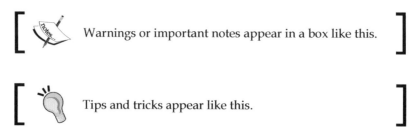

Warnings or important notes appear in a box like this.

Tips and tricks appear like this.

Reader feedback

Feedback from our readers is always welcome. Let us know what you think about this book—what you liked or may have disliked. Reader feedback is important for us to develop titles that you really get the most out of.

To send us general feedback, simply send an e-mail to feedback@packtpub.com, and mention the book title via the subject of your message.

If there is a topic that you have expertise in and you are interested in either writing or contributing to a book, see our author guide on www.packtpub.com/authors.

Customer support

Now that you are the proud owner of a Packt book, we have a number of things to help you to get the most from your purchase.

Downloading the example code

You can download the example code files for all Packt books you have purchased from your account at http://www.PacktPub.com. If you purchased this book elsewhere, you can visit http://www.PacktPub.com/support and register to have the files e-mailed directly to you.

Errata

Although we have taken every care to ensure the accuracy of our content, mistakes do happen. If you find a mistake in one of our books—maybe a mistake in the text or the code—we would be grateful if you would report this to us. By doing so, you can save other readers from frustration and help us improve subsequent versions of this book. If you find any errata, please report them by visiting http://www.packtpub.com/support, selecting your book, clicking on the **errata submission form** link, and entering the details of your errata. Once your errata are verified, your submission will be accepted and the errata will be uploaded on our website, or added to any list of existing errata, under the Errata section of that title. Any existing errata can be viewed by selecting your title from http://www.packtpub.com/support.

Piracy

Piracy of copyright material on the Internet is an ongoing problem across all media. At Packt, we take the protection of our copyright and licenses very seriously. If you come across any illegal copies of our works, in any form, on the Internet, please provide us with the location address or website name immediately so that we can pursue a remedy.

Please contact us at `copyright@packtpub.com` with a link to the suspected pirated material.

We appreciate your help in protecting our authors, and our ability to bring you valuable content.

Questions

You can contact us at `questions@packtpub.com` if you are having a problem with any aspect of the book, and we will do our best to address it.

1
Web Charts

In this chapter you will learn the general background of web charts. This includes a short history of how web charts used to be made before Ajax and HTML5 became the new standard. The recent advancement in JavaScript programming will be briefly discussed. Then the new HTML5 features—SVG and canvas, which are the main drive behind JavaScript charts, are introduced and demonstrated. This is followed by a quick guide on the other JavaScript graphing packages that are available on the market. Finally, an introduction of Highcharts is given, which explains the advantages of Highcharts over the other products. In this chapter we will cover the following:

- A short history of web charting
- The uprising of JavaScript and HTML5
- JavaScript charts on the market
- Why Highcharts?

A short history of web charting

Before diving into Highcharts, it is worth mentioning how web charts evolved from pure HTML with server-side technology to the current client side.

HTML image map (server-side technology)

This technique has been used since the early days of HTML, when server-side operations were the main drive. Charts were only HTML images generated from the web server. Before there was any server-side scripting language such as PHP, one of the common approaches was to use **Common Gateway Interface (CGI)**, which executes plotting programs (such as gnuplot) to output the images. Later, when PHP became popular, the GD graphic module was used for plotting. One product that uses this technique is JpGraph. The following is an example of how to include a chart image in an HTML page:

```
<img src="pie_chart.php" border=0 align="left">
```

The chart script file—pie_chart.php—is embedded inside an HTML img tag. When the page is loaded, the browser sees the img src attribute and sends an HTTP request for pie_chart.php. As far as the web browser is concerned, it has no knowledge whether the .php file is an image file or not. When the web server (with PHP support) receives the request, it recognizes the .php extension and executes the PHP scripts. The following is the cut down JpGraph example; the script outputs the image content and streams it back as an HTTP response, in the same way as normal image content would be sent back.

```
// Create new graph
$graph = new Graph(350, 250);
// Add data points in array of x-axis and y-axis values
$p1 = new LinePlot($datay,$datax);
$graph->Add($p1);
// Output line chart in image format back to the client
$graph->Stroke();
```

Furthermore, this technology combines with an HTML map tag for chart navigation, so that when users click on a certain area of a graph, for example a slice in a pie chart, it can load a new page with another graph.

This technology has the following advantages:

- Server-side technology, which means chart creation does not necessarily require user interaction to initiate.

- Ideal for automation tasks, for example scheduled reports or e-mail alerts with the graph attached.

- Doesn't require JavaScript. It is robust, pure HTML, and is light on the client.

It has the following disadvantages:

- More workload on the server side
- Pure HTML, a limited technology — little interactions can be put on the graphs and no animations

Java applet (client side) and servlet (server side)

Java applet enables the web browser to execute multiplatform Java Byte Code to achieve what HTML cannot do, such as graphics display, animations, and advanced user interactions. This was the first technology to extend traditional server-based work to the client side. To include a Java applet in an HTML page, HTML applet (deprecated) or object tags are used and require a Java plugin to be installed for the browser.

The following is an example of including a Java applet inside an object tag. As Java does not run on the same environment in Internet Explorer as other browsers, the conditional comments for IE were used:

```
<!--[if !IE]> Non Internet Explorer way of loading applet -->
<object classid="Java:chart.class" type="application/x-java-applet"
 height="300" width="550" >
<!--<![endif] Internet way of loading applet -->
  <object classid="clsid:8AD9C840..." codebase="/classes/">
  <param name="code" value="chart.class" />
  </object>
<!--[if !IE]> -->
</object>
<!--<![endif]-->
```

Generally, the Java 2D chart products are built from the java.awt.Graphics2D class and the java.awt.geom package from Java **Abstract Window Toolkit (AWT)**. Then, the main chart library allows the users to have the option of using it on a browser extending from the Applet class or running it on the server side extending from the Servlet class.

An example of a Java product is JFreeChart. It comes with 2D and 3D solutions and is free for nonprofit use. JFreeChart can be run as an applet, servlet, or standalone application. The following shows part of the code used to plot data points within an applet:

```
public class AppletGraph extends JApplet {
  // Create X and Y axis plot dataset and populate
  // with data.
  XYPlot xyPlot = new XYPlot();
  xyPlot.setDataset(defaultXYDataset);
  CombinedDomainXYPlot combinedDomainXYPlot =
    new CombinedDomainXYPlot();
  combinedDomainXYPlot.add(xyPlot);
  // Create a jFreeChart object with the dataset
  JFreeChart jFreeChart = new JFreeChart(combinedDomainXYPlot);
  // Put the jFreeChart in a chartPanel
  ChartPanel chartPanel = new ChartPanel(jFreeChart);
  chartPanel.setPreferredSize(new Dimension(900,600));
  // Add the chart panel into the display
  getContentPane().add(chartPanel);
}
```

To run a chart application on the server side, a servlet container is needed, for example Apache Tomcat. The standard `web.xml` file is defined to bind a URL to a servlet:

```
<?xml version="1.0" encoding="UTF-8"?>
<web-app id="server_charts" version="2.4" xmlns="..." xmlns:xsi="..."
  xsi:schemaLocation="...">
  <servlet>
    <servlet-name>PieChartServlet</servlet-name>
    <servlet-class>charts.PieChartServlet</servlet-class>
  </servlet>
  <servlet-mapping>
    <servlet-name>PieChartServlet</servlet-name>
    <url-pattern>/servlets/piechart</url-pattern>
  </servlet-mapping>
</web-app>
```

When the servlet container, such as Tomcat, receives an HTTP request with the URL `http://localhost/servlets/piechart`, it resolves the request into a servlet application. The web server then executes the chart servlet, formats the output into an image, and returns the image content as an HTTP response.

This technology has the following advantages:

- Advanced graphics, animations, and user interfaces
- Reusable core code for different deployment options — client side, server side, or standalone applications

It has the following disadvantages:

- Applet security issues
- If the plugin crashes, it can hang or crash the browser
- Very CPU intensive
- Requires Java plugin
- Long startup time
- Standardization problem

Adobe Shockwave Flash (client side)

Flash is widely used because it offers audio, graphics, animation, and video capabilities on web browsers. Browsers are required to have the Adobe Flash Player plugin installed. As for plotting graphs, this technique is the common choice (because there weren't many other options) before the HTML5 standard became popular.

Graphing software adopting this technology basically ship with their own exported **Shockwave Flash (SWF)** files. These SWF files contain compressed vector-based graphics and compiled ActionScript instructions to create a chart. In order for the Flash Player to display the graphs, the SWF file is needed to be loaded from an HTML page. To do that, an HTML `object` tag is needed. The tag is internally created and injected into the document's DOM by the software's own JavaScript routines.

Inside this `object` tag, it contains dimension and SWF path information for plotting the graph, and the graph variable data is also passed inside this tag. So, as soon as the browser sees an `object` tag with specific parameters, it calls the installed Flash Player to process both the SWF file and the parameters. To pass the graph's plot data from the server side to the client side's Flash Player, `flashVars` is embedded inside a `param` tag with the data type. The following is an example from Yahoo YUI 2:

```
<object id="yuiswf1" type="..." data="charts.swf" width="100%"
height="100%">
<param name="allowscriptaccess" value="always">
<param name="flashVars" value="param1=value1&param2=value2">
</object>
```

This technology has the following advantage:

- Pretty graphics and animations with rich user interactions

It has the following disadvantage:

- Similar to applets

The uprising of JavaScript and HTML5

The role of JavaScript has been shifted significantly from a few simple client routines to a dominant language for creating and managing web user interfaces. The programming technique is nothing like what it was a decade ago. This is driven by a group of pioneers such as Douglas Crockford who is responsible for transforming the language for educating and making JavaScript a better language with his book *JavaScript: The Good Parts, O'Reilly Media / Yahoo Press*; and both Sam Stephenson, creator of Prototype JavaScript library (`http://www.prototypejs.org`), and John Resig, creator of JQuery library (`http://jquery.com`), who brought JavaScript into a framework for building more complicated web frontend software.

To give an introduction of the new programming style is beyond the scope of this book. However, throughout this book, we will see examples in jQuery (because Highcharts uses a jQuery library as the default choice and jQuery is the most popular JavaScript framework). Readers are expected to know the basics of jQuery and CSS selector syntax. Readers should also be familiar with advanced JavaScript scripting described in the book *JavaScript: The Good Parts*, such as prototypes, closure, inheritance, and function objects.

HTML5 (SVG and canvas)

In this section, two HTML5 technologies, SVG and canvas, are covered with examples.

SVG (Scalable Vector Graphics)

HTML5 is the biggest advancement so far in the HTML standard. The adoption of the standard is growing fast (also fuelled by Apple mobile devices, which stopped supporting Adobe Flash). HTML5 comes with many new features. Again, it is beyond the scope of this book to cover them. However, the most relevant part to web charting is **Scalable Vector Graphics (SVG)**. SVG is an XML format for describing vector-based graphics, which is composed of components such as paths, text, shapes, color, and so on. The technology is similar to PostScript except that PostScript is a stack-based language. As implied by its name, one of the major advantages of SVG is that it is a lossless technology (same as PostScript); it doesn't suffer from any pixelation effect by enlarging the image. A reduced image size will not suffer from loss of original content.

Furthermore, the SVG can be scripted with timing animation **Synchronized Multimedia Integration Language (SMIL)** and event handling. SVG technology is supported by all the major browsers.

The following is a simple example of SVG code — a single curved line between two points:

```
<svg xmlns="http://www.w3.org/2000/svg" version="1.1">
  <path id="curveAB" d="M 100 350 q 150 -300 300 0" stroke="blue"
stroke-width="5" fill="none" />
  <!-- Mark relevant points -->
  <g stroke="black" stroke-width="3" fill="black">
    <circle id="pointA" cx="100" cy="350" r="3" />
    <circle id="pointB" cx="400" cy="350" r="3" />
  </g>
  <!-- Label the points -->
  <g font-size="30" font="sans-serif" fill="black" stroke="none" text-
anchor="middle">
    <text x="100" y="350" dx="-30">A</text>
    <text x="400" y="350" dx="30">B</text>
  </g>
</svg>
```

The preceding SVG code is executed in the following steps:

1. Draw a path with `id="curveAB"` with data (d). First, move M to an absolute coordinate (100, 350), then draw a Bézier quadratic curve from the current position to (150, -300) and finish at (300, 0).

2. Group (g) the two circle elements — "pointA" and "pointB" — with the center coordinates (100, 350) and (400, 350) respectively with a radius of 3 pixels. Then fill both circles in black.

3. Group the two text elements A and B, started at (100, 350) and (400, 350), which display with the sans-serif font in black, and then shift along the x axis (dx) 30 pixels left and right, respectively.

The following is the final graph from the SVG script:

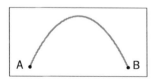

Canvas

Canvas is another new HTML5 standard, which is used by some JavaScript chart software. The purpose of canvas is as its name implies; you declare a drawing area in the canvas tag, then use the new JavaScript APIs to draw lines and shapes in pixels. Canvas has no built-in animation routine, so the API calls in timing sequences are used to simulate an animation. Also, there is no event handling support; developers need to manually attach event handlers to certain regions in the canvas. Hence, fancy chart animation may prove more complicated to implement.

The following is an example of canvas code, which achieves the same effect as the preceding SVG curve:

```
<canvas id="myCanvas" width="500" height="300" style="border:1px solid
#d3d3d3;">Canvas tag not supported</canvas>
<script type="text/javascript">
var c=document.getElementById("myCanvas");
var ctx=c.getContext("2d");
// Draw the quadratic curve from Point A to B
ctx.beginPath();
ctx.moveTo(100, 250);
ctx.quadraticCurveTo(250, 0, 400, 250);
ctx.strokeStyle="blue";
ctx.lineWidth=5;
ctx.stroke();
// Draw a black circle attached to the start of the curve
ctx.fillStyle="black";
ctx.strokeStyle="black";
ctx.lineWidth=3;
ctx.beginPath();
ctx.arc(100,250,3, 0, 2* Math.PI);
ctx.stroke();
ctx.fill();
// Draw a black circle attached to the end of the curve
ctx.beginPath();
ctx.arc(400,250,3, 0, 2* Math.PI);
ctx.stroke();
ctx.fill();
// Display 'A' and 'B' text next to the points
ctx.font="30px 'sans-serif'";
ctx.textAlign="center";
ctx.fillText("A", 70, 250);
ctx.fillText("B", 430, 250);
</script>
```

As you can see, both canvas and SVG can do the same task whereas canvas takes more instructions:

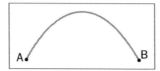

Instead of a continuous path description in SVG, a sequence of JavaScript drawing methods are called. Instead of a single tag with multiple attributes, multiple attribute setting routines are called. SVG is mostly declarative, while canvas enforces an imperative programming approach.

JavaScript charts on the market

There are many different chart libraries on offer on the market. It is impossible to discuss each one of them. They are open source, but some of them are short-lived in terms of not having a comprehensive set of basic charts, such as pie, line, and bar charts and they look rather unfinished. Here, a handful of commercial and open source products are discussed, including all the basic charts (and some with extras). Some of them still support the Flash plugin, which is an option for backward compatibility, the reason being SVG and canvas are not supported in older browsers. Although some of them are not free for commercial development, which is understandable, they do offer a very affordable price.

 See http://code.google.com/p/explorercanvas/. Many libraries use this add-on to emulate canvas prior to IE 9.

jqPlot

jqPlot is packaged with all the basic charts, as well as gauges and candlestick. The software is open source and totally free. jqPlot is based on the jQuery library and uses the canvas approach for plotting charts. This product has a very similar look and feel to Flot/Flotr. Additionally, jqPlot supports animations for column and line charts, but not pie charts, which could be the general issue on canvas approach to produce fancy implementations. In terms of documentation, it is probably the most complete, compared to other free software.

amCharts

amCharts offers a full set of charts in both 2D and 3D with other interesting charts such as radar, bubble, candlestick, and polar. All the charts look pretty and support animations. amCharts is free for commercial use but a credit label will be displayed in the upper-left corner of the charts. The only minor drawback is that the constructor API style seems a bit clumsy. Each attribute assignment has to be done either by calling a method or as an assignment statement explicitly, but not by the object specifier's style.

Ext JS 4 Charts

Ext JS is a very popular Ajax application framework developed by Sencha, a pioneer company specializing in web application development. In Ext JS 4, it comes with the pure JavaScript charts library unlike its predecessor Ext JS 3, which uses the YUI 2 Flash chart library. As the market trend is moving away from Adobe Flash, Sencha responds with a home brew charting library. Ext JS 4 covers all the basic 2D charts plus the gauge and radar charts, and all the charts support animations. The license is free for open source and noncommercial usage, and a developer license is needed for commercial development. A great benefit of Ext JS 4 charts is the integration with the comprehensive set of UI components, for example, for a chart with a storage framework, displaying/updating both the chart and the table of data with editors is very simple to do.

YUI 3 Charts

YUI 3 is another popular Ajax application framework under BSD license. YUI 3 has removed their support for Flash and implemented their own JavaScript charts. The new version comes with all the basic charts in 2D without any animation's support. However, the line charts look just above average, and the column and pie charts look plain and basic. Like Sencha's Ext JS, charts in YUI can be integrated with other components supplied by the framework.

FusionCharts

FusionCharts is probably one of the most impressive looking and has the most comprehensive charts out there in the market. Not only does it come with a full-range variety of interesting 2D charts (radar, dial, map, and candlestick) available as a separate product, but it also offers fully interactive 3D charts. All the chart animations are very professionally done. Basically, FusionCharts can be run in two modes, Flash or JavaScript. For the JavaScript mode, FusionCharts use their own extended Highcharts library to achieve the same 2D and 3D effect, and look the same as their Flash version. Although FusionCharts comes with a higher price tag, this is the only product that has the best looking charts and rotatable 3D charts.

JS Charts

JS Charts offers all the basic charts in both 2D and 3D looks. JS Charts uses the HTML5 canvas technology to render charts. The bars and lines look good with animations, however, the presentation of a pie chart is slightly behind and it offers no animation support. The product is free for noncommercial use and commercial license is on per domain basis. The constructor API is similar to amCharts done via method calls.

Flot and Flotr

Flot is an MIT licensed freeware offering 2D charts but without any animation at the time of writing. It is a canvas-based product built on the jQuery framework. The software produces nice-looking line charts but not the bar and pie charts (which require a plugin). Documentation is not very comprehensive and there are not many update activities within the product. There is also another chart package, Flotr, which is inspired by the Flot line chart style and is based on the Prototype framework. Flotr offers all the basic canvas charts with better looking bar and pie charts, and includes candlestick and radar charts. However, Flotr has even fewer activities than Flot; both products seem to be heading towards the end of their lifecycle.

Why Highcharts?

Although Highcharts only has the basic 2D charts, it offers very appealing and professional looking charts in the market. It is a product which stands out by paying attention to details, not only on the presentation side but also in other areas that are described later on. The product was released in late 2009 and developed by a Norwegian company called Highsoft Solutions AS, created and founded by Torstein Hønsi. Highcharts is not their first product, but by far their best selling one.

Highcharts and JavaScript frameworks

Although Highcharts is built with the JavaScript framework library, it is implemented in such a way that it doesn't totally rely on one particular framework. Highcharts is packaged with adapters, to make its interfaces to framework, pluggable.

As a result, Highcharts can be incorporated under MooTools, Prototype, or jQuery JavaScript frameworks. This empowers users without compromising their already developed product or allows them to decide on using the framework which is best suited to their projects. Highcharts uses jQuery as the default framework implementation, hence it only requires users to load the jQuery library before Highcharts.

To use Highcharts under the MooTools environment, users simply do the following:

```
<script src="//ajax.googleapis.com/ajax/libs/mootools/1.4.5/mootools-
yui-compressed.js"></script>
<script type="text/javascript"
        src="Highcharts-2.2.2/js/adapters/mootools-adapter.js"></
script>
<script type="text/javascript"
        src="Highcharts-2.2.2/js/highcharts.js"></script>
```

And to use Highcharts under Prototype, users need to do the following:

```
<script src="//ajax.googleapis.com/ajax/libs/prototype/1.7.1.0/
prototype.js"></script>
<script type="text/javascript"
        src="Highcharts-2.2.2/js/adapters/prototype-adapter.js"></
script>
<script type="text/javascript"
        src="Highcharts-2.2.2/js/highcharts.js"></script>
```

Presentation

Highcharts strikes the right balance of look and feel. The charts themselves are visually pleasant and yet the style is simple. The default choices of color are soothing without a sharp contrast conflicting each other, which is aided by the subtle shadow and white border effects. None of the text nor the colors of the axes are in black or any dark color, which keeps the viewers' attention centered to the colored data presentation.

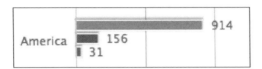

All the animations (initial, update, tooltip) in Highcharts are finely tuned—smooth with a gradual slowdown motion. For instance, the initial animation of the donut chart, which is a multiseries pie chart, is the most impressive one. This is the area where Highcharts is clearly better; the animations in other charts are too mechanical, too much, and sometimes off-putting.

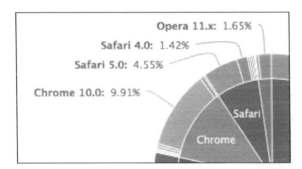

The round corners of tooltip and legends (both inner and outer) with a simple border do not fight for the viewers' attention and nicely blend inside the chart. The following is a tooltip sample:

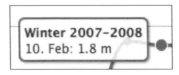

The following is a legend example with two series:

In a nutshell, every element in Highcharts does not compete with each other for viewers' attention; they share the load equally and work together as a chart.

License

Highcharts has free noncommercial as well as commercial licenses. The free license for personal and nonprofit purposes is Creative Commons – Attribution NonCommercial 3.0. Highcharts offers different flavors of commercial licenses for different purposes. They have a one-off single website license and, thankfully, developer licenses. For web development products, a developer license is a better model than charging in units of website basis or a very high priced OEM license because of the following reasons:

- It is easy for the software companies to work out the math in their development plans
- There is less worry regarding how many copies are being sold, so as to not violate the license

As usual, the developer license does not automatically grant the use of Highcharts indefinitely. The license only permits the unlimited use of all the versions released within a year from the license purchase date. Thereafter, an update license is required if developers decide to use a newer version and so on. Moreover, any condition can be negotiated for the OEM license, and most commonly, the quote is based on the number of developers on the project and the number of deployments.

Simple API model

Highcharts has a very simple API model. For creating a chart, the constructor API expects an object specifier with all the necessary settings. As for dynamically updating an existing chart, Highcharts comes with a small set of APIs. The configuration properties are described in detail in *Chapter 2, Highcharts Configurations*. The API calls are discussed in *Chapter 7, Highcharts APIs*.

Documentations

Highcharts' online documentation is one of the areas that really outshines the others. It is not just a simple documentation page to dump all the definitions and examples. It's a documentation page built with thought. Here is why.

The left-hand side of the documentation page is organized in an object structure as how you would pass it to create a chart. You can expand and collapse the object's attributes further like in a JavaScript console. This has helped the users to become familiar with the product by using it naturally.

```
series : [{
    data                        :  "",
    dataParser                  :  ,
    dataURL                     :  null,
    legendIndex                 :  undefined,
    name                        :  "",
    stack                       :  null,
    type                        :  "line",
    xAxis                       :  0,
    yAxis                       :  0
}],
```

The well thought out part of the documentation is on the right-hand side with the definitions of the attributes. Each definition comes with a description and an online demonstration for each setting linking to the jsFiddle website.

```
type : String
The type of series. Can be one of area, areaspline, bar, column, line, pie,
scatter or spline. Defaults to "line".
Try it: Line and column in the same chart
```

This instant jsFiddle demo invites users to explore different property values and observes the effect on the chart. Hence, the whole documentation browsing process becomes very effective and fluid.

Openness (feature request with user voice)

One unusual way of how Highcharts decides new features for every major release is via the users' voice (this is not unusual in open source project practices but it is one of the areas where Highcharts is better than the others). Users can submit new feature requests and then vote for them. The company then reviews the feature requests with the highest votes and draws up a development plan for the new features. The details of the plan are then published on the Highcharts website.

In addition, Highcharts is hosted on GitHub, an online public source control service, which allows JavaScript developers to contribute and clone their own versions.

Highcharts – a quick tutorial

In this section, you will see how to implement your first Highcharts graph. First, download the latest version from the Highcharts website.

Directories structure

When you unpack the downloaded ZIP file, you should see the following directories' structure under the **Highcharts-2.x.x** top-level directory:

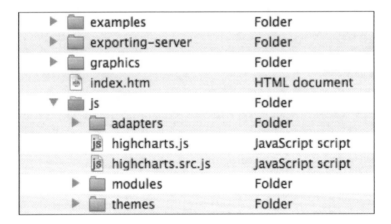

The following is what each directory contains and is used for:

- `index.html`: This is the demo HTML page, which is the same as the demo page on the Highcharts website, so that you can still experiment with Highcharts offline.
- `examples`: This contains all the source files for the examples.
- `graphics`: This contains image files used by the examples.

- exporting-server: This is a directory for the server-side function to export charts into an image file using Batik, which is a Java-based toolkit for managing SVG content, and exporting the server is one of its usages.

- js: This is the main directory with Highcharts code. Each JavaScript filename has two suffixes, .src.js, which contains the source code with comments in it, and .js, which is the minification of JavaScript source files.

- adapters: This has the adapter facility for using with MooTools or Prototype modules. It contains the following files:

  - exporting.js for client-side exporting and printing functions

  - canvas-tools.js – we need to use a third-party tool, canvg, to support Android 2.x, as the native browser has no SVG support but can display the canvas

- themes: This has a set of JavaScript files pre-built with settings such as background colors, font styles, axis layouts, and so on. Users can load one of these files in their charts for different styles.

All you need to do is move the top-level Highcharts-2.x.x/js directory inside your web server document's root directory.

To use Highcharts, you need to include Highcharts-2.x.x/js/highcharts.js and a jQuery library in your HTML file. The following is an example showing the percentage of web browsers' usage for a public website. The example uses the minimal configuration settings for getting you started quickly. The following is the top half of the example:

```
<!DOCTYPE HTML>
<html>
  <head>
    <meta http-equiv="Content-Type"
          content="text/html; charset=utf-8">
    <title>Highcharts First Example</title>
    <script src="//ajax.googleapis.com/ajax/libs/jquery/1.7.1/jquery.
min.js"></script>
    <script type="text/javascript"
          src="Highcharts-2.2.2/js/highcharts.js"></script>
```

We use the Google public library service to load the jQuery library Version 1.7.1 before loading the Highcharts library.

The second half of the example is the main Highcharts code, as follows:

```
<script type="text/javascript">
    $(document).ready(function() {
        var chart = new Highcharts.Chart({
            chart: {
                renderTo: 'container',
                type: 'spline'
            },
            title: {
                text: 'Web browsers statistics'
            },
            subtitle: {
                text: 'From 2008 to present'
            },
            xAxis: {
                categories: [ 'Jan 2008', 'Feb', .... ],
                tickInterval: 3
            },
            yAxis: {
                title: {
                    text: 'Percentage %'
                },
                min: 0
            },
            plotOptions: {
                series: {
                    lineWidth: 2
                }
            },
            series: [{
                name: 'Internet Explorer',
                data: [54.7, 54.7, 53.9, 54.8, 54.4, ... ]
            }, {
                name: 'FireFox',
                data: [36.4, 36.5, 37.0, 39.1, 39.8, ... ]
            }, {
                // Chrome started until late 2008
                name: 'Chrome',
                data: [ null, null, null, null, null, null,
                        null, null, 3.1, 3.0, 3.1, 3.6, ... ]
            }, {
                name: 'Safari',
                data: [ 1.9, 2.0, 2.1, 2.2, 2.4, 2.6, ... ]
            }, {
                name: 'Opera',
```

```
            data: [ 1.4, 1.4, 1.4, 1.4, 1.5, 1.7, ... ]
        }]
    });
});
</script>
  </head>
  <body>
  <div>
    <!-- Highcharts rendering takes place inside this DIV -->
    <div id="container"></div>
  </div>
</body>
</html>
```

The spline graph is created via an object specifier that contains all the properties and
series data required. Once the `chart` object is created, the graph is displayed in the
browser. Within this object specifier, there are major components corresponding to
the structure of the chart.

```
var chart = new Highcharts.Chart({
    chart: {
        ...
    },
    title: '...'
    ...
});
```

The `renderTo` option instructs Highcharts to display the graph onto the HTML
`<div>` element with `'container'` as the ID value, which is defined in the HTML
`<body>` section. The `type` option is set to the default presentation type as `'spline'`
for any series data, as follows:

```
chart: {
    renderTo: 'container',
    type: 'spline'
}
```

Next is to set `title` and `subtitle`, which appears at the center part at the top
of the chart:

```
title: {
    text: 'Web browsers ... '
},
subtitle: {
    text: 'From 2008 to present'
},
```

The categories option in the xAxis property contains an array of x axis labels for each data point. Since the graph has at least 50 data points, printing each x axis label will make the text overlap each other. Rotating the labels still results in the axis looking very packed. The best compromise is to print every third label, (tickIntervals: 3) which causes the labels to be nicely spaced out from each other.

 For the sake of simplicity, we use 50 entries in xAxis.categories to represent the time. However, we will see a more optimal and logical way to display date time data in the next chapter.

```
xAxis: {
    categories: [ 'Jan 2008', 'Feb', .... ],
    tickInterval: 3
},
```

The options in yAxis are to assign the title of the y axis and set the minimum possible value to zero, otherwise Highcharts will display a negative percentage range along the y axis, which is unwanted for this dataset.

```
yAxis: {
    title: {
        text: 'Percentage %'
    },
    min: 0
},
```

The plotOptions property is to control how each series is displayed according to its type (line, pie, bar, and so on). The plotOptions.series option is the general configuration applied to all the series type instead of defining each setting inside the series array. In this example, the default lineWidth for all the series is set to 2 pixels wide, as follows:

```
plotOptions: {
    series: {
        lineWidth: 2
    }
},
```

The `series` property is the heart of the whole configuration object, which defines all the series data. It is an array of the series configuration objects. For this example, the name option is the name of the series that appears in the chart legend and tooltip. The data is an array of y axis values, which has the same length as the `xAxis`. `categories` array to form (x,y) data points.

```
series: [{
    name: 'Internet Explorer',
    data: [54.7, 54.7, 53.9, 54.8, 54.4, ... ]
}, {
    name: 'FireFox',
    data: [36.4, 36.5, 37.0, 39.1, 39.8, ... ]
}, {
```

The following screenshot shows how the final Highcharts should look on a Safari browser:

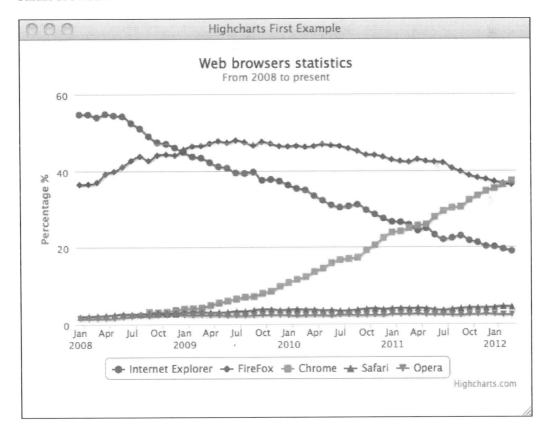

The following screenshot shows how it should look on an Internet Explorer 9 browser:

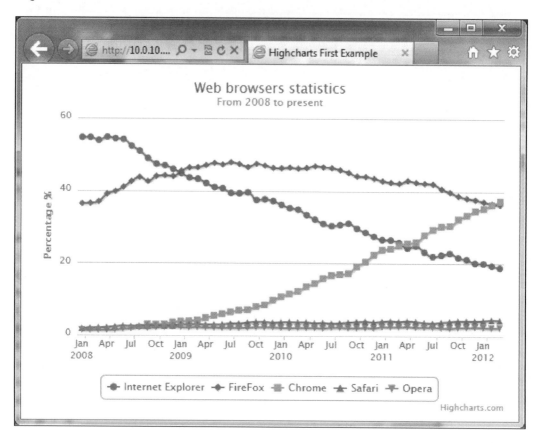

The following screenshot shows how it should look on a Chrome browser:

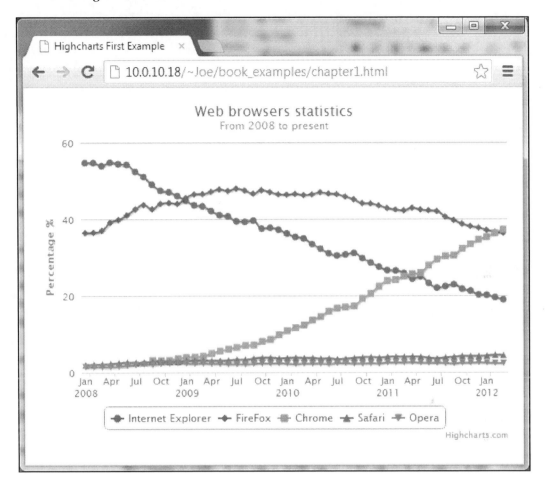

The following screenshot shows how it should look on a Firefox browser:

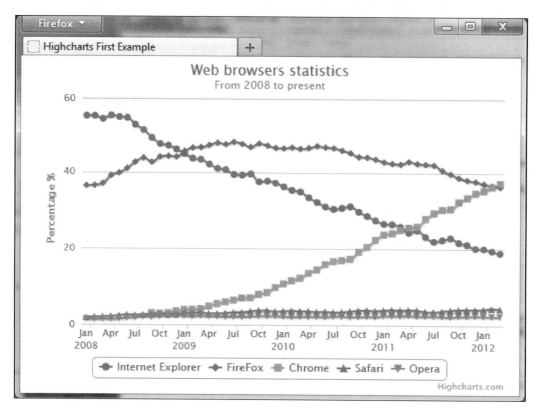

Summary

Web charting has been around since the early days of HTML, emerging from server-side technology to client-side. During this period, several solutions have been adopted to work around the shortcomings of HTML. Now, with the new HTML5, which is rich in features, web charting has come back to HTML and this time it is for good, with the aid of unleashed JavaScript.

A number of JavaScript chart products were mentioned in this chapter..
Among these, Highcharts emerges with a distinct graphical style and smooth user interactions.

In the next chapter, we will explore the Highcharts configuration object in greater detail with plenty more examples. The configuration object is the core part of the product that the structure serves as the common prototype for all the charts.

2
Highcharts Configurations

All Highcharts graphs share the same configuration structure and it is crucial for us to get familiar with the core components. However, it is not possible to go through all the configurations in this book. In this chapter, we will explore the properties that are mostly used from a functional point of view and demonstrate them with ongoing examples. We will learn the concept of how Highcharts manages layout, and then explore how to configure axes, specify single series and multiple series data, followed by formatting and styling tooltips in both JavaScript and HTML. Finally, we will get to know how to polish our charts with various types of animations and to apply color gradients. In this chapter we will cover the following:

- Understanding Highcharts layouts
- Framing the chart with axes
- Revisiting the series configuration
- Styling the tooltips
- Animating charts
- Expanding colors with gradients

Configuration structure

In the Highcharts configuration object, the components at the top level represent the skeleton structure of a chart. The following is a list of the major components that are covered in this chapter. For the references of all the configurations, go to `http://api.highcharts.com/highcharts`.

The following is a list of the major components:

- `chart`: Configurations for the top-level chart properties such as layouts, dimensions, events, animations, and user interactions

- `series`: Array of series objects (consisting of data and specific options) for single and multiple series, where the series data can be specified in a number of ways

- `xAxis`/`yAxis`: Configurations for all the axis properties such as labels, styles, intervals, plotlines, plot bands, and backgrounds

- `tooltip`: Layout and format style configurations for the series data tooltips

- `title`/`subtitle`: Layout and style configurations for the chart title and subtitle

- `legend`: Layout and format style configurations for the chart legend

- `plotOptions`: Contains all the plotting options, such as display, animation, and user interactions for common series and specific series types

- `exporting`: Configurations control the layout and the function of print and export features

Understanding Highcharts layouts

Before we start to learn how Highcharts layouts work, it is imperative that we understand some basic concepts first. To do that, let us first recall the chart example used in *Chapter 1, Web Charts*, and set a couple of borders to be visible. First, set a border around the plot area; to do that we can set the options of `plotBorderWidth` and `plotBorderColor` in the `chart` section, as follows:

```
chart: {
        renderTo: 'container',
        type: 'spline',
        plotBorderWidth: 1,
        plotBorderColor: '#3F4044'
},
```

The second border is set around the Highcharts container. Next, we extend the preceding `chart` section with additional settings:

```
chart: {
        renderTo: 'container',
        ....
        borderColor: '#a1a1a1',
        borderWidth: 2,
        borderRadius: 3
},
```

Basically, this sets the container border color with the width of 2 pixels and the corner radius to 3 pixels.

As we can see, there is a border around the container, and this is the boundary that the Highcharts display cannot exceed:

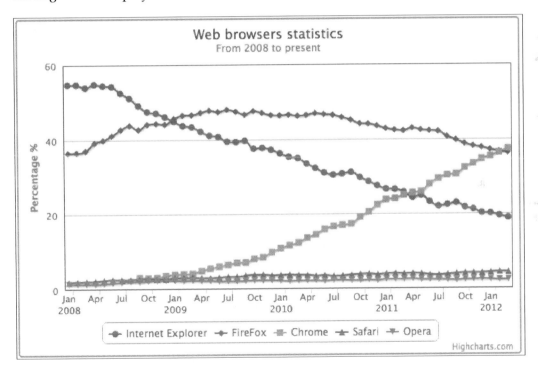

By default, Highcharts displays have three different areas—spacing area, labeling area, and plot area. The plot area is the area inside the inner rectangle that contains all the plot graphics. The labeling area is the area where labels such as title, subtitle, axis title, legend, and credits go around the plot area, so that it is between the edge of the plot area and the inner edge of the spacing area. The spacing area is the area between the container border and the outer edge of the labeling area. The following screenshot shows three different kinds of areas. A gray dotted line is inserted to illustrate the boundary between the spacing and labeling areas.

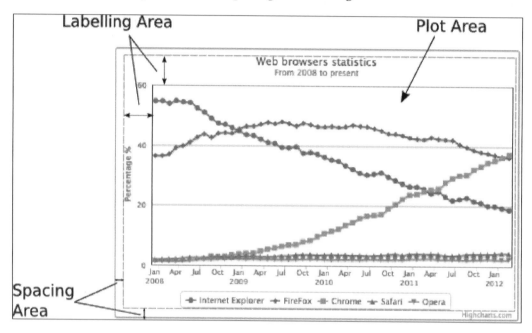

Each chart label positioning can be operated in one of the following two layouts:

- **Automatic layout**: Highcharts automatically adjusts the plot area size based on the labels' positions in the labeling area, that is, the plot area does not overlap with the label element at all. Automatic layout is the simplest way to configure, but has less control; this is the default way of positioning the chart elements.

- **Fixed layout**: There is no concept of labeling area. The chart label is specified in a fixed location such that it has a floating effect on the plot area. In other words, the plot area side does not automatically adjust itself to the adjacent label position. This gives users full control of exactly how to display the chart.

The spacing area controls the offset of the Highcharts display on each side. As long as the chart margins are not defined, increasing or decreasing the spacing area has the global effect on the plot area measurement in both automatic and fixed layouts.

Chart margins and spacings

In this section, we will see how chart margins and spacing settings have an effect on the overall layout. Chart margins can be configured with the properties `margin`, `marginTop`, `marginLeft`, `marginRight`, and `marginBottom`, and they are not enabled by default. Setting chart margins has a global effect on the plot area, so that none of the label positions nor the chart spacing configurations can affect the plot area size. Hence, all the chart elements are in a fixed layout mode with respect to the plot area. The `margin` option is an array of four margin values covered for each direction, the same as CSS starting from north and going clockwise. Also, the `margin` option has a lower precedence than any of the directional `margin` options, regardless of the order in the `chart` section.

Spacing configurations are enabled by default with a fixed value on each side. These can be configured in the `chart` section with the property names `spacingTop`, `spacingLeft`, `spacingBottom`, and `spacingRight`.

In this example, we are going to increase or decrease the `margin` or `spacing` property on each side of the chart and observe the effect. The following are the chart settings:

```
chart: {
    renderTo: 'container',
    type: ...
    marginTop: 10,
    marginRight: 0,
    spacingLeft: 30,
    spacingBottom: 0
},
```

The following screenshot shows what the chart looks like:

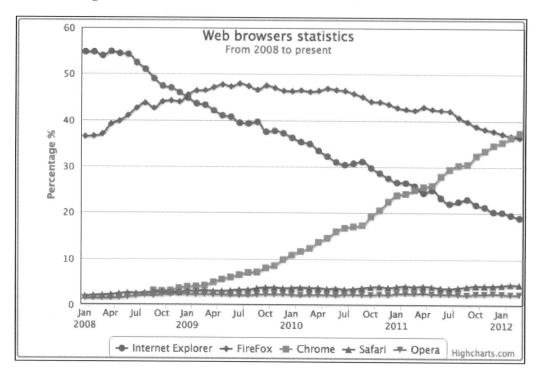

The `marginTop` property fixates the plot area's top border `10` pixels away from the container border. It also changes the top border into fixed layout to any label elements, hence the chart title and subtitle float on top of the plot area. The `spacingLeft` property increases the spacing area on the left-hand side, hence it pushes the y-axis title further in. As it is in the automatic layout (without declaring `marginLeft`), it also pushes the plot area's west border in. Setting `marginRight` to `0` will override all the default spacing on the chart's right-hand side and turn it into fixed layout mode. Finally, setting `spacingBottom` to `0` makes the legend touch the lower bar of the container. Hence, it also stretches the plot area downwards. This is because the bottom edge is still in automatic layout even though `spacingBottom` is set to `0`.

Chart label properties

Chart labels such as `xAxis.title`, `yAxis.title`, `legend`, `title`, `subtitle`, and `credits` share the common property names, which are as follows:

- `align`: This is for horizontal alignment for the label; possible keywords are `'left'`, `'center'`, and `'right'`. As for the axis title, it is `'low'`, `'middle'`, and `'high'`.

- `floating`: This is for the label position having a floating effect in the plot area. Setting this to `true` will cause the label position to have no effect on the adjacent plot area's boundary.

- `margin`: This is the margin setting between the label and the side of the plot area adjacent to it. Only certain label types have this setting.

- `verticalAlign`: This is for vertical alignment for the label; keywords are `'top'`, `'middle'`, and `'bottom'`.

- `x`: This is for horizontal positioning in relation to alignment.

- `y`: This is for vertical positioning in relation to alignment.

As for the labels' `x` and `y` positioning, they are not used for absolute positioning within the chart. They are designed for fine adjustment with the label alignment. The following diagram shows the coordinate directions, where the center represents the label location:

We can experiment with these properties with a simple example of the `align` and `y` position settings, by placing both title and subtitle next to each other. The title is shifted to the left with `align` set to `'left'`, whereas the subtitle alignment is set to `'right'`. In order to make both titles appear on the same line, we change the subtitle's `y` position to `15`, which is the same as the title's default `y` value:

```
title: {
    text: 'Web browsers ...',
    align: 'left'
},
subtitle: {
    text: 'From 2008 to present',
    align: 'right',
    y: 15
},
```

The following is a screenshot showing both titles aligning on the same line:

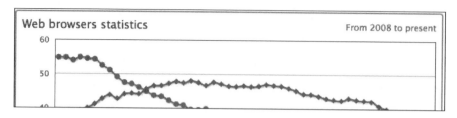

In the following subsections, we will experiment with how the changes in alignment for each label element will affect the layout behaviors towards the plot area.

Title and subtitle alignments

Title and subtitle have the same layout properties, and the only difference is that the default values and title have the `margin` setting. Specifying `verticalAlign` to any value can change from the default automatic layout to the fixed layout (internally this switches `floating` to `true`). However, manually setting the subtitle's `floating` property to `false` does not switch it back to automatic layout. The following is an example of having `title` in automatic layout and `subtitle` in fixed layout:

```
title: {
    text: 'Web browsers statistics'
},
subtitle: {
    text: 'From 2008 to present',
    verticalAlign: 'top',
    y: 60     },
```

The `verticalAlign` property for the subtitle is set to `'top'`, which switches the layout into the fixed layout and the `y` offset is increased to `60`. The `y` offset pushes the subtitle's position further down. Due to the fact that the plot area is not in an automatic layout relationship to the subtitle anymore, the top border of the plot area goes above the subtitle. However, the plot area is still in the automatic layout towards the title, hence the title is still above the plot area:

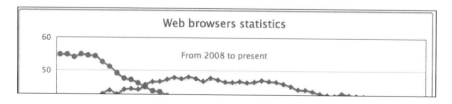

This is currently a defect reported in Highcharts. The assignment in `verticalAlign` forces both title and subtitle into fixed layout (that is, `floating` is `true`). You can find the bug report at `http://github.com/highslide-software/highcharts.com/issues/962`.

Legend alignment

Legends show different behaviors for the `verticalAlign` and `align` properties. Apart from setting the alignment to `'center'`, all other settings in `verticalAlign` and `align` remain in automatic positioning. The following is an example of the legend located on the right-hand side of the chart. The `verticalAlign` property is switched to the middle of the chart, where the horizontal `align` is set to `'right'`:

```
legend: {
    align: 'right',
    verticalAlign: 'middle',
    layout: 'vertical',
},
```

The `layout` property is assigned to `'vertical'` so that it causes the items inside the legend box to be displayed in a vertical manner. As we can see, the plot area is automatically resized for the legend box:

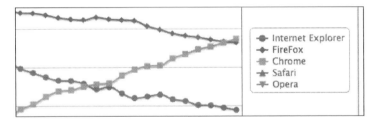

Axis title alignment

Axis titles do not use `verticalAlign`. Instead, they use the `align` setting, which is either `'low'`, `'middle'`, or `'high'`. The title's `margin` value is the distance between the axis title and the axis line. The following is an example of showing the y-axis title rotated horizontally instead of vertically (which it does by default), and displayed on the top of the axis line instead of next to it. Moreover, we use the `y` property to finely tune the title location:

```
yAxis: {
    title: {
        text: 'Percentage %',
        rotation: 0,
```

```
            y: -15,
            margin: -70,
            align: 'high'
        },
        min: 0
    },
```

The following is a screenshot of the upper-left corner of the chart showing that the title is aligned horizontally at the top of the y axis. Alternatively, we can use the `offset` option instead of `margin` to achieve the same result.

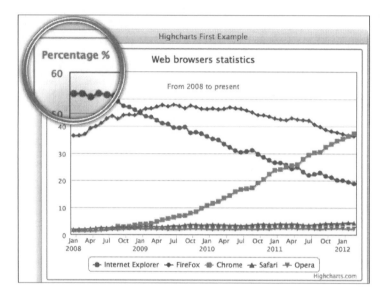

Credits alignment

Credits is a bit different than other label elements. It only supports the `align`, `verticalAlign`, `x`, and `y` properties in the `credits.position` property (shorthand for `credits: { position: ... }`), and is also not affected by any spacing settings. Suppose we have a graph without a legend and we have to move the credits to the lower-left area of the chart; the following code snippet shows how to do it:

```
legend: {
    enabled: false
},
credits: {
    position: {
        align: 'left'
    },
    text: 'Joe Kuan',
    href: 'http://joekuan.wordpress.com'
},
```

However, the credits text is off the edge of the chart, as shown in the following screenshot:

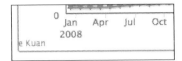

Even if we move the `credits` label to the right with x positioning, the label is still a bit too close to the x-axis interval label. We can introduce extra `spacingBottom` to put a gap between both labels, as follows:

```
chart: {
      spacingBottom: 30,
         ....
},
credits: {
      position: {
         align: 'left',
         x: 20,
         y: -7
      },
```

The following is a screenshot of the credits with the final adjustments:

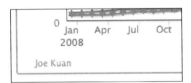

Experimenting with the automatic layout

In this section, we will examine the automatic layout feature in more detail. For the sake of simplifying the example, we will start only with the chart title and without any chart spacing settings:

```
chart: {
      renderTo: 'container',
      // border and plotBorder settings
      .....
},
title: {
      text: 'Web browsers statistics,
},
```

From the preceding example, the chart title should appear as expected between the container and the plot area's borders:

Web browsers statistics

The space between the title and the top border of the container has the default setting `spacingTop` for the spacing area (default value of 10 pixels high). The gap between the title and the top border of the plot area is the default setting for `title.margin`, which is 15 pixels high.

By setting `spacingTop` in the `chart` section to `0`, the chart title moves up next to the container top border. Hence the size of the plot area is automatically expanded upwards, as follows:

Web browsers statistics

Then we set `title.margin` to `0`; the plot area border moves further up, hence the height of the plot area increases further, as follows:

Web browsers statistics

As you may notice, there is still a gap of a few pixels between the top border and the chart title. This is actually due to the default value of the title's y position setting, which is 15 pixels, large enough for the default title font size.

The following is the chart configuration for setting all the spaces between the container and the plot area to `0`:

```
chart: {
    renderTo: 'container',
    // border and plotBorder settings
    .....
    spacingTop: 0
},
title: {
    text: 'Web browsers statistics',
    margin: 0,
    y: 0
}
```

If we set title.y to 0, all the gaps between the top edge of the plot area and the top container edge close up. The following is the final screenshot of the upper-left corner of the chart, to show the effect. The chart title is not visible anymore as it has been shifted above the container:

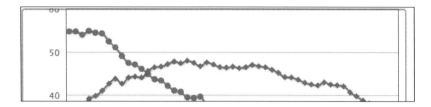

Interestingly, if we work backwards to the first example, the default distance between the top of the plot area and the top of the container is calculated, as follows:

spacingTop + title.margin + title.y = 10 + 15 + 15 = 40

Therefore, changing any of these three variables will automatically adjust the plot area from the top container bar. Each of these offset variables actually has its own purpose in the automatic layout. Spacing is for the gap between the container and the chart content. So, if we want to display a chart nicely spaced with other elements on a web page, spacing elements should be used. Equally, if we want to use a specific font size for the label elements, we should consider adjusting the y offset. Hence, the labels are still maintained at a distance and do not interfere with other components in the chart.

Experimenting with the fixed layout

In the preceding section we have learned how the plot area dynamically adjusted itself. In this section, we will see how we can manually position the chart labels. First, we will start with the example code from the beginning of the *Experimenting with the automatic layout* section and set the chart title's verticalAlign to 'bottom', as follows:

```
chart: {
    renderTo: 'container',
    // border and plotBorder settings    .....
},
title: {
    text: 'Web browsers statistics',
    verticalAlign: 'bottom'
},
```

The chart title is moved to the bottom of the chart, next to the lower border of the container. Notice that this setting has changed the title into floating mode, and more importantly the legend still remains in the default automatic layout to the plot area:

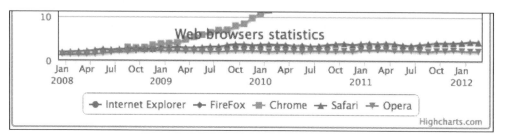

Beware that we haven't specified `spacingBottom`, which has a default value of 15 pixels height applied to the chart. This means that there should be a gap between the title and the container bottom border, but none is shown. This is because the `title.y` position has a default value of 15 pixels in relation to spacing. According to the diagram in the *Chart label properties* section, this positive y value pushes the title towards the bottom border's direction, which compensates for the space created by `spacingBottom`.

Let's make a bigger change on the y offset position this time to show that `verticalAlign` is floating on top of the plot area:

```
title: {
    text: 'Web browsers statistics',
    verticalAlign: 'bottom',
    y: -90
},
```

The negative y value moves the title up, as shown in the following screenshot:

Now the title is overlapping the plot area. To demonstrate that the legend is still in automatic layout towards the plot area, here we change the legend's y position and the margin settings, which is the distance from the axis label:

```
legend: {
    margin: 70,
    y: -10
},
```

This has pushed up the bottom side of the plot area. However, the chart title still remains in the fixed layout and its position within the chart hasn't been changed at all after applying the new legend setting, as shown in the following screenshot:

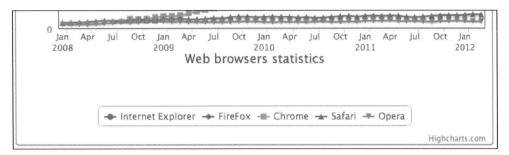

By now we should have a better understanding of how to position label elements, and their layout policy relating to the plot area.

Framing the chart with axes

In this section, we are going to look into Highcharts axis configuration in terms of their functional area. Throughout this section, we will start off with a plain line graph and gradually apply more options to the chart to demonstrate the effects.

Accessing the axis data type

There are two ways to specify data for a chart—categories and series data. For displaying intervals with specific names, we should use the categories field that expects an array of strings. Each entry in the categories array is then associated with the series data array. Alternatively, the axis interval values are embedded inside the series data array. Then Highcharts extracts the series data for both axes, interprets the data type, and formats and labels the values appropriately.

The following is a straightforward example showing the usage of categories:

```
chart: {
    renderTo: 'container',
    height: 250,
    spacingRight: 20
},
title: {
    text: 'Market Data: Nasdaq 100'
},
subtitle: {
```

```
                text: 'May 11, 2012'
        },
        xAxis: {
            categories: [ '9:30 am', '10:00 am', '10:30 am',
                          '11:00 am', '11:30 am', '12:00 pm',
                          '12:30 pm', '1:00 pm', '1:30 pm',
                          '2:00 pm', '2:30 pm', '3:00 pm',
                          '3:30 pm', '4:00 pm' ],
            labels: {
                step: 3
            }
        },
        yAxis: {
            title: {
                text: null
            }
        },
        legend: {
            enabled: false
        },
        credits: {
            enabled: false
        },
        series: [{
            name: 'Nasdaq',
            data: [ 2606.01, 2622.08, 2636.03, 2637.78, 2639.15,
                    2637.09, 2633.38, 2632.23, 2632.33, 2632.59,
                    2630.34, 2626.89, 2624.59, 2615.98 ]
        }]
```

The preceding code snippet produces a graph that looks like the following screenshot:

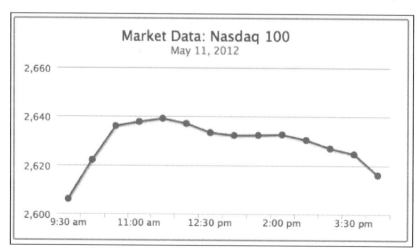

The first name, **9:30 am**, in the categories field corresponds to the first value, 2606.01, in the series data array, and so on.

Alternatively, we can specify the time values inside the series data and use the type property of the x axis to format the time. The type property supports 'linear' (default), 'logarithmic', or 'datetime'. The 'datetime' setting automatically interprets the time in the series data into human-readable form. Moreover, we can use the dateTimeLabelFormats property to predefine the custom format for the time unit. The option can also accept multiple time unit formats; this is for when we don't know in advance how long the time span is in the series data, that is, each unit in the resulting graph can be in per hour, per day, and so on. The following example shows how the graph is specified with predefined hourly and minute formats. The syntax of the format string is based on the PHP strftime function:

```
xAxis: {
    type: 'datetime',
    // Format 24 hour time to AM/PM
    dateTimeLabelFormats: {

        hour: '%I:%M %P',
        minute: '%I %M'
    }
},
series: [{
    name: 'Nasdaq',
    data: [ [ Date.UTC(2012, 4, 11, 9, 30), 2606.01 ],
            [ Date.UTC(2012, 4, 11, 10), 2622.08 ],
            [ Date.UTC(2012, 4, 11, 10, 30), 2636.03 ],
            .....
        ]
}]
```

Note that the x axis is in the 12-hour time format:

Instead, we can define the format handler for the xAxis.labels.formatter property to achieve a similar effect. Highcharts provides a utility routine, Highcharts.dateFormat, which converts the timestamp in milliseconds to a readable format. In the following code snippet, we define the formatter function using dateFormat and this.value. The keyword this is the axis's interval object, whereas this.value is the UTC time value for the instance of the interval.

```
xAxis: {
    type: 'datetime',
    labels: {
        formatter: function() {
            return Highcharts.dateFormat('%I:%M %P', this.value);
        }
    }
},
```

Since the time values of our data points are in fixed intervals, they can also be arranged in a cut down version. All it needs is to define the starting point of time, pointStart, and the regular interval between them, pointInterval, in milliseconds.

```
series: [{
    name: 'Nasdaq',
    pointStart: Date.UTC(2012, 4, 11, 9, 30),
    pointInterval: 30 * 60 * 1000,
    data: [ 2606.01, 2622.08, 2636.03, 2637.78,
            2639.15, 2637.09, 2633.38, 2632.23,
            2632.33, 2632.59, 2630.34, 2626.89,
            2624.59, 2615.98 ]
}]
```

Adjusting intervals and background

We have learned how to use the axis's categories and series data array in the last section. In this section, we will see how to format interval lines and the background style to produce a graph with more clarity.

So, let's continue from the previous example. First, let's create some interval lines along the y axis. In the chart, the interval is automatically set to 20. However, it would be clearer to double the number of interval lines. To do that, simply assign the tickInterval value to 10. Then, we use minorTickInterval to put another line in between the intervals to indicate a semi-interval. In order to distinguish between interval and semi-interval lines, we set the semi-interval lines, minorGridLineDashStyle, to dashed and dotted style.

There are nearly a dozen line style settings available in Highcharts, from `'Solid'` to `'LongDashDotDot'`. Readers can refer to the online manual for possible values.

The following is the first step for creating the new settings:

```
yAxis: {
    title: {
        text: null
    },
    tickInterval: 10,
    minorTickInterval: 5,
    minorGridLineColor: '#ADADAD',
    minorGridLineDashStyle: 'dashdot'
}
```

The interval lines should look like the following screenshot:

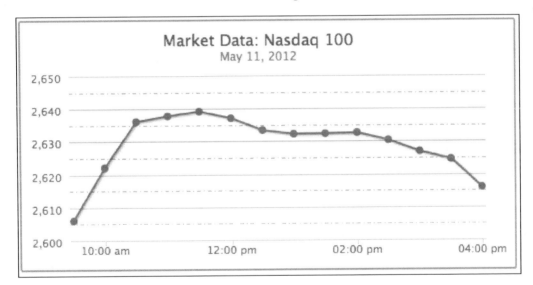

To make the graph even more presentable, we add some striping effect with shading—`alternateGridColor`. Then we change the interval line color, `gridLineColor`, to a similar range with the stripes. The following code snippet is added into the `yAxis` configuration:

```
gridLineColor: '#8AB8E6',
alternateGridColor: {
    linearGradient: {
        x1: 0, y1: 1,
```

```
        x2: 1, y2: 1
    },
    stops: [ [0, '#FAFCFF' ],
             [0.5, '#F5FAFF'] ,
             [0.8, '#E0F0FF'] ,
             [1, '#D6EBFF'] ]
}
```

We will discuss the color gradient later in this chapter. The following is the graph with the new shading background:

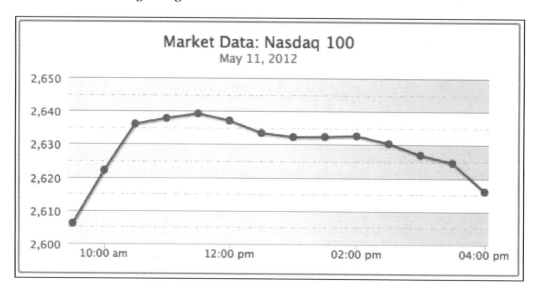

The next step is to apply a more professional look onto the y-axis line. We are going to draw a line on the y axis with the lineWidth property and add some measurement marks along the interval lines with the following code snippet:

```
lineWidth: 2,
lineColor: '#92A8CD',
tickWidth: 3,
tickLength: 6,
tickColor: '#92A8CD',
minorTickLength: 3,
minorTickWidth: 1,
minorTickColor: '#D8D8D8'
```

`tickWidth` and `tickLength` add the effect of little marks at the start of each interval line. We apply the same color on both the interval mark and the axis line. Then add ticks—`minorTickLength` and `minorTickWidth`—into the semi-interval lines with a smaller size. This gives a nice measurement mark effect along the axis, as shown in the following screenshot:

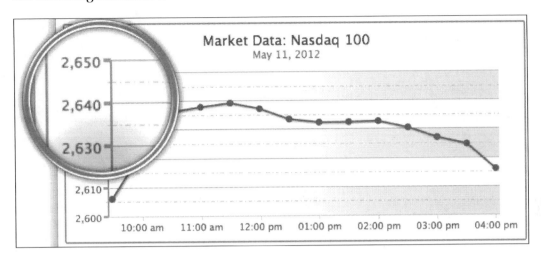

Now we apply a similar polish to the `xAxis` configuration, as follows:

```
xAxis: {
    type: 'datetime',
    labels: {
        formatter: function() {
            return Highcharts.dateFormat('%I:%M %P', this.
value);
        },
    },
    gridLineDashStyle: 'dot',
    gridLineWidth: 1,
    tickInterval: 60 * 60 * 1000,
    lineWidth: 2,
    lineColor: '#92A8CD',
    tickWidth: 3,
    tickLength: 6,
    tickColor: '#92A8CD',
},
```

We set the x-axis interval lines into the hourly format and switch the line style to a dotted line. Then we apply the same color, thickness, and interval ticks as in the y axis. The following is the screenshot:

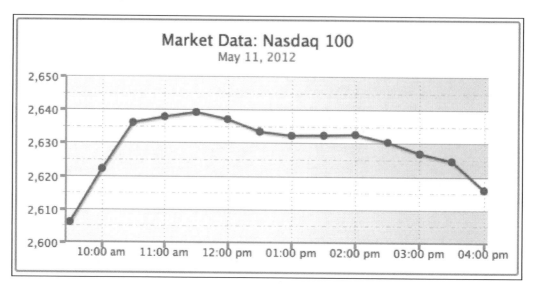

However, there are some defects along the x-axis line. To begin with, the meeting point between the x-axis and y-axis lines does not align properly. Secondly, the interval labels at the x axis are touching the interval ticks. Finally, part of the first data point is covered by the y-axis line. The following is an enlarged screenshot showing the issues:

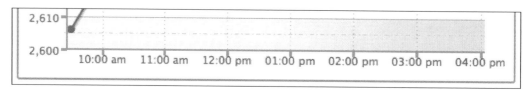

There are two ways to resolve the axis lines' alignment problem, as follows:

- Shift the plot area 1 pixel away from the x axis. This can be achieved by setting the offset property of xAxis to 1.
- Increase the x-axis line width to 3 pixels, which is the same width as the y-axis tick interval.

As for the x-axis label, we can simply solve the problem by introducing the y offset value inside the labels setting.

Finally, to avoid the first data point touching the y-axis line, we can impose `minPadding` on the x axis. What this does is to add padding space at the minimum value of the axis, that is, the first point. The `minPadding` value is based on the ratio of the graph width. In this case, setting the property to 0.02 is equivalent to shifting along the x axis 5 pixels to the right (250px * 0.02). The following are the additional settings to smooth the chart:

```
xAxis: {
    ....
    labels: {
            formatter: ...,
            y: 17
    },
    .....
    minPadding: 0.02,
    offset: 1
}
```

The following screenshot shows that the issues have been addressed:

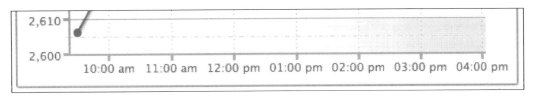

As we can see, Highcharts has a comprehensive set of configurable variables with such flexibility.

Using plot lines and plot bands

In this section, we are going to see how we can use Highcharts to place any lines or bands along the axis. We will continue with the example from the previous section. Let's draw a couple of lines to indicate the day's highest and lowest index points on the y axis. The `plotLines` field accepts an array of object configurations for each plot line. There are no width and color default values for `plotLines`, so we need to specify them explicitly in order to see the line. The following is the code snippet for the plot lines:

```
yAxis: {
        ... ,
        plotLines: [{
            value: 2606.01,
            width: 2,
            color: '#821740',
```

```
                    label: {
                        text: 'Lowest: 2606.01',
                        style: {
                            color: '#898989'
                        }
                    }
                }
            }, {
                value: 2639.15,
                width: 2,
                color: '#4A9338',
                label: {
                    text: 'Highest: 2639.15',
                    style: {
                        color: '#898989'
                    }
                }
            }]
        }
```

The following screenshot shows what it should look like:

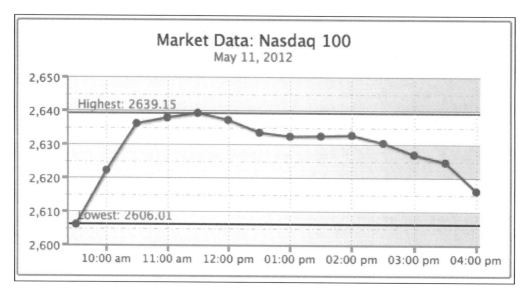

We can improve the look of the chart slightly. Firstly, the text label for the top plot line should be next to the highest point, and secondly the label for the bottom line should not be remotely covered by the series and interval lines, as follows:

To resolve these issues, we can assign the plot line's `zIndex` to `1`, which brings the text label above the interval lines. We also set the `x` position of the label to shift the texts next to the point. The following are the new changes:

```
plotLines: [{
    ... ,
    label: {
        ... ,
        x: 25
    },
    zIndex: 1
}, {
    ... ,
    label: {
        ... ,
        x: 130
    },
    zIndex: 1
}]
```

The following graph shows the label has been moved away from the plot line and over the interval line:

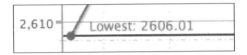

Now we are going to change the preceding example with a plot band area that shows the index change between the market opening and closing. The plot band configuration is very similar to plot lines, except that it uses the `to` and `from` properties and also the `color` property accepts gradient settings or color code. We create a plot band with a triangle text symbol and values to signify a positive close. Instead of using the `x` and `y` properties to fine-tune the label position, we use the `align` option to adjust the text to the center of the plot area:

```
plotBands: [{
    from: 2606.01,
    to: 2615.98,
    label: {
        text: '▲ 9.97 (0.38%)',
        align: 'center',
        style: {
            color: '#007A3D'
        }
    },
```

```
            zIndex: 1,
            color: {
                linearGradient: {
                    x1: 0, y1: 1,
                    x2: 1, y2: 1
                },
                stops: [ [0, '#EBFAEB' ],
                         [0.5, '#C2F0C2'] ,
                         [0.8, '#ADEBAD'] ,
                         [1, '#99E699']
                ]
            }
        }
    }]
```

 The triangle is an alt-code character; hold down the left *Alt* key and enter 30 in the number keypad. See http://www.alt-codes. net for more details.

This produces a chart with a green plot band highlighting a positive close in the market, as shown in the following screenshot:

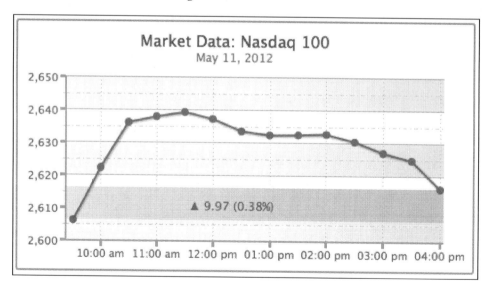

Extending to multiple axes

Previously, we have run through most of the axis configurations. Here, we explore how we can use multiple axes, which is just an array of objects containing axis configurations.

Continuing from the previous stock market example, suppose now we want to include
another market index, Dow Jones, along with Nasdaq. However, both indices are
different in nature, hence their value ranges are vastly different. First let us examine
the outcome by displaying both indices with the common y axis. We change the title,
remove the fixed interval setting on the y axis, and include another series data:

```
chart: ... ,
title: {
    text: 'Market Data: Nasdaq & Dow Jones'
},
subtitle: ... ,
xAxis: ... ,
credits: ... ,
yAxis: {
    title: {
        text: null
    },
    minorGridLineColor: '#D8D8D8',
    minorGridLineDashStyle: 'dashdot',
    gridLineColor: '#8AB8E6',
    alternateGridColor: {
        linearGradient: {
            x1: 0, y1: 1,
            x2: 1, y2: 1
        },
        stops: [ [0, '#FAFCFF' ],
                 [0.5, '#F5FAFF'] ,
                 [0.8, '#E0F0FF'] ,
                 [1, '#D6EBFF'] ]
    },
    lineWidth: 2,
    lineColor: '#92A8CD',
    tickWidth: 3,
    tickLength: 6,
    tickColor: '#92A8CD',
    minorTickLength: 3,
    minorTickWidth: 1,
    minorTickColor: '#D8D8D8',
},
series: [{
  name: 'Nasdaq',
  data: [ [ Date.UTC(2012, 4, 11, 9, 30), 2606.01 ],
          [ Date.UTC(2012, 4, 11, 10), 2622.08 ],
          [ Date.UTC(2012, 4, 11, 10, 30), 2636.03 ],
              ...
          ]
}, {
```

```
      name: 'Dow Jones',
      data: [ [ Date.UTC(2012, 4, 11, 9, 30), 12598.32 ],
                [ Date.UTC(2012, 4, 11, 10), 12538.61 ],
                [ Date.UTC(2012, 4, 11, 10, 30), 12549.89 ],
                ...
              ]
    }]
```

The following is the chart showing both market indices:

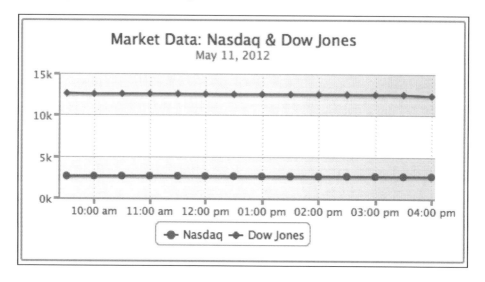

As expected, the index changes during the day have been normalized by the vast differences. Both lines look roughly straight, which falsely implies that the indices have hardly changed.

Let us now explore putting both indices onto separate y axes. We should remove any background decoration on the y axis, because we now have a different range of data shares on the same background.

The following is the new setup for yAxis:

```
yAxis: [{
    title: {
        text: 'Nasdaq'
    },
}, {
    title: {
        text: 'Dow Jones'
    },
    opposite: true
}],
```

Now `yAxis` is an array of axis configurations. The first entry in the array is for Nasdaq and the second one is for Dow Jones. This time we display the axis title to distinguish between both. The `opposite` property is to put the Dow Jones y axis onto the other side of the graph for clarity. Otherwise, both y axes appear on the left-hand side.

The next step is to align indices from the y-axis array to the series data array, as follows:

```
series: [{
    name: 'Nasdaq',
    yAxis: 0,
    data: [ ... ]
}, {
    name: 'Dow Jones',
    yAxis: 1,
    data: [ ... ]
}]
```

We can clearly see the indices' movement in the new graph, as follows:

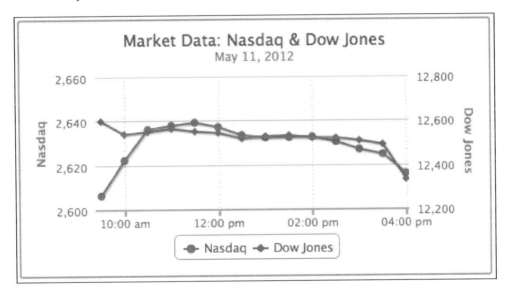

Moreover, we can improve the final view by color matching the series to the axis lines. The `Highcharts.colors` property contains a list of default colors for the series, so we use the first two entries for our indices. Another improvement is to set `maxPadding` for the x axis, because the new y-axis line covers parts of the data points at the high end of the x axis:

```
xAxis: {
    ... ,
    minPadding: 0.02,
```

```
        maxPadding: 0.02
    },
yAxis: [{
    title: {
        text: 'Nasdaq'
    },
    lineWidth: 2,
    lineColor: '#4572A7',
    tickWidth: 3,
    tickLength: 6,
    tickColor: '#4572A7'
}, {
    title: {
        text: 'Dow Jones'
    },
    opposite: true,
    lineWidth: 2,
    lineColor: '#AA4643',
    tickWidth: 3,
    tickLength: 6,
    tickColor: '#AA4643'
}],
```

The following screenshot shows the improved look of the chart:

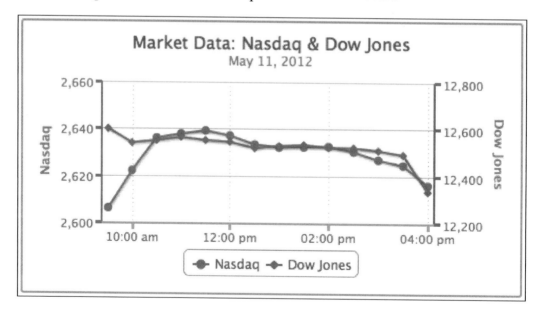

We can extend the preceding example and have more than a couple of axes, simply by adding entries into the yAxis and series arrays and mapping both together. The following screenshot shows a four-axes line graph:

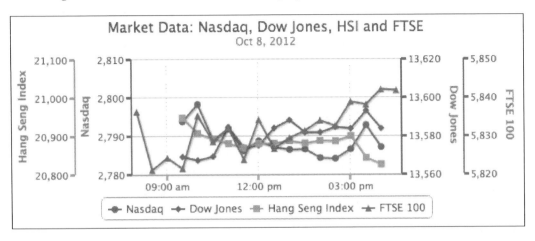

Revisiting the series configuration

By now, we should have an idea of what series properties do. In this section we are going to examine it in more detail.

The series property is an array of series configuration objects that contain data- and series-specific options. It allows us to specify single series data and multiple series data. The purpose of series objects is to inform Highcharts of the format of the data and how the data is presented in the chart.

All the data values in the chart are specified through the data field. The data field is highly flexible, and it can take an array in a number of forms, as follows:

- Numerical values
- An array with x and y values
- Point object with properties describing the data point

The first two options have already been examined in the *Accessing axis data type* section. In this section we will explore the third option. Let's use the single series Nasdaq example and we will specify the series data through a mixture of numerical values and objects:

```
series: [{
    name: 'Nasdaq',
    pointStart: Date.UTC(2012, 4, 11, 9, 30),
    pointInterval: 30 * 60 * 1000,
    data: [{
        // First data point
        y: 2606.01,
        marker: {
            symbol: 'url(./sun.png)'
            }
        }, 2622.08, 2636.03, 2637.78,
    {
        // Highest data point
        y: 2639.15,
        dataLabels: {
            enabled: true
        },
        marker: {
            fillColor: '#33CC33',
            radius: 5
        }
    }, 2637.09, 2633.38, 2632.23, 2632.33,
        2632.59, 2630.34, 2626.89, 2624.59,
    {
        // Last data point
        y: 2615.98,
        marker: {
            symbol: 'url(./moon.png)'
            }
        }]
    }]
```

The first and the last data points are objects that have y-axis values and image files to indicate the opening and closing of the market. The highest data point is configured with a different color and data label. The size of the data point is also set slightly larger than default. The rest of the data arrays are just numerical values, as shown in the following screenshot:

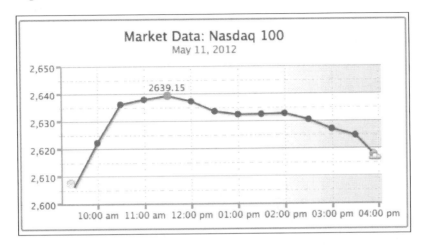

There is currently a minor defect in aligning a single data point with an image. However, it helps in perfecting with assigning image properties to the whole series (http://github.com/highslide-software/highcharts.com/issues/969).

Exploring PlotOptions

plotOptions is a wrapper object for config objects for each series type, which are area, areaspline, bar, column, pie, scatter, spline gauge, and range. These configurations have properties such as plotOptions.line.lineWidth, common to other series types, as well as other configurations such as plotOptions.pie. center, which is only specific to the pie series type. Among the specific series, there is plotOptions.series, which is used for common plotting options shared by the whole series.

The preceding plotOptions can form a chain of precedence between plotOptions. series, plotOptions.{series-type}, and the series configuration. For example, series[x].shadow (where series[x].type is 'pie') has a higher precedence than plotOptions.pie.shadow, which in turn has a higher precedence than plotOptions.series.shadow.

The purpose of this is the chart composed of multiple different series types. For example, a chart with multiple series of columns and a single line series, so the common properties between column and line can be defined in `plotOptions.series.*`, whereas `plotOptions.column` and `plotOptions.line` hold their own specific property values. Moreover, properties in `plotOptions.{series-type}.*` can be further overridden by the same series type specified in the series array.

The following is a reference for the configurations in precedence. The higher-level ones have lower precedence, which means configurations defined in a lower chain can override the defined properties in the higher level of the chain. For the series array, preference is valid if `series[x].type` or the default series type value is the same as the series type in `plotOptions`.

```
chart.defaultSeriesType or chart.type
    series[x].type

plotOptions.series.{seriesProperty}
    plotOptions.{series-type}.{seriesProperty}
        series[x].{seriesProperty}

plotOptions.points.events.*
        series[x].data[y].events.*

plotOptions.series.marker.*
        series[x].data[y].marker.*
```

`plotOptions` contains properties controlling how a series type is presented in the chart; for example, inverted charts, series colors, stacked column charts, user interactions to the series, and so on. All these options will be covered in detail when we study each type of chart. Meanwhile, we will explore the concept of `plotOptions` with a monthly Nasdaq graph. The graph has five different series data — open, close, high, low, and volume. Normally, this data is used for plotting daily stock charts (OHLCV). We compact them into a single chart for the purpose of demonstrating `plotOptions`.

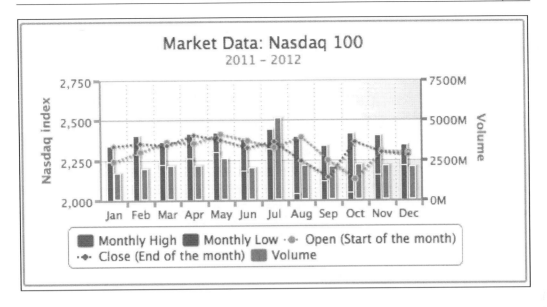

The following is the chart configuration code for generating the preceding graph:

```
chart: {
    renderTo: 'container',
    height: 250,
    spacingRight: 30
},
title: {
    text: 'Market Data: Nasdaq 100'
},
subtitle: {
    text: '2011 - 2012'
},
xAxis: {
    categories: [ 'Jan', 'Feb', 'Mar', 'Apr',
                  'May', 'Jun', 'Jul', 'Aug',
                  'Sep', 'Oct', 'Nov', 'Dec' ],
    labels: {
        y: 17
    },
    gridLineDashStyle: 'dot',
    gridLineWidth: 1,
    lineWidth: 2,
    lineColor: '#92A8CD',
    tickWidth: 3,
    tickLength: 6,
    tickColor: '#92A8CD',
```

```
        minPadding: 0.04,
        offset: 1
    },
    yAxis: [{
        title: {
            text: 'Nasdaq index'
        },
        min: 2000,
        minorGridLineColor: '#D8D8D8',
        minorGridLineDashStyle: 'dashdot',
        gridLineColor: '#8AB8E6',
        alternateGridColor: {
            linearGradient: {
                x1: 0, y1: 1,
                x2: 1, y2: 1
            },
            stops: [ [0, '#FAFCFF' ],

                     [0.5, '#F5FAFF'] ,
                     [0.8, '#E0F0FF'] ,
                     [1, '#D6EBFF'] ]
        },
        lineWidth: 2,
        lineColor: '#92A8CD',
        tickWidth: 3,
        tickLength: 6,
        tickColor: '#92A8CD'
    }, {
        title: {
            text: 'Volume'
        },
        lineWidth: 2,
        lineColor: '#3D96AE',
        tickWidth: 3,
        tickLength: 6,
        tickColor: '#3D96AE',
        opposite: true
    }],
    credits: {
        enabled: false
    },
    plotOptions: {
        column: {
            stacking: 'normal'
        },
        line: {
            zIndex: 2,
```

```
                    marker: {
                        radius: 3,
                        lineColor: '#D9D9D9',
                        lineWidth: 1
                    },
                    dashStyle: 'ShortDot'
                }
            },
            series: [{
                name: 'Monthly High',
                // Use stacking column chart - values on
                // top of monthly low to simulate monthly
                // high
                data: [ 98.31, 118.08, 142.55, 160.68, ... ],
                type: 'column'
            }, {
                name: 'Monthly Low',
                data: [ 2237.73, 2285.44, 2217.43, ... ],
                type: 'column'
            }, {
                name: 'Open (Start of the month)',
                data: [ 2238.66, 2298.37, 2359.78, ... ]
            }, {
                name: 'Close (End of the month)',
                data: [ 2336.04, 2350.99, 2338.99, ... ]
            }, {
                name: 'Volume',
                data: [ 1630203800, 1944674700, 2121923300, ... ],
                yAxis: 1,
                type: 'column',
                stacking: null
            }]
        }
```

Although the graph looks slightly complicated, we will go through the code step-by-step to make it clearer. First, there are two entries in the yAxis array: the first one is for the Nasdaq index, the second y axis, displayed on the right-hand side (opposite: true), is for the volume trade. In the series array, the first and second series are specified as column series types (type: 'column'), which override the default series type 'line'. Then the stacking option is defined as 'normal' in plotOptions.column, which stacks the monthly high on top of the monthly low column (blue and red columns). Strictly speaking, the stacked column chart is used for displaying the ratio of data belonging to the same category. For the sake of demonstrating plotOptions, we use the stacked column chart to show the upper and lower end of monthly trade. To do that, we take the difference between monthly high and monthly low and substitute the differences back into the monthly high series. Hence, in the code, we can see that the data values in the monthly high series are much smaller than the monthly low.

The third and fourth series are the market open and market close index; both take the default line series type and inherit options defined from `plotOptions.line`. The `zIndex` option is assigned to 2 for overlaying both line series on top of the fifth volume series, otherwise both lines are covered by the volume columns. The `marker` object configurations are to reduce the default data point size, as the whole graph is already compacted with columns and lines.

The last column series is the volume trade, and the `stacking` option in the series is manually set to `null`, which overrides the inherited option from `plotOptions.column`. This resets the series back to the non-stacking option, that is, displaying as a separate column. Finally, the `yAxis` index option is set to align with the y axis of the **Volume** series (`yAxis: 1`).

Styling the tooltips

Tooltips in Highcharts are enabled by the boolean option `tooltip.enabled`, which is `true` by default. Their content formats are flexible, which can be defined via a callback handler or in HTML style. We will continue from the example in the previous section. As the chart is packed with multiple lines and columns, first we can enable the crosshair tooltip for helping us align the data points onto the axes. The `crosshairs` configuration can take either a Boolean value to activate the feature or an object style for the crosshair line style. The following is the code snippet to set up crosshairs with an array of x- and y-axis configurations for the gray color and dash line styles.

```
tooltip : {
    crosshairs: [{
        color: '#5D5D5D',
        dashStyle: 'dash',
        width: 2
    }, {
        color: '#5D5D5D',
        dashStyle: 'dash',
        width: 2
    }]
},
```

 Again, the `dashStyle` option uses the same common line style values in Highcharts. See the crosshairs reference manual for all the possible values.

The following screenshot shows the cursor hovering over a data point of the market close series. We can see a tooltip box appearing next to the pointer and gray crosshairs for both axes:

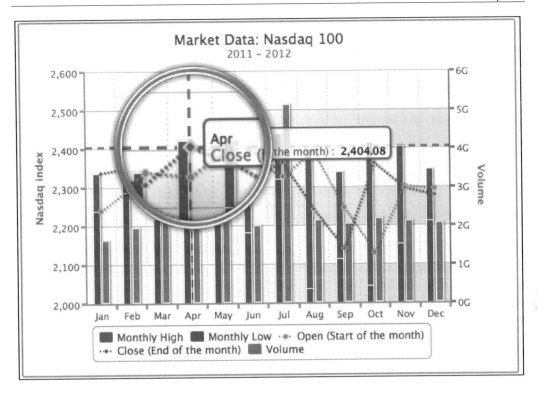

Formatting the tooltips in HTML

Highcharts provides template options such as `headerFormat`, `pointFormat`, and `footerFormat` to construct the tooltip by specific template variables (or macros). These specific variables are series and point, and we can use their properties, such as `point.x`, `point.y`, `series.name`, and `series.color`, within the template. For instance, the default tooltip setting uses `pointFormat`, which has the default value of the following code snippet:

```
<span style="color:{series.color}">{series.name}</span>:
<b>{point.y}</b><br/>
```

Highcharts internally translates the preceding expression into SVG text markups, hence only a subset of HTML syntax can be supported, which is `<b>`, `<br>`, `<strong>`, `<em>`, `<i>`, `<span>`, `<href>`, and font style attributes in CSS. However, if we want to have more flexibility in polishing the content and the capability to include image files, we need to use the `useHTML` option for a full HTML tooltip. This option allows us to do the following:

- Use other HTML tags such as `<img>` inside the tooltip
- Create a tooltip in real HTML content, so that it is outside the SVG markups

Here, we are going to format an HTML table inside a tooltip. We will use `headerFormat` to create a header column for the category and a bottom border to separate between header and data. Then we will use `pointFormat` to set up an icon image along with the series name and data. The image file is based on the `series.index` macro, so different series have different image icons. We use the `series.color` macro to highlight the series name with the same color in the chart and apply the `series.data` macro for the series value.

```
tooltip : {
    useHTML: true,
    headerFormat: '<table><thead><tr>' +
        '<th style="border-bottom: 2px solid #6678b1; color:
#039" ' +
            'colspan=2 >{point.key}</th></tr></thead><tbody>',
        pointFormat: '<tr><td style="color: {series.color}">' +
            '<img src="./series_{series.index}.png" ' +
            'style="vertical-align:text-bottom; margin-right: 5px" >'
+
            '{series.name}: </td><td style="text-align: right; color:
#669;">' +
            '<b>{point.y}</b></td></tr>',
        footerFormat: '</tbody></table>'
},
```

So when we hover over a data point, the template variable `point` is substituted internally by the hovered point object, and the series is replaced by the `series` object containing the data point.

The following is the screenshot of the new tooltip. The icon next to the series name indicates market close:

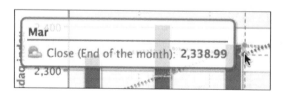

Using the callback handler

Alternatively, we can implement the tooltip through the callback handler in JavaScript. The tooltip handler is declared through the `formatter` option. The major difference between template options and handler is that we can disable the tooltip display for certain points by setting conditions and return `false`, whereas for template options we cannot. In the callback example, we use the `this.series` and `this.point` variables for the series name and values for the data point that is hovered over.

The following is an example of the handler:

```
formatter: function() {
        return '<span style="color:#039;font-weight:bold">' +
            this.point.category +
            '</span><br/><span style="color:' +
            this.series.color + '">' + this.series.name +
            '</span>: <span style="color:#669;font-weight:bold">'
 + this.point.y + '</span>';
    }
```

The preceding handler code returns an SVG text tooltip with the series name, category, and value, as shown in the following screenshot:

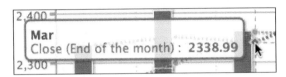

Applying a multiple series tooltip

Another flexible tooltip feature is to allow all the series data to be displayed inside the same tooltip. This simplifies user interaction to look up for multiple series data in one action. To enable this feature, we need to set the `shared` option to `true`.

We will continue with the previous example for the multiple series tooltip. The following is the new tooltip code:

```
shared: true,
useHTML: true,
headerFormat: '<table><thead><tr><th colspan=2 >' +
              '{point.key}</th></tr></thead><tbody>',
pointFormat:    '<tr><td style="color: {series.color}">' +
              '{series.name}: </td>' +
              '<td style="text-align: right; color: #669;"> '
 + '<b>{point.y}</b></td></tr>',
footerFormat: '</tbody></table>'
```

The preceding code snippet will produce the following screenshot:

Mar	
Monthly High:	142.55
Monthly Low:	2,217.43
Open (Start of the month):	2,359.78
Close (End of the month):	2,338.99
Volume:	2,121,923,300

As previously discussed, we will use the monthly high and monthly low series to plot stacked columns, which is actually used for plotting data within the same category. Therefore, the tooltip for the monthly high series is showing the subtracted values that we previously put in. To correct this within the tooltip, we can use the handler to apply different properties for the monthly high series, as follows:

```
shared: true,

formatter: function() {
    return '<span style="color:#039;font-weight:bold">' +
        this.x + '</span><br/>' +
        this.points.map(function(point, idx) {
            return '<span style="color:' + point.series.color +
                '">' + point.series.name +
                '</span>: <span style="color:#669;font-
weight:bold">' +
                    Highcharts.numberFormat((idx == 0) ? point.total
: point.y) + '</span>';
            }).join('<br/>');
        }
```

`point.total` is the total of the difference and the monthly low series value. The following screenshot shows the new corrected **Monthly High** value:

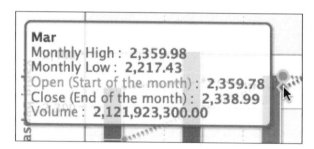

Animating charts

There are two types of animations in Highcharts—initial and update animations. Initial animation is the animation when series data is ready and the chart is displayed; update animation is after the initial animation and when the series data or any parts of the chart anatomy have been changed.

The initial animation configurations can be specified through `plotOptions.series.animation` or `plotOptions.{series-type}.animation`, whereas the update animation is configured via the `chart.animation` property.

All the Highcharts animations use jQuery implementation. The `animation` property can be a boolean value or a set of animation options. Highcharts uses jQuery swing animation. The following are the options:

- `duration`: The time, in milliseconds, to complete the animation.

- `easing`: The type of animation jQuery provided. The variety of animations can be extended by importing the jQuery UI plugin. A good source of reference can be found at `http://plugindetector.com/demo/easing-jquery-ui/`.

Here, we continue the example from the previous section. We will apply the animation settings into `plotOptions.column` and `plotOptions.line`, as follows:

```
plotOptions: {
    column: {
        ... ,
        animation: {
            duration: 2000,
            easing: 'swing'
        }
    },
    line: {
        .... ,
        animation: {
            duration: 3000,
            easing: 'linear'
        }
    }
},
```

The animations are tuned into at a much slower pace, so we can notice the difference between linear and swing animations. The line series appears in a linear speed along the x axis, whereas the column series expands upwards in a linear speed and then decelerates sharply when approaching the end of the display. The following is a screenshot showing an ongoing linear animation:

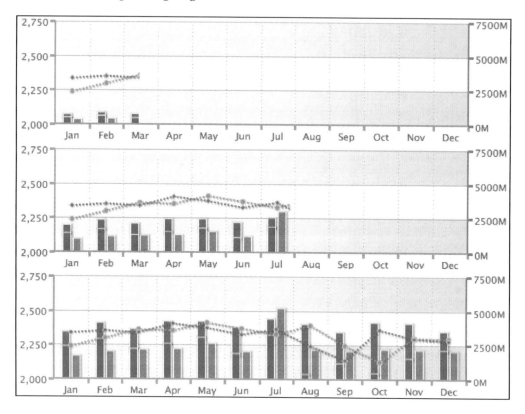

Expanding colors with gradients

Highcharts not only supports single color values, but also allows complex color gradient definitions. Highcharts supports linear gradient, which is a directional color shading as well as radial (or circular) gradient. In this section, we will experiment with linear gradient, and the radial gradient will be explored in *Chapter 6, Gauge, Polar, and Range Charts*. In Highcharts, the color gradient is based on the SVG linear color gradient standard, which is composed of two sets of information, as follows:

- `linearGradient`: This gives a gradient direction for the color spectrum made up of two sets of x and y coordinates; ratio values are between 0 and 1, or in percentages

- `stops`: This gives a sequence of colors to be filled in the spectrum and their ratio positions within the gradient direction

We use the previous stock market example with only the **Volume** series, and redefine `yAxis.alternateGridColor` as follows:

```
yAxis: [{
    title: { text: 'Nasdaq index' },
    ....
    alternateGridColor: {
        linearGradient: [ 10, 250, 400, 250 ],
            stops: [
                [ 0, 'red' ],
                [ 0.2, 'orange' ],
                [ 0.5, 'yellow' ] ,
                [ 0.8, 'green' ] ,
                [ 1, 'lime' ] ]
    }
```

`linearGradient` is an array of coordinate values that are arranged in the x1, y1, x2, and y2 order. The values can be absolute coordinates, percentage strings, or ratio values between 0 and 1. The difference is that colors defined in coordinate values can be affected by the chart size, whereas percentage and ratio values can avoid that.

> The array syntax for absolute position gradients is deprecated because it doesn't work similarly between SVG and VML, and also it doesn't scale well with varying sizes of the charts.

The `stops` property has an array of tuples; the first value is the offset ranging from 0 to 1 and the second value is the color definition. The offset and color values define where the color is positioned within the spectrum. For example, `[0, 'red' ]` and `[0.2, 'orange' ]` mean starting with the red color at the beginning and gradually changing the color to orange in the horizontal direction towards the position at x = 80 (0.2 * 400), and then changing from the orange color at x = 80 to the yellow color at x = 200, and so on. The following is a screenshot of the multicolor gradient:

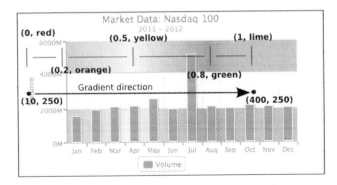

As we can see, the red and orange colors are not appearing in the chart because the gradient is based on coordinates. Hence, depending on the size of the chart, the position of the x axis exceeds the red and orange coordinates in this example. Alternatively, we can specify `linearGradient` in terms of percentage, as follows:

```
linearGradient: [ '20%', 250, '90%', 250 ]
```

This means `linearGradient` stretches from 20% of the width of the chart to 90%, so that the color bands are not limited to the size of the chart. The following screenshot shows the effect of the new `linearGradient` setting:

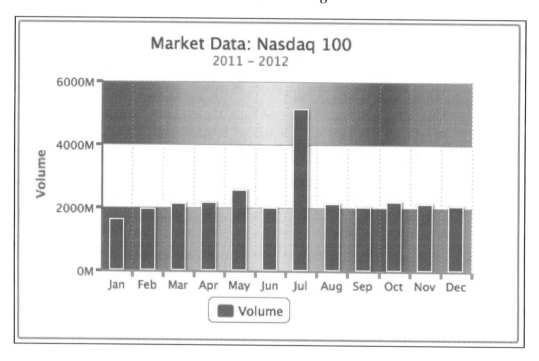

The chart background now has the complete color spectrum. As for specifying ratio values between 0 and 1, `linearGradient` must be defined in an object style, otherwise the values will be treated as coordinates. Note that the ratio values are referred to as the fraction over the plot area only, and not the whole chart.

```
linearGradient: { x1: 0, y1: 0, x2: 1, y2: 0 }
```

The preceding line of code is an alternative way for setting the horizontal gradient.

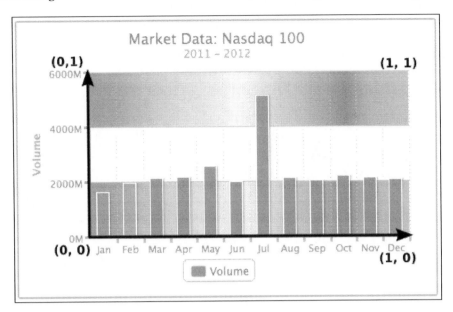

The following line of code adjusts the vertical gradient:

```
linearGradient: { x1: 0, y1: 0, x2: 0, y2: 1 }
```

This produces a gradient background in the vertical direction. We also set the `'Jan'` and `'Jul'` data points individually as point objects with linear shading in the vertical direction.

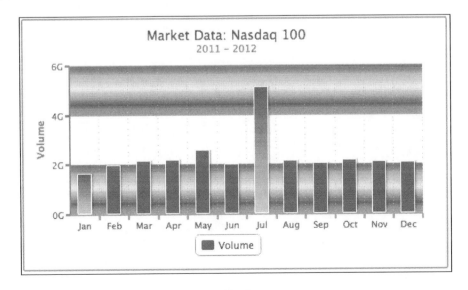

Moreover, we can manipulate Highcharts' standard colors to trigger the color gradient on the series plot. This approach is taken from a post in a Highcharts forum experimenting on a 3D charts look. Before plotting a chart, we need to overwrite the default series color with a gradient color. The following code snippet replaces the first series color with horizontal blue gradient shading. Note that the ratio gradient values in this example are referring to the width of the series column:

```
$(document).ready(function() {

    Highcharts.getOptions().colors[0] = {
            linearGradient: { x1: 0, y1: 0, x2: 1, y2: 0 },
            stops: [ [ 0, '#4572A7' ],
                     [ 0.7, '#CCFFFF' ],
                     [ 1, '#4572A7' ] ]
    };

    var chart = new Highcharts.Chart({   ...
```

The following is the screenshot of a column chart with color shading:

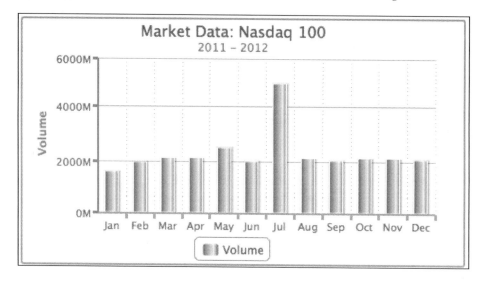

Summary

In this chapter, major configuration components were discussed and experimented with examples shown. By now, we should be comfortable and ready to plot some of the basic graphs with more elaborate styles. In the next chapter, we will explore line, area, and scatter graphs supported by Highcharts. We will apply configurations that we have learned in this chapter and explore the series-specific style options to plot charts in an artistic style.

3
Line, Area, and Scatter Charts

In this chapter, we will learn about line, area, and scatter charts and explore their plotting options in more details. We will also learn how to create stacked chart and projection charts. Then, we will attempt to plot the charts in a slightly more artistic style. The reason for that is to provide us with an opportunity to utilize various plotting options. In this chapter we will cover the following:

- Introducing line charts
- Sketching an area chart
- Mixing line and area series
- Combining scatter and area series

Introducing line charts

First let's start with a single series line chart. We will use one of the many data provided by The World Bank organization at www.worldbank.org. The following is the code snippet to create a simple line chart which shows the percentage of population ages, 65 and above, in Japan for the past three decades:

```
var chart = new Highcharts.Chart({
    chart: {
        renderTo: 'container'
    },
    title: {
        text: 'Population ages 65 and over (% of total)',
    },
    credits: {
        position: {
```

```
            align: 'left',
            x: 20
        },
        text: 'Data from The World Bank'
    },
    yAxis: {
        title: {
            text: 'Percentage %'
        }
    },
    xAxis: {
        categories: ['1980', '1981',
        '1982', ... ],
        labels: {
            step: 5
        }
    },
    series: [{
        name: 'Japan - 65 and over',
        data: [  9, 9, 9, 10, 10, 10, 10 ... ]
    }]
});
```

The following is the display of the simple chart:

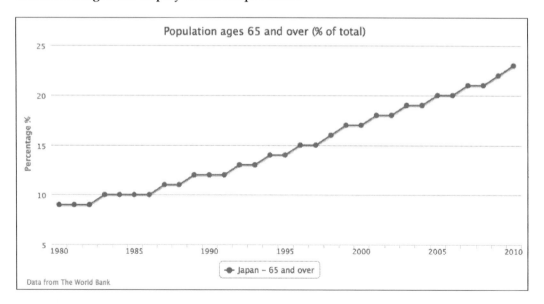

Instead of specifying the year number manually as strings in categories, we can use the `pointStart` option in the `series` config to initiate the x-axis value for the first point. So we have an empty xAxis config and `series` config, as follows:

```
xAxis: {
},
series: [{
    pointStart: 1980,
    name: 'Japan - 65 and over',
    data: [  9, 9, 9, 10, 10, 10, 10 ... ]
}]
```

Although this simplifies the example, the x-axis labels are automatically formatted by Highcharts utility method, `numberFormat`, which adds a comma after every three digits. The following is the outcome on the x axis:

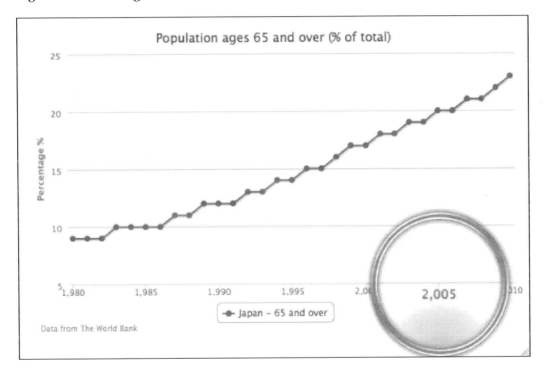

To resolve the x-axis label, we overwrite the label's `formatter` option by simply returning the value to bypass the `numberFormat` method being called. Also we need to set the `allowDecimals` option to `false`. The reason for that is when the chart is resized to elongate the x axis, decimal values are shown. The following is the final change to use `pointStart` for the year values:

```
xAxis: {
    labels:{
        formatter: function() {
            // 'this' keyword is the label object
            return this.value;
        }
    },
    allowDecimals: false
},
series: [{
    pointStart: 1980,
    name: 'Japan - 65 and over',
    data: [  9, 9, 9, 10, 10, 10, 10 ... ]
}]
```

Extending to multiple series line charts

We can include several more line series and set the Japan series by increasing the line width to be 6 pixels wide, as follows:

```
series: [{
    lineWidth: 6,
    name: 'Japan',
    data: [  9, 9, 9, 10, 10, 10, 10 ... ]
}, {
    Name: 'Singapore',
    data: [ 5, 5, 5, 5, ... ]
}, {
    ...
}]
```

The line series for Japanese population becomes the focus in the chart, as shown in the following screenshot:

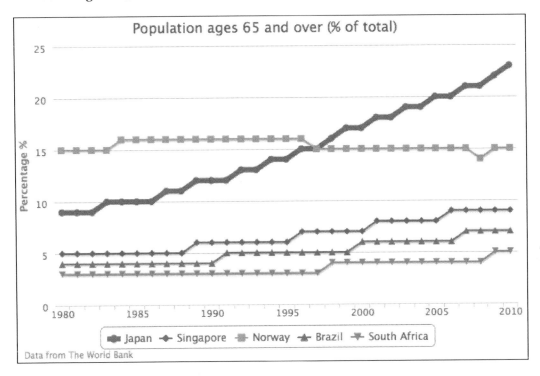

Let's move on to a more complicated line graph. For the sake of demonstrating inverted line graphs, we use the `chart.inverted` option to flip the y and x axes to opposite orientations. Then we change the line colors of the axes to match the same series colors as we did in previous chapter. We also disable data point markers for all the series and finally align the second series to the second entry in the y-axis array, as follows:

```
chart: {
    renderTo: 'container',
    inverted: true,
},
yAxis: [{
    title: {
        text: 'Percentage %'
    },
    lineWidth: 2,
    lineColor: '#4572A7'
}, {
```

```
            title: {
                text: 'Age'
            },
            opposite: true,
            lineWidth: 2,
            lineColor: '#AA4643'
        }],
        plotOptions: {
            series: {
                marker: {
                    enabled: false
                }
            }
        },
        series: [{
            name: 'Japan - 65 and over',
            type: 'spline',
            data: [ 9, 9, 9, ... ]
        }, {
            name: 'Japan - Life Expectancy',
            yAxis: 1,
            data: [ 76, 76, 77, ... ]
        }]
```

The following is the inverted graph with double y axes:

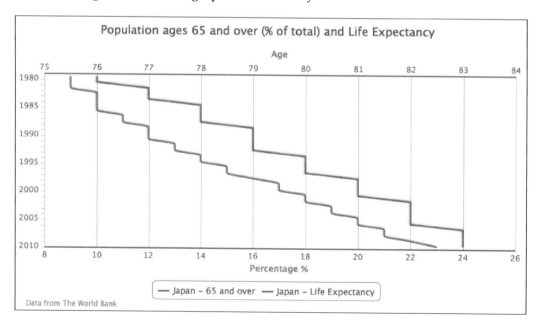

The data representation of the chart may look slightly odd as the usual time labels are swapped to the y axis and the data trend is awkward to comprehend. The `inverted` option is normally used for showing data in a noncontinuous form and in bar format. If we interpret the data from the graph, 12 percent of the population is 65 and over, and the life expectancy is 79 in 1990.

By setting `plotOptions.series.marker.enabled` to `false` it switches off all the data point markers. If we want to display a point marker for a particular series, we can either switch off the marker globally and then set the marker on an individual series, or the other way round.

```
plotOptions: {
    series: {
        marker: {
            enabled: false
        }
    }
},
series: [{
    marker: {
        enabled: true
    },
    name: 'Japan - 65 and over',
    type: 'spline',
    data: [ 9, 9, 9, ... ]
}, {
```

The following graph demonstrates that only the **65 and over** series has point markers:

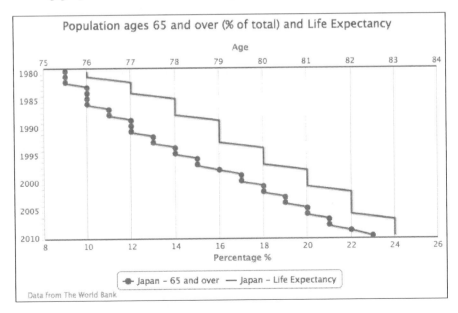

Sketching an area chart

In this section, we are going to use our very first example and turn it into a more stylish graph (based on the design of wind energy poster by Kristin Clute), which is an area spline chart. An **area spline chart** is generated using the combined properties of area and spline charts. The main data line is plotted as a spline curve and the region underneath the line is filled in a similar color with a gradient and an opaque style.

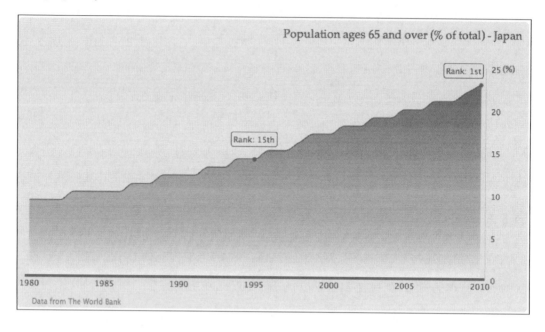

Firstly, we want to make the graph easier for viewers to look up the values for the current trend, so we move the y axis next to the latest year, that is, to the opposite side of the chart:

```
yAxis: {  ....
    opposite:true
}
```

The next thing is to remove the interval lines and have a thin axis line along the y axis:

```
yAxis: { ....
    gridLineWidth: 0,
    lineWidth: 1,
}
```

Then we simplify the y-axis title with a percentage sign and align it to the top of the axis:

```
yAxis: { ....
    title: {
        text: '(%)',
        rotation: 0,
        x: 10,
        y: 5,
        align: 'high'
    },
}
```

As for the x axis, we thicken the axis line with a red color and remove the interval ticks:

```
xAxis: { ....
    lineColor: '#CC2929',
    lineWidth: 4,
    tickWidth: 0,
    offset:    2
}
```

For the chart title, we move the title to the right of the chart, increase the margin between the chart and the title, and then adopt a different font for the title:

```
title: {
    text: 'Population ages 65 and over (% of total) -
Japan ',
    margin: 40,
    align: 'right',
    style: {
        fontFamily: 'palatino'
    }
}
```

After that we are going to modify the whole series presentation, we first set the `chart.type` property from `'line'` to `'areaspline'`. Notice that setting the properties inside this `series` object will overwrite the same properties defined in `plotOptions.areaspline` and so on in `plotOptions.series`.

Since so far there is only one series in the graph, there is no need to display the legend box. We can disable it with the showInLegend property. We then smarten the area part with gradient color and the spline with a darker color:

```
series: [{
    showInLegend: false,
    lineColor: '#145252',
    fillColor: {
        linearGradient: {
            x1: 0, y1: 0,
            x2: 0, y2: 1
        },
        stops:[ [ 0.0, '#248F8F' ] ,
                [ 0.7, '#70DBDB' ],
                [ 1.0, '#EBFAFA' ] ]
    },
    data: [ ... ]
}]
```

After that, we introduce a couple of data labels along the line to indicate that the ranking of old age population has increased over time. We use the values in the series data array corresponding to the year 1995 and 2010, and then convert the numerical value entries into data point objects. Since we only want to show point markers for these two years, we turn off markers globally in plotOptions.series. marker.enabled and set the marker on, individually inside the point objects accompanied with style settings:

```
plotOptions: {
    series: {
        marker: {
            enabled: false
        }
    }
},
series: [{ ...,
    data:[ 9, 9, 9, ...,
            { marker: {
                radius: 2,
                lineColor: '#CC2929',
                lineWidth: 2,
                fillColor: '#CC2929',
                enabled: true
            },
            y: 14
        }, 15, 15, 16, ... ]
}]
```

We then set a bounding box around the data labels with round corners (borderRadius) in the same border color (borderColor) as the x axis. The data label positions are then finely adjusted with the x and y options. Finally, we change the default implementation of the data label formatter. Instead of returning the point value, we print the country ranking.

```
series: [{ ...,
    data:[ 9, 9, 9, ...,
         { marker: {
             ...
         },
         dataLabels: {
             enabled: true,
             borderRadius: 3,
             borderColor: '#CC2929',
             borderWidth: 1,
             y: -23,
             formatter: function() {
                 return "Rank: 15th";
             }
         },
         y: 14
    }, 15, 15, 16, ... ]
}]
```

The final touch is to apply a gray background to the chart and add extra space into spacingBottom. The extra space for spacingBottom is to avoid the credit label and x-axis label getting too close together, because we have disabled the legend box.

```
chart: {
    renderTo: 'container',
    spacingBottom: 30,
    backgroundColor: '#EAEAEA'
},
```

When all these configurations are put together, it produces the exact chart, as shown in the screenshot at the start of this section.

Mixing line and area series

In this section we are going to explore different plots including line and area series together, as follows:

- Projection chart, where a single trend line is joined with two series in different line styles

- Plotting an area spline chart with another step line series

- Exploring a stacked area spline chart, where two area spline series are stacked on top of each other

Simulating a projection chart

The projection chart has spline area with the section of real data and continues in a dashed line with projection data. To do that we separate the data into two series, one for real data and the other for projection data. The following is the series configuration code for the future data up to 2024. This data is based on the National Institute of Population and Social Security Research report (http://www.ipss.go.jp/pp-newest/e/ppfj02/ppfj02.pdf).

```
series: [{
    name: 'project data',
    type: 'spline',
    showInLegend: false,
    lineColor: '#145252',
    dashStyle: 'Dash',
    data: [ [ 2010, 23 ], [ 2011, 22.8 ],
            ... [ 2024, 28.5 ] ]
}]
```

The future series is configured as a spline in a dashed line style and the legend box is disabled, because we want to show both series as being from the same series. Then we set the future (second) series color the same as the first series. The final part is to construct the series data. As we specify the x-axis time data with the pointStart property, we need to align the projection data after 2010. There are two approaches that we can use to specify the time data in a continuous form, as follows:

- Insert null values into the second series data array for padding to align with the real data series

- Specify the second series data in tuples, which is an array with both time and projection data

Next we are going to use the second approach because the series presentation is simpler. The following is the screenshot only for the future data series:

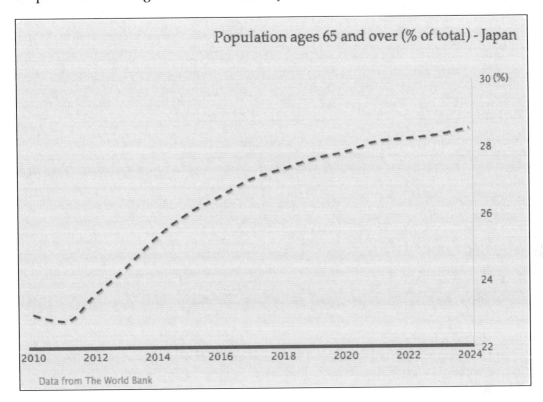

The real data series is exactly the same as the graph in the screenshot at the start of the *Sketching an area chart* section, except without the point markers and data label decorations. The next step is to join both series together, as follows:

```
series: [{
    name: 'real data',
    type: 'areaspline',
    ....
}, {
    name: 'project data',
    type: 'spline',
    ....
}]
```

Since there is no overlap between both series data, they produce a smooth projection graph:

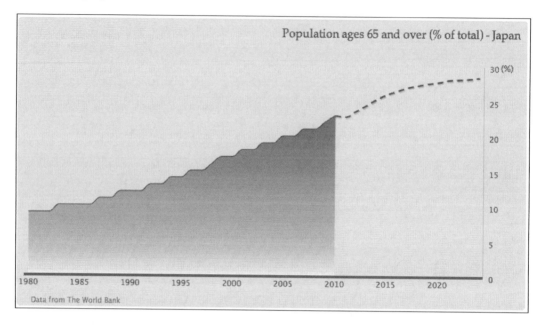

Contrasting spline with step line

In this section we are going to plot an area spline series with another line series but in a step presentation. The step line transverses vertically and horizontally only according to the changes in series data. It is generally used for presenting discrete data, that is, data without continuous/gradual movement.

For the purpose of showing a step line, we will continue from the first area spline example. First of all, we need to enable the legend by removing the disabled showInLegend setting and also remove dataLabels in the series data.

Next is to include a new series, **Ages 0 to 14**, in the chart with a default line type. Then we will change the line style slightly differently into steps. The following is the configuration for both series:

```
series: [{
    name: 'Ages 65 and over',
    type: 'areaspline',
    lineColor: '#145252',
    pointStart: 1980,
    fillColor: {
        ....
    },
```

```
        data: [ 9, 9, 9, 10, ...., 23 ]
}, {
    name: 'Ages 0 to 14',
    // default type is line series
    step: true,
    pointStart: 1980,
    data: [ 24, 23, 23, 23, 22, 22, 21,
            20, 20, 19, 18, 18, 17, 17, 16, 16, 16,
            15, 15, 15, 15, 14, 14, 14, 14, 14, 14,
            14, 14, 13, 13 ]
}]
```

The following screenshot shows the second series in the stepped line style:

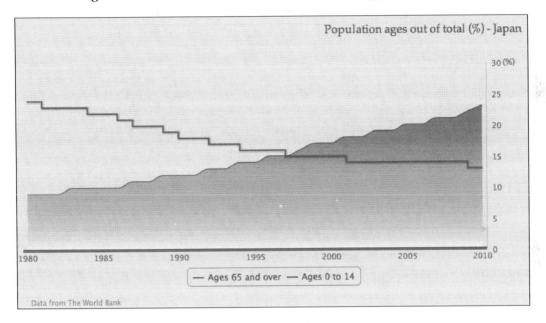

Extending to a stacked area chart

In this section we are going to turn both series into area splines and stack them on top of each other to create a stacked area chart. As the data series are stacked together, we can observe the series quantity roughly in individual, proportional, and total formats.

Let's change the second series into another `'areaspline'` type:

```
name: 'Ages 0 to 14',
type: 'areaspline',
pointStart: 1980,
data: [ 24, 23, 23, ... ]
```

Set the `stacking` option to `'normal'` as a default setting for `areaspline`, as follows:

```
plotOptions: {
    areaspline: {
        stacking: 'normal'
    }
}
```

This sets both area graphs stacked on top of each other. By doing so we can observe from the data that both age groups of population roughly compensate each other to make up a total of around 33 percent of the total population and the **Ages 65 and over** group is increasingly outpaced in the later stage:

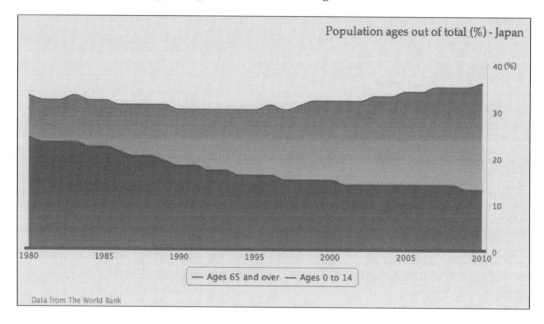

Suppose we have three area spline series and we only want to stack two of them (although it is clearer to do that in a columns chart than in an area spline chart). As described in the *Exploring PlotOptions* section in *Chapter 2, Highcharts Configurations*, we can set the `stacking` option in `plotOptions.series` to `'normal'`, and manually turn off `stacking` in the third series configuration. The following is the series configuration with another series:

```
plotOptions: {
    series: {
        marker: {
            enabled: false
        },
        stacking: 'normal'
```

```
            }
        },
        series: [{
            name: 'Ages 65 and over',
            ....
        }, {
            name: 'Ages 0 to 14',
            ....
        }, {
            name: 'Ages 15 to 64',
            type: 'areaspline',
            pointStart: 1980,
            stacking: null,
            data: [ 67, 67, 68, 68, .... ]
        }]
```

This creates an area spline graph with the third series, **Ages 15 to 64**, covering the other two stacked series, as shown in the following screenshot:

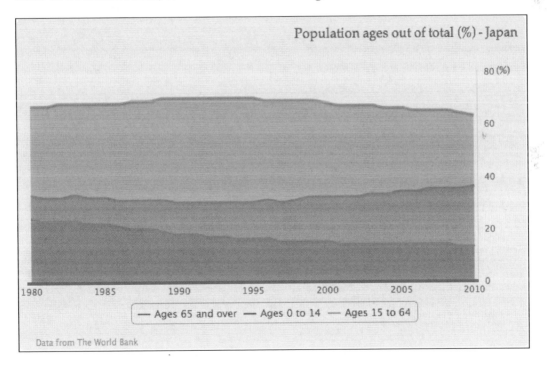

Plotting charts with missing data

If a series has missing data, then Highcharts' default action is to display the series as a broken line. There is an option, `connectNulls`, which allows the series line to continue even if there is missing data. The default value for this option is `false`. Let's examine the default behavior by setting two spline series with null data points. Also, we enable the point markers, so that we can clearly view the missing data points:

```
series: [{
        name: 'Ages 65 and over',
        connectNulls: true,
        ....,
        // Missing data from 2004 - 2009
        data: [ 9, 9, 9, ...., 23 ]

    }, {
        name: 'Ages 0 to 14',
        ....,
        // Missing data from 1989 - 1994
        data: [ 24, 23, 23, ...., 13 ]
    }]
```

The following is a chart with a spline series presenting missing points in different styles:

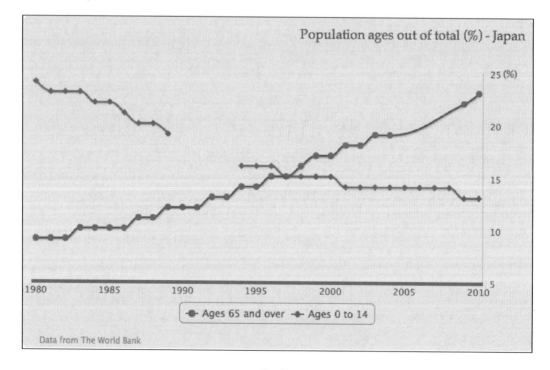

As we can see the **Ages 0 to 14** series has a clear broken line, whereas **Ages 65 and over** is configured with setting `connectNulls` to `true`, which joins the missing points with a spline curve. If the point marker is not enabled, we won't be able to notice the difference.

However, we should use this option with caution and should especially never enable it with the `stacking` option. Suppose we have a stacked area chart with both series and there is missing data only in the **Ages 0 to 14** series, which is the bottom series. The default action for the missing data will make the graph look like the following screenshot:

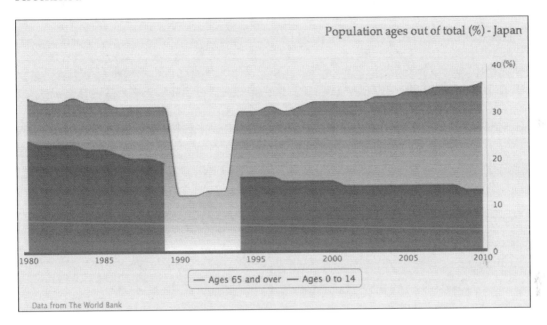

Although the bottom series does show the broken part, the stack graph overall still remains correct. The same area of the top series drops back to single series values and the overall percentage is still intact.

The problem arises when we set the `connectNulls` option to `true` and do not realize that there is missing data in the series. This results in an inconsistent graph, as follows:

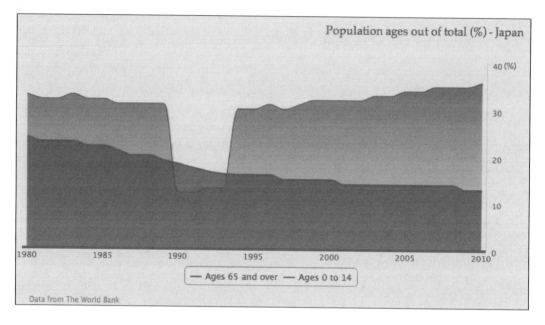

The bottom series covers a hole left from the top series, which contradicts the stack graph's overall percentage.

Combining scatter and area series

Highcharts also supports scatter charts that enable us to plot the data trend from a large set of data samples. In here we are going to use scatter series differently which makes our chart a bit like a poster chart.

First, we are going to use a subset of the `'Ages 0 to 14'` data and set the series to the `scatter` type:

```
name: 'Ages 0 to 14',
type: 'scatter',
data: [ [ 1982, 23 ], [ 1989, 19 ],
        [ 2007, 14 ], [ 2004, 14 ],
        [ 1997, 15 ], [ 2002, 14 ],
        [ 2009, 13 ], [ 2010, 13 ] ]
```

Then we will enable the data labels for the `scatter` series and make sure the `marker` shape is always `'circle'`, as follows:

```
plotOptions: {
    scatter: {
        marker: {
            symbol: 'circle'
        },
        dataLabels: {
            enabled: true
        }
    }
}
```

The preceding code snippet gives us the following graph:

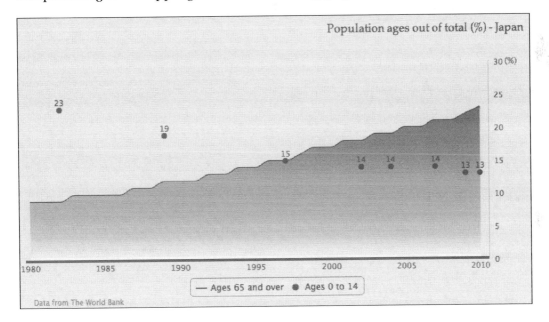

Highcharts provides a list of marker symbols as well as allowing users to supply their own marker icons (see *Chapter 2, Highcharts Configurations*). The list of supported symbols contains `circle`, `square`, `diamond`, `triangle`, and `triangle-down`.

Polishing a chart with an artistic style

The next step is to format each scatter point into a bubble style with the `radius` property and manually set the data label font size proportional to the percentage value. Then use the `verticalAlign` property to adjust the labels to center inside the enlarged scatter points. The various sizes of the scatter points require us to present each data point with different attributes. Hence, we need to change the series data definition into an array of point object configurations, such as:

```
plotOptions: {
  scatter: {
      marker: {
          symbol: 'circle'
      },
      dataLabels: {
          enabled: true,
          verticalAlign: 'middle'
      }
  }
},
data: [ {
    dataLabels: {
        style: {
            fontSize: '25px'
        }
    },
    marker: { radius: 31 },
    y: 23,
    x: 1982
    }, {
    dataLabels: {
        style: {
            fontSize: '22px'
        }
    },
    marker: { radius: 23 },
    y: 19,
    x: 1989
}, .....
```

The following screenshot shows a graph with a sequence of data points from a large marker size and font, gradually becoming smaller according to their percentage values:

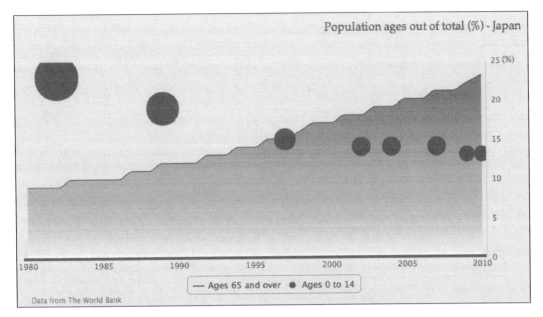

Now we have two issues with the preceding graph. Firstly, the scatter series color (default second series color) clashes with the gray text label inside the markers making it hard to read.

To resolve the first issue we will change the scatter series to a lighter color with the following gradient setting:

```
color: {
    linearGradient: { x1: 0, y1: 0, x2: 0, y2: 1 },
    stops: [ [ 0, '#FF944D' ],
             [ 1, '#FFC299' ] ]
},
```

Then we give the scatter points a darker outline in `plotOptions`, as follows:

```
plotOptions: {
    scatter: {
        marker: {
            symbol: 'circle',
            lineColor: '#E65C00',
            lineWidth: 1
        },
```

Secondly, the data points are blocked by the end of the axes range. The issue can be resolved by introducing extra padding spaces into both axes:

```
yAxis: {
        ....,
        maxPadding: 0.09
},
xAxis: {
        ....,
        maxPadding: 0.02
}
```

The following is the new outlook of the graph:

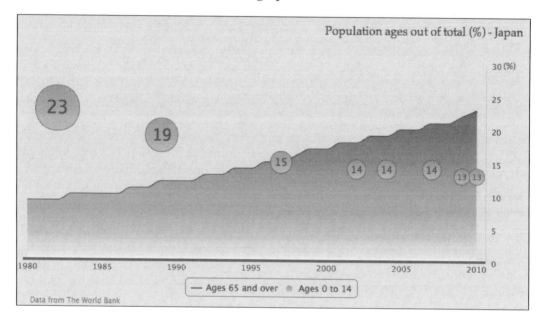

For the next part we will put up a logo and some decorative texts. There are two ways to import an image into a chart—the `plotBackgroundImage` option or the `renderer.image` API call. The `plotBackgroundImage` option brings the whole image into the chart background which is not what we intend to do. The `renderer.image` method offers more control on the location and the size of the image. The following is the call after the chart is created:

```
var chart = new Highcharts.Chart({
        ...
});
chart.renderer.image('logo.png', 240, 10, 187, 92).add();
```

`logo.png` is the URL path for the logo image file; the next two parameters are the x and y positions (starting from 0, where 0 is the upper-left corner) of the chart where the image will be displayed; the last two parameters are the width and height of the image file. The `image` call basically returns an `element` object and the subsequent `.add` call puts the returned image object into the renderer.

As for the decorative text, it is a red circle with white bold text in a different size. They are all created from the renderer. In the following code snippet the first renderer call is to create a red circle with x and y locations, and radius size. Then immediately the SVG attributes with the `attr` method are set, which configures the transparency and outline in a darker color. The next three renderer calls are to create text inside the red circle and the it is set up by using the `css` method for font size, style, and color. We will revisit `chart.renderer` as part of the Highcharts API in *Chapter 7, Highcharts APIs*.

```
// Red circle at the back
chart.renderer.circle(220, 65, 45).attr({
        fill: '#FF7575',
        'fill-opacity': 0.6,
        stroke: '#B24747',
        'stroke-width': 1
}).add();
// Large percentage text with special font
chart.renderer.text('37.5%', 182, 63).css({
        fontWeight: 'bold',
        color: #FFFFFF',
        fontSize: '30px',
        fontFamily: 'palatino'
}).add();
// Align subject in the circle
chart.renderer.text('65 and over', 184, 82).css({
        'fontWeight': 'bold',
}).add();
chart.renderer.text('by 2050', 193, 96).css({
        'fontWeight': 'bold',
}).add();
```

Finally, we move the legend box to the top of the chart. In order to locate the legend inside the plot area, we need to set the `floating` property to `true` which forces the legend into a fixed layout mode. Then we remove the default border line and set the legend items' list into a vertical direction:

```
legend: {
    floating: true,
    verticalAlign: 'top',
    align: 'center',
```

```
        x: 130,
        y: 40,
        borderWidth: 0,
        layout: 'vertical',
    },
```

The following is our final graph with the decorations:

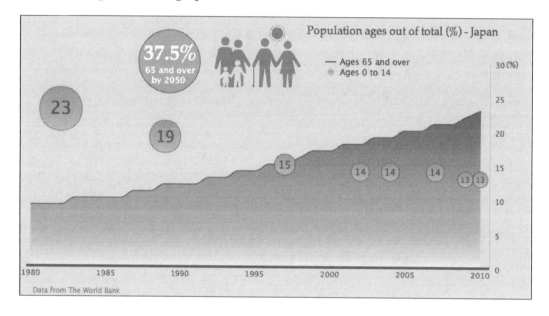

Summary

In this chapter we have explored the usage of line, area, and scatter charts. We can see how much flexibility Highcharts can offer to make a poster-like chart. In the next chapter we will learn how to plot column and bar charts and learn about their plotting options.

4
Bar and Column Charts

In this chapter we will start off by learning the column charts and their plotting options. Then we will apply more advanced options for stacking and grouping columns together. After that, we will move on to bar charts by following the same example. Then we will learn how to polish up a bar chart and apply tricks to turn a bar chart into mirror and horizontal gauge charts. Finally, a web page of multiple charts will be put together as a concluding exercise. In this chapter we will cover the following:

- Introducing column charts
- Stacking and grouping a column chart
- Adjusting column colors and data labels
- Introducing bar charts
- Constructing a mirror chart
- Converting a single bar chart into a horizontal gauge chart
- Sticking the charts together

Introducing column charts

The difference between column and bar charts is trivial. The data in column charts is aligned vertically whereas it is aligned horizontally in bar charts. Column and bar charts are generally used for plotting data with categories along the x axis. In this section we are going to demonstrate plotting column charts. The dataset we are going to use is offered by the U.S. Patent and Trademark Office. The graph just after the following code snippet shows a column chart for the number of patents granted to the United Kingdom for the last 10 years. The following is the chart configuration code:

```
chart: {
    renderTo: 'container',
    type: 'column',
    borderWidth: 1
},
title: {
    text: 'Number of Patents Granted',
},
credits: {
    position: {
        align: 'left',
        x: 20
    },
    href: 'http://www.uspto.gov',
    text: 'Source: U.S. Patent & Trademark Office'
},
xAxis: {
    categories: [
        '2001', '2002', '2003', '2004', '2005',
        '2006', '2007', '2008', '2009', '2010',
        '2011' ]
},
yAxis: {
    title: {
        text: 'No. of Patents'
    }
},
plotOptions: {
},
series: [{
    name: 'UK',
    data: [ 4351, 4190, 4028, 3895, 3553,
            4323, 4029, 3834, 4009, 5038, 4924 ]
}]
```

The following is the result that we get from the preceding code snippet:

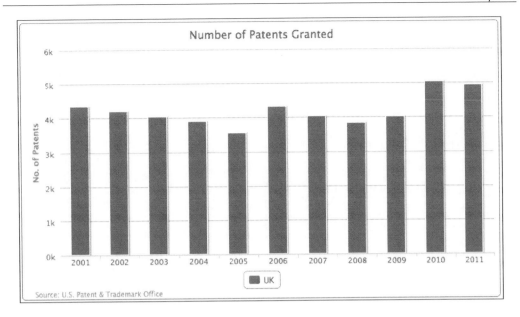

 Data can be found from the online report *All Patents, All Types Report* by Patent Technology Monitoring Team at `http://www.uspto.gov/web/offices/ac/ido/oeip/taf/apat.htm`.

Let's add another series, **France**. The following chart shows both series aligned with each other side by side finally:

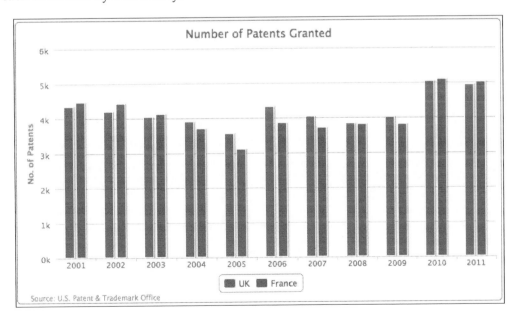

Overlapped column chart

Another way to present multiseries columns is to overlap the columns. The main reason for this type of presentation is to avoid columns becoming too thin and overpacked if there are too many categories in the chart. As a result, it is difficult to observe the values and compare them. Overlapping the columns provides more space between each category; hence each column can still retain the width.

We can make both series partially overlap each other with the padding options, as follows:

```
plotOptions: {
    series: {
        pointPadding: -0.2,
        groupPadding: 0.3
    }
},
```

The default setting for padding between columns (also for bars) is 0.2 which is a fraction value of the width of each category. In this example we are going to set `pointPadding` to a negative value, which means instead of having padding distance between neighboring columns, we bring the columns together to overlap each other. `groupPadding` is the distance of group values relative to each category width, that is, the distance between the pair of **UK** and **France** columns in **2005** and **2006**. In this example, we have set it to 0.3 to make sure the columns don't automatically become wider, because overlapping produces more spaces between each group. The following is the screenshot of the overlapping columns:

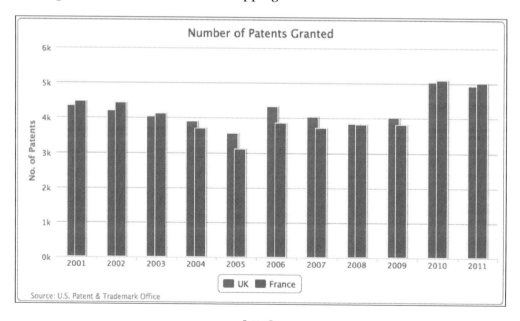

Stacking and grouping a column chart

Instead of aligning columns side by side, we can stack the columns on top of each other. Although this would make it slightly harder to visualize each column's values, we can instantly observe the total values of each category and the change of ratios between the series. Another powerful feature with stacked columns is to group them selectively when we have more than a couple of series. This can give a sense of proportions between multiple groups of stacked series.

Let's start a new column chart with the UK, Germany, Japan, and South Korea.

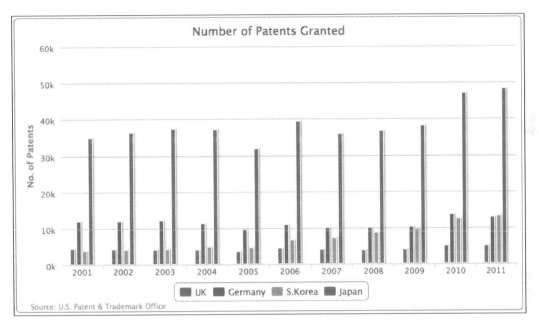

The number of patents granted for Japan has gone off the scale compared to other countries. Let's group and stack the multiple series into Europe and Asia with the following series configuration:

```
plotOptions: {
    column: {
        stacking: 'normal'
    }
},
series: [{
    name: 'UK',
    data: [ 4351, 4190, 4028, .... ],
    stack: 'Europe'
}, {
```

```
            name: 'Germany',
            data: [ 11894, 11957, 12140, ... ],
            stack: 'Europe'
        }, {
            name: 'S.Korea',
            data: [ 3763, 4009, 4132, ... ],
            stack: 'Asia'
        }, {
            name: 'Japan',
            data: [ 34890, 36339, 37248, ... ],
            stack: 'Asia'
        }]
```

We declare column `stacking` in `plotOptions` as `'normal'` and then for each column series assign a stack group name, `'Europe'` and `'Asia'`, which produces the following graph:

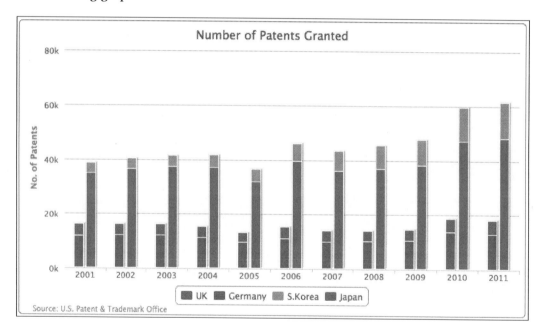

As we can see, the chart reduces four vertical bars into two and each column is comprised of two series. The first vertical bar is the `'Europe'` group and the second one is `'Asia'`.

Mixing the stacked and single columns

In the last section we acknowledged the benefit of grouping and stacking multiple series. There are also occasions when multiple series can belong to a group and there are individual series in their own groups. Highcharts offers the flexibility to mix the stacked and grouped series with single series.

Let's look at an example of mixing a stacked column and single column together. First remove the stack group assignment in each series; that is, the default action for all the column series is to remain stacked together. Then we introduce a new column series, US, and manually declare the stacking option as null in the series configuration to override the default plotOptions setting:

```
plotOptions: {
    column: {
        stacking: 'normal'
    }
},
series: [{
    name: 'UK',
    data: [ 4351, 4190, 4028, .... ]
}, {
    name: 'Germany',
    data: [ 11894, 11957, 12140, ... ]
}, {
    name: 'S.Korea',
    data: [ 3763, 4009, 4132, ... ]
}, {
    name: 'Japan',
    data: [ 34890, 36339, 37248, ... ]
}, {
    name: 'US',
    data: [ 98655, 97125, 98590, ... ],
    stacking: null
}]
```

The new series array produces the following graph:

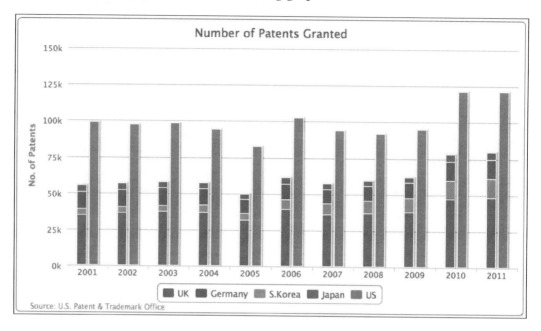

The first four series—**UK**, **Germany**, **S. Korea**, and **Japan**—are stacked together as a single column and **US** is displayed as a separate column. We can easily observe by stacking the series together that the number of patents of the four countries put together is less than two-thirds of the number of patents of the **US** (the US is nearly 25 times of the UK).

Comparing the columns in stacked percentages

Alternatively, we can see how each country compares by normalizing the values into percentages and stacking them together. This can be achieved by removing the manual `stacking` setting in the US series and setting the global column `stacking` as 'percent':

```
plotOptions: {
    column: {
        stacking: 'percent'
    }
}
```

All the series are put into a single column and their values are normalized into percentages, as shown in the following screenshot:

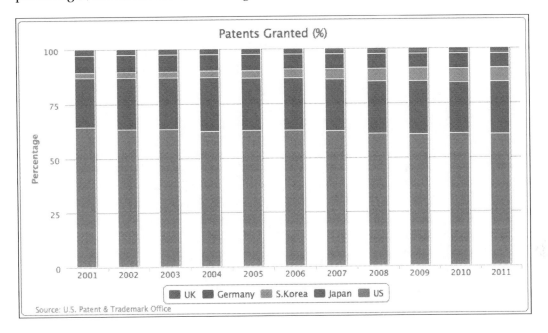

Adjusting column colors and data labels

Let's make another chart, and this time we will plot the top ten countries with patents granted. The following is the code to produce the chart:

```
chart: {
    renderTo: 'container',
    type: 'column',
    borderWidth: 1
},
title: {
    text: 'Number of Patents Filed in 2011'
},
credits: { ... },
xAxis: {
    categories: [
        'United States', 'Japan',
        'South Korea', 'Germany', 'Taiwan',
        'Canada', 'France', 'United Kingdom',
        'China', 'Italy' ]
},
yAxis: {
```

```
        title: {
            text: 'No. of Patents'
        }
    },
    series: [{
        showInLegend: false,
        data: [ 121261, 48256, 13239, 12968, 9907,
                5754, 5022, 4924, 3786, 2333 ]
    }]
```

The preceding code snippet generates the following graph:

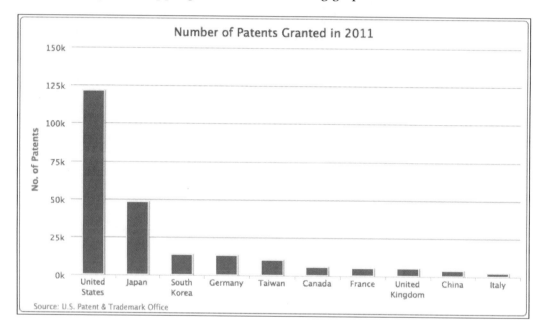

There are several areas that we would like to change in the preceding graph. First there are word wraps in the country names. In order to avoid that we can apply rotation on the x-axis labels, as follows:

```
xAxis: {
    categories: [
        'United States', 'Japan',
        'South Korea',   ... ],
    labels: {
        rotation: -45,
        align: 'right'
    }
},
```

Secondly, the large value from `'United States'` has gone off the scale compared to values from other countries, so we cannot really identify their values. To resolve this issue we can apply a logarithmic scale onto the y axis, as follows:

```
yAxis: {
    title: ... ,
    type: 'logarithmic'
},
```

Finally, we would like to print the value labels along the columns and decorate the chart with different colors for each column, as follows:

```
plotOptions: {
    column: {
        colorByPoint: true,
        dataLabels: {
            enabled: true,
            rotation: -90,
            y: 25,
            color: '#F4F4F4',
                formatter: function() {
                    return
                    Highcharts.numberFormat(this.y, 0);
                },
                x: 10,
                style: {
                    fontWeight: 'bold'
                }
        }
    }
},
```

The following is the graph showing all the improvements:

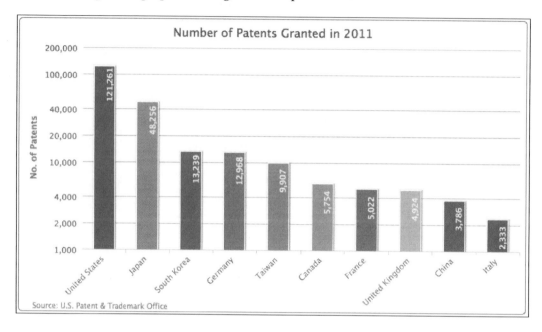

Introducing bar charts

In Highcharts there are two ways to specify bar charts—setting series' `type` to `'bar'` or setting the `chart.inverted` option to `true` with column series (also true for switching from bar to column). Switching between column and bar is simply a case of swapping the display orientation between the y and x axes; all the label rotations are still intact. Moreover, the actual configurations still remain in the x and y axes. To demonstrate this we will use the previous example along with the `inverted` option set to `true`, as follows:

```
chart: {
    .... ,
    type: 'column',
    inverted: true
},
```

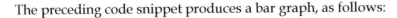

The preceding code snippet produces a bar graph, as follows:

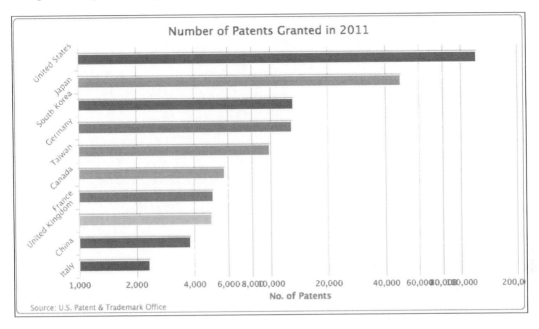

The rotation of the country name and the logarithmic axis labels still remain the same. In fact, now the value labels are muddled together and the category names are not aligning properly to the bars. The next step is to reset the label orientations to restore the graph to a readable form; we will simply swap the label setting from the y axis to the x axis:

```
xAxis: {
    categories: [ 'United States',
                  'Japan', 'South Korea', ... ]
},
yAxis: {
    .... ,
    labels: {
        rotation: -45,
        align: 'right'
    }
},
```

Then we will reset the default column `dataLabel` settings by removing the rotation option and re-adjusting the x and y positioning to align inside the bars:

```
plotOptions: {
    column: {
        ..... ,
        dataLabels: {
```

```
                enabled: true,
                color: '#F4F4F4',
                x: -40,
                y: 5,
                formatter: ....
                style: ...
            }
        }
```

The following is the graph with fixed data labels:

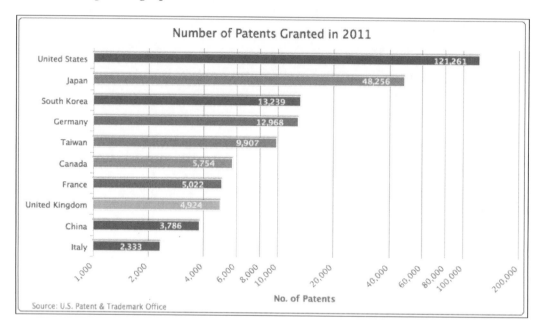

Giving the bar chart a simpler look

Here we are going to strip the axes back for a minimal, bare presentation. We remove the whole y axis and adjust the category name above the bar. To strip off the y axis we will use the following code snippet:

```
yAxis: {
    title: {
        text: null
    },
    labels: {
        enabled: false
    },
    gridLineWidth: 0,
    type: 'logarithmic'
},
```

Then we move the country labels above the bars. This is accompanied by removing the axis line and the interval tick line, then change the label alignments and their x and y positioning:

```
xAxis: {
    categories: [ 'United States', 'Japan',
                  'South Korea', ... ],
    lineWidth: 0,
    tickLength: 0,
    labels: {
        align: 'left',
        x: 0,
        y: -13,
        style: {
            fontWeight: 'bold'
        }
    }
},
```

Since we changed the label alignments to go above the bars, the horizontal position of the bars (plot area) has shifted to the left-hand side of the chart to take over the old label positions. Therefore we need to increase the spacing on the left to avoid the chart looking too packed. Finally, we add a background image to the plot area just to fill up the empty spaces, as follows:

```
chart: {
    renderTo: 'container',
    type: 'column',
    spacingLeft: 20,
    plotBackgroundImage: 'chartBg.png',
    inverted: true
},
title: {
    text:  null
},
```

The following screenshot shows the new simple look of our bar chart:

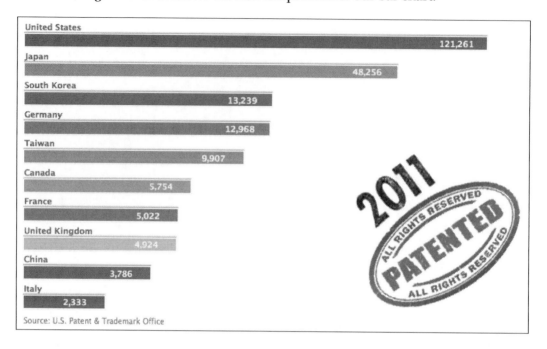

Source: U.S. Patent & Trademark Office

Constructing a mirror chart

Using a mirror chart is another way of comparing two column series. Instead of aligning the two series as columns adjacent to each other, mirror charts align them in bars opposite to each other. Sometimes this is used as a preferred way for presenting the trend between the two series.

In Highcharts we can make use of a stacked bar chart and change it slightly into a mirror chart for comparing two sets of data horizontally side by side. To do that let's start with a new data series from Patents Granted, which shows the comparison between the United Kingdom and China with respect to the number of patents granted for the past decade.

The way we configure the chart is really a column-stacked bar chart, with one set of data being positive and another set being manually converted to negative values, such that the zero value axis is in the middle of the chart. Then we invert the column chart into a bar chart and label the negative range as positive. To demonstrate this concept let's create a stacked column chart first with both positive and self-made negative ranges, as follows:

```
chart: {
    renderTo: 'container',
    type: 'column',
    borderWidth: 1
},
title: {
    text: 'Number of Patents Granted',
},
credits: { ... },
xAxis: {
    categories: [ '2001', '2002', '2003', ... ],
},
yAxis: {
    title: {
        text: 'No. of Patents'
    }
},
plotOptions: {
    series: {
        stacking: 'normal'
    }
},
series: [{
    name: 'UK',
    data: [ 4351, 4190, 4028, ... ]
    }, {
    name: 'China',
    data: [ -265, -391, -424, ... ]
}]
```

The following screenshot shows the stacked-column chart with the zero value in the middle of the y axis:

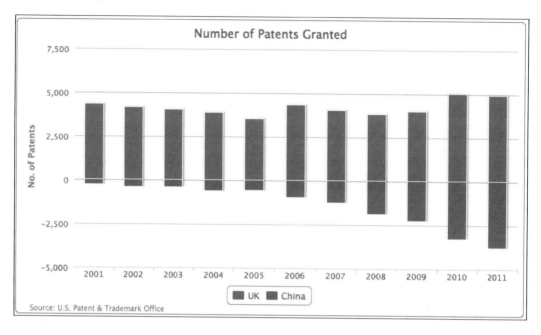

Then we change the configuration into a bar chart with two x axes showing on each side with the same range. The last step is to define the y-axis label's `formatter` function to turn the negative labels into positive ones, as follows:

```
chart: {
    .... ,
    type: 'bar',
},
xAxis: [{
    categories: [ '2001', '2002', '2003', ... ],
}, {
    categories: [ '2001', '2002', '2003', ... ],
    opposite: true,
    linkedTo: 0,
}],
yAxis: {
    .... ,
```

```
        labels: {
            formatter: function() {
                return
            Highcharts.numberFormat(Math.abs(this.value), 0);
                }
            }
        },
```

The following is the final bar chart for comparing the number of patents granted between the UK and China for the past decade:

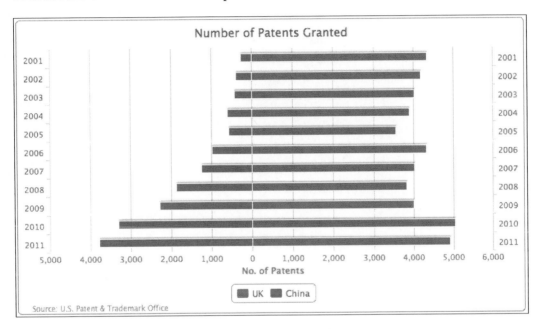

Extending to a stacked mirror chart

We can also apply the same principle from the column example to stacked and grouped series charts. Instead of having two groups of stacked columns displayed next to each other, we can have all the series stacked together with zero value to divide both groups. The following screenshot demonstrates the comparison between the European and Asian stacked groups in a bar chart:

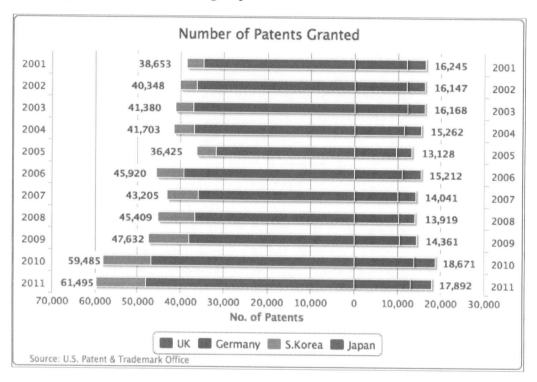

The South Korean and Japanese series are stacked together on the left-hand side (the negative side), whereas the UK and Germany are grouped on the right-hand side (the positive side). The only tricky bit to producing the preceding graph is how to output the data labels.

First of all, the South Korean and Japanese series data is manually set to negative values. Secondly, since South Korea and the UK are both the outer series of their own group, we enable the data label for these series. The following code snippet shows the series array configuration:

```
series: [{
    name: 'UK',
    data: [ 4351, 4190, 4028, ... ],
    dataLabels : {
```

```
                    enabled: true,
                    backgroundColor: '#FFFFFF',
                    x: 40,
                    formatter: function() {
                            return
        Highcharts.numberFormat(Math.abs(this.total), 0);
                    },
                    style: {
                        fontWeight: 'bold'
                    }
                }
            }, {
            name: 'Germany',
            data: [ 11894, 11957, 12140, ... ],
            }, {
            name: 'S.Korea',
            data: [ -3763, -4009, -4132, ... ],
            dataLabels : {
                    enabled: true,
                    x: -48,
                    backgroundColor: '#FFFFFF',
                    formatter: function() {
                            return
        Highcharts.numberFormat(Math.abs(this.total), 0);
                    },
                    style: {
                        fontWeight: 'bold'
                    }
                }
            }, {
            name: 'Japan',
            data: [ -34890, -36339, -37248, ... ],
        }]
```

Note that the definition for the `formatter` function is using `this.total` and not
`this.y`, because we are using the position of the outer series to print the group's
total value. The white background settings for the data labels are to avoid the
interfering of the y-axis interval lines.

Converting a single bar chart into a horizontal gauge chart

A horizontal gauge chart is generally used as an indicator for the current threshold level, meaning the extreme values in the y axis are fixed. Another characteristic is the single value (one dimension) in the x axis which is the current time.

Next we are going to learn how to turn a chart with a single bar into a gauge-level chart. The basic idea is to diminish the plot area to the same size as the bar. This means we have to fix the size of both the plot area and the bar, disregarding the dimension of the container. To do that we set `chart.width` and `chart.height` to some values. Then we decorate the plot area with a border and background color for making it resemble a container for the gauge:

```
chart: {
    renderTo: 'container',
    type: 'bar',
    plotBorderWidth: 2,
    plotBackgroundColor: '#D6D6EB',
    plotBorderColor: '#D8D8D8',
    plotShadow: true,
    spacingBottom: 43,
    width: 350,
    height: 120
},
```

We then switch off the y-axis title and set up a regular interval within the percentage, as follows:

```
xAxis: {
    categories: [ 'US' ],
    tickLength: 0
},
yAxis: {
    title: {
        text: null
    },
    labels: {
        y: 20
    },
    min: 0,
    max: 100,
    tickInterval: 20,
    minorTickInterval: 10,
```

```
    tickWidth: 1,
    tickLength: 8,
    minorTickLength: 5,
    minorTickWidth: 1,
    minorGridLineWidth: 0
},
```

The final part is to configure the bar series, so that the bar width fits perfectly within the plot area. The rest of the series configuration is to brush up the bar with an SVG gradient effect, as follows:

```
series: [{
    borderColor: '#7070B8',
    borderRadius: 3,
    borderWidth: 1,
    color: {
        linearGradient:
            { x1: 0, y1: 0, x2: 1, y2: 0 },
        stops: [
                [ 0, '#D6D6EB' ],
                [ 0.3, '#5C5CAD' ],
                [ 0.45, '#5C5C9C' ],
                [ 0.55, '#5C5C9C' ],
                [ 0.7, '#5C5CAD' ],
                [ 1, '#D6D6EB'] ]
    },
    pointWidth: 50,
    data: [ 48.9 ]
}]
```

 The multiple of stop gradients are supported by SVG, but not by VML. For VML browsers, such as Internet Explorer 8, the number of stop gradients should be restricted to two.

The following is the final polished look of the gauge chart:

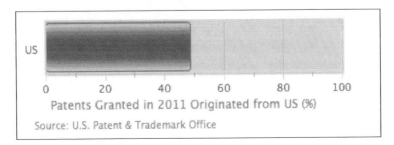

Sticking the charts together

In this section we are building a page with a mixture of charts. The main chart is displayed on the left-hand side panel and three mini charts are displayed on the right-hand side panel in top-down order. The layout is achieved by HTML `div` boxes and CSS styles.

The left-hand side chart is from the multicolored column chart example that we discussed previously. All the axes lines and labels are disabled in the mini charts.

The first mini chart from the top is a two-series line chart with `dataLabels` enabled only for the last point in each series, that is, the last point in the data array is a data object instead. The label color is set to the same color as its series. Then `plotLine` is inserted into the y axis at the 50 percent value mark. The following is a sample of one of the series configurations:

```
pointStart: 2001,
marker: {
    enabled: false
},
data: [ 53.6, 52.7, 52.7, 51.9, 52.4,
        52.1, 51.2, 49.7, 49.5, 49.6,
        { y: 48.9,
          name: 'US',
          dataLabels: {
              color: '#4572A7',
              enabled: true,
              x: -10,
              y: 14,
              formatter: function() {
                  return
            this.point.name + ": " + this.y + '%';
              }
          }
        }]
```

The second mini chart is a simple bar with data labels outside the categories. The style for the data label is set to a larger, bold font.

The last mini chart is basically a scatter chart with each series having a single point, so that each series can appear in the right-hand side legend. Moreover, we set the x value for each series to zero, so that we can have different sizes of data points as well, and stacked on top of each other. The following is an example for one of the scatter series configurations:

```
zIndex: 1,
legendIndex: 0,
color: {
    linearGradient:
        { x1: 0, y1: 0, x2: 0, y2: 1 },
        stops: [ [ 0, '#FF6600' ],
                 [ 0.6, '#FFB280' ] ]
},
name: 'America - 49%',
marker: {
    symbol: 'circle',
        lineColor: '#B24700',
        lineWidth: 1
},
data: [
    { x: 0, y: 49, name: 'America',
      marker: { radius: 74 }
} ]
```

The following is the screenshot of these multiple charts displayed next to each other:

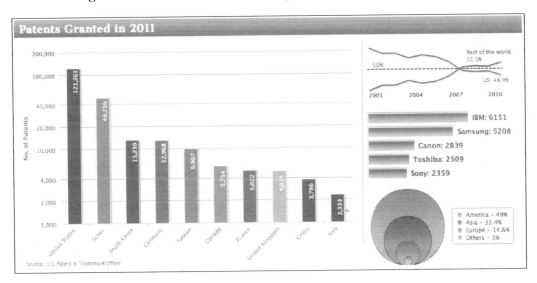

Summary

In this chapter we have learned how to use both column and bar charts. We utilized their options to achieve various presentations of columns and bars for the ease of comparison between data. We also advanced the configurations for different chart appearances such as mirror and horizontal gauge charts. In the next chapter we will explore the pie chart series.

5
Pie Charts

In this chapter, we will learn how to plot pie charts and explore their various options. We will then examine how to put multiple pies inside a chart. After that we will find out how to create a donut chart. We then end the chapter by sketching a chart containing all the series types that we have learned so far — column, line, and pie series types. In this chapter, we will be covering the following topics:

- Understanding the relationship of chart, pie, and series
- Plotting simple pie charts — single series
- Plotting multiple pies in a chart — multiple series
- Preparing a donut chart — multiple series
- Building a chart with multiple series types

Understanding the relationship of chart, pie, and series

Pie charts are simple to plot; they have no axes to configure and all they need is data with categories. Generally, the term **pie chart** refers to a chart with a single pie series. In Highcharts, a chart can handle multiple pie series. In this case, a chart can display more than one pie; each pie associates with a series of data. Instead of showing multiple pies, Highcharts can display a donut chart that is basically a pie chart with multiple concentric rings lying on top of each other. Each concentric ring is a pie series, similar to a stacked pie chart. We will first learn how to plot a chart with a single pie, and then later on in the chapter, we will explore the plotting with multiple pie series in separate pies and a donut chart.

Plotting simple pie charts – single series

In this chapter, we are going to use video gaming data supplied by **vgchartz** (www.vgchartz.com). The following is the pie chart configuration and the data is the number of games sold in 2011 according to the publishers, based on the top 100 games sold. Wii Sports is taken out of the dataset because it is free with the Wii console.

```
chart: {
    renderTo: 'container',
    type: 'pie',
    borderWidth: 1
},
title: {
    text: 'Number of Software Games Sold in 2011 Grouped by
Publishers',
},
credits: {
    ...
},
series: [{
    data: [ [ 'Nintendo', 54030288 ],
          [ 'Electronic Arts', 31367739 ],
          ... ]
}]
```

Here is a simple pie chart screenshot with the first data point (Nintendo) starting from the 12 o'clock position. The first slice always starts from 12 o'clock position and this cannot be changed.

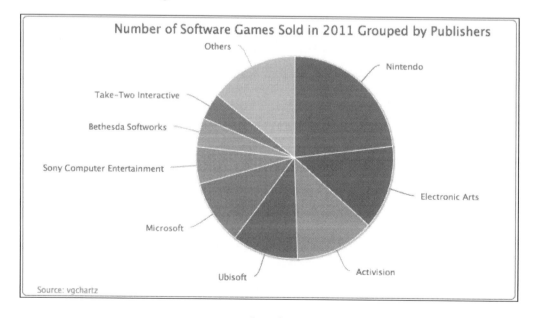

Configuring the pie with sliced off sections

We can improve the previous pie chart to include values in the labels and word wrap some of the long names of the publisher. Instead of redefining the `dataLabels.formatter` option, we will predefine a method, `formatWithLineBreaks` and use it inside the `formatter` option because we will reuse this method in other examples:

```
function formatWithLineBreaks(str) {
    var words = str.split(' ');
    var lines = [];
    var line = '';

    $.each(words, function(idx, word) {
        if (line.length + word.length > 25) {
            lines.push(line);
            line = '';
        }
        line += word + ' ';
    });
    lines.push(line);
    return lines.join('<br/>');

}
```

The following is the configuration code for the pie series. `allowPointSelect` allows the users to interact with the chart by clicking on the data points. As for the pie series, this is used for slicing off a section of the pie chart (see the following screenshot). The `slicedOffset` option is to adjust how far the section is sliced off from the pie chart.

```
plotOptions: {
    pie: {
        slicedOffset: 20,
        allowPointSelect: true,
        dataLabels: {
            formatter: function() {
                var str = this.point.name + ': ' +
                    Highcharts.numberFormat(this.y, 0);
                return formatWithLineBreaks(str);
            }
        }
    }
},
```

Additionally, we would like to slice off the largest section in the initial display; its label is shown in bold type font. To do that, we will need to change the largest data point into object configuration as shown in the following screenshot. Then we put the `sliced` property into the object and change from the default, `false`, to `true`, which forces the slice to part from the center. Furthermore, we set the `dataLabels` with the assignment of the `fontWeight` option to overwrite the default settings:

```
series: [{
  data: [ {
    name: 'Nintendo',
    y: 54030288,
    sliced: true,
    dataLabels: {
      style: {
      fontWeight: 'bold'
      }
    }
  }, [ 'Electronic Arts', 31367739 ],
    [ 'Activision', 30230170 ], .... ]
}]
```

The following is the chart with the refined labels:

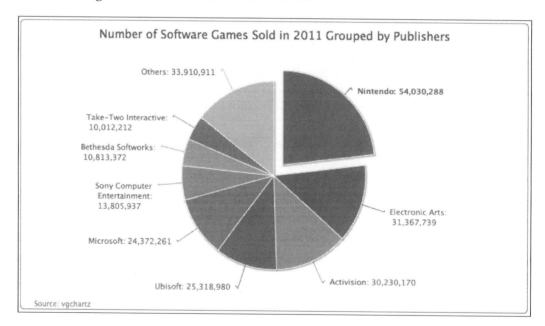

As mentioned before, the `slicedOffset` option has also pushed the sliced off section further than the default distance, which is 10 pixels. The `slicedOffset` applies to all the sliced off sections, which means that we cannot control the distance of individually parted sections. It is also worth noticing that the connectors (the lines between the slice and the data label) become crooked as a result of that. In the next example, we demonstrate that the `sliced` property can be applied to as many data points as we want and remove the `slicedOffset` option to resume the default settings to show the difference. The following chart illustrates this with three parted slices by repeating the data object settings (Nintendo) to two other points:

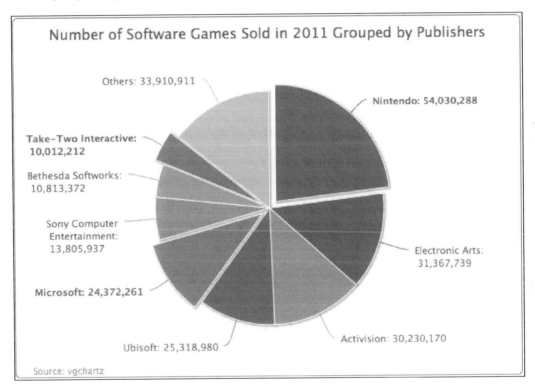

Notice that the connectors resume back to being smooth lines. However, there is another interesting behavior for the `sliced` option. For those slices with `sliced` as the default setting (`false`), only one of them can be sliced off. For instance, the user clicks on the **Others** section and it moves away from the chart. Then clicking on the **Activision** will slice off the section and the **Others** section moves back towards the center, whereas the three configured `sliced: true` sections maintain their parted positions. In other words, with the `sliced` option set to `true`, this enables its state to be independent of others with the `false` setting.

Applying a legend to a pie chart

So far the chart contains large numbers; it is confusing to really comprehend how much larger one section is than the other. We can print all the labels in percentages. Let's put all the publisher names inside a legend box and the percentage values printed inside each slice.

The plotting configuration is redefined as follows. To enable the legend box, we set `showInLegend` to `true`. Then we set the data labels' font color and style to bold and white respectively, and change the `formatter` function slightly to use the `this.percentage` variable that is only available for the pie series. The `distance` option is the distance between the data label and the outer edge of the pie. A positive value will shift the data label outside of the edge and a negative value will do the same in the opposite direction.

```
plotOptions: {
  pie: {
    showInLegend: true,
    dataLabels: {
      distance: -24,
      color: 'white',
      style: {
        fontWeight: 'bold'
      },
      formatter: function() {
        return Highcharts.numberFormat(this.percentage) + '%';
      }
    }
  }
},
```

Then for the legend box, we add in some padding as there are more than a few legend items, and set the legend box closer to the pie, as follows:

```
legend: {
  align: 'right',
  layout: 'vertical',
  verticalAlign: 'middle',
  itemMarginBottom: 4,
  itemMarginTop: 4,
  x: -40
},
```

The following is another presentation of the chart:

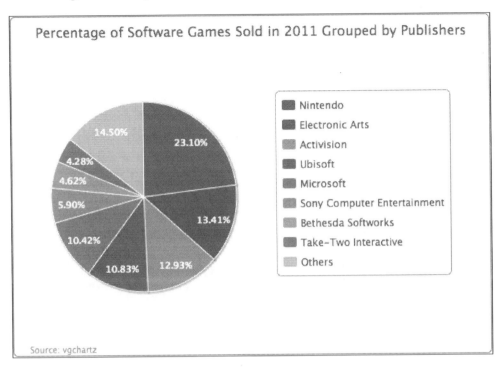

Plotting multiple pies in a chart – multiple series

With pie charts, we can do something more informative by displaying another pie chart side by side for the comparison of data. This can be done by simply specifying two series configurations in the series array.

We continue to use the previous example for the chart on the left-hand side and we create a new category series from the same dataset, but grouped by platforms this time. The following is the series configuration for doing so:

```
series: [{
  center: [ '25%', '50%' ],
  data: [ [ 'Nintendo', 54030288 ],
      [ 'Electronic Arts', 31367739 ],
      .... ]
}, {
  center: [ '75%', '50%' ],
  dataLabels: {
```

```
        formatter: function() {
            var str = this.point.name + ': ' +
    Highcharts.numberFormat(this.percentage, 0) + '%';
            return formatWithLineBreaks(str);
        }
    },
    data: [ [ 'Xbox', 80627548 ],
           [ 'PS3', 64788830 ],
           . . . ] ]
}]
```

As we can see, we use a new option, `center`, to position the pie chart. The option contains an array of two percentage values— the first is the ratio of the "x" position to the whole container width, whereas the second percentage value is the "y" ratio. The default value is `['50%', '50%']`, which is in the middle of the container. In this example, we specify the first percentage values to `'25%'` and `'75%'`, which are in the middle of the left- and the right-hand side halves respectively.

In the second series, we will choose to display the pie chart with percentage data labels instead of unit values. The following is the screenshot of a chart with double pies:

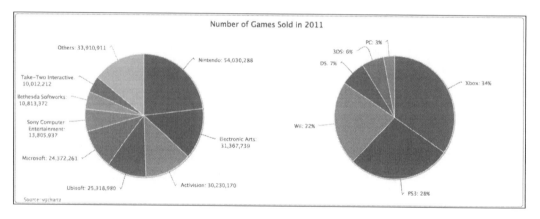

On the surface, this is not much different to plotting two separate pie charts in an individual `<div>` tag, apart from sharing the same title. The main benefit is that we can combine different series type presentations under the same chart. For instance, we want to present the distribution in ratio in pie series directly above each group of multiple column series. We will learn how to do this later in the chapter.

Preparing a donut chart – multiple series

Highcharts offers another type of pie chart—a **donut chart**. It has the drill-down effect on a category into sub-categories and is a convenient way of viewing data in greater detail. This drill-down effect can be applied on multiple levels. In this section, we will create a simple donut chart that has an outer ring of subcategories (game titles) that align with the inner categories (publishers).

For the sake of simplicity, we only use the top three game publishers for the inner pie chart. The following is the series array configuration for the donut chart:

```
series: [{
    name: 'Publishers',
    dataLabels : {
      distance: -70,
      color: 'white',
      formatter: function() {
         return this.point.name + ':<br/> ' +
Highcharts.numberFormat(this.y / 1000000, 2);
      },
      style: {
         fontWeight: 'bold'
      }
    },
    data: [ [ 'Nintendo', 54030288 ], [ 'Electronic Arts',
31367739 ],
         [ 'Activision', 30230170 ] ]
  }, {
    name: 'Titles',
    innerSize: '60%',
    dataLabels: {
      formatter: function() {
        var str = '<b>' + this.point.name  '</b>: ' + Highcharts.
numberFormat(this.y / 1000000, 2);
         return formatWithLineBreaks(str);
      }
    },
    data: [ // Nintendo
        { name: 'Pokemon B&W', y: 8541422,
         color: colorBrightness("#4572A7",
                  0.05) },
        { name: 'Mario Kart', y: 5349103,
         color: colorBrightness('#4572A7',
                  0.1) },
        ....

        // EA
        { name: 'Battlefield 3', y: 11178806,
         color: colorBrightness('#AA4643',
```

```
                             0.05) },
          ....

          // Activision
          { name: 'COD: Modern Warfare 3',
            y: 23981182,
            color: colorBrightness('#89A54E',
                         0.1) },
          ....
      }]
   }]
```

First, we have two series—the inner pie series, or the **Publishers**, and the outer ring series, or the **Titles**. The Titles series has all the subcategories data together and it aligns with the Publisher series. The order is such that the values of the subcategories for the **Nintendo** category are before the subcategory data of **Electronic Arts** and so on (see the order of data array in the Title series).

Each data point in the subcategories series is declared as a data point object for assigning the color in similar range to their main category. This can be achieved by following the Highcharts demo to fiddle with the color brightness:

```
color: Highcharts.Color(color).brighten(brightness).get()
```

Basically, what this does is to use the main category color value to create a `Color` object and then adjust the color code with the brightness parameter. This parameter is derived from the ratio of the subcategory value. We rewrite this example into a function known as `colorBrightness`, and call it in the chart configuration.

```
function colorBrightness(color, brightness) {
   return
      Highcharts.Color(color).brighten(brightness).get();
}
```

The next part is to specify which series goes to the inner pie and which goes to the outer ring. The `innerSize` option is used by the outer series, Title, to create an inner circle. As a result, the Title series forms a donut/concentric ring. The value for the `innerSize` option can be either in pixels or percentage values of the plot area size.

The final part is to decorate the chart with data labels. Obviously we want to position the data labels of the inner charts to be over the inner pie, so that we assign a negative value to the `dataLabels.distance` option. Instead of printing long values, we define the `formatter` to convert them into units of millions.

The following is the display of the donut chart:

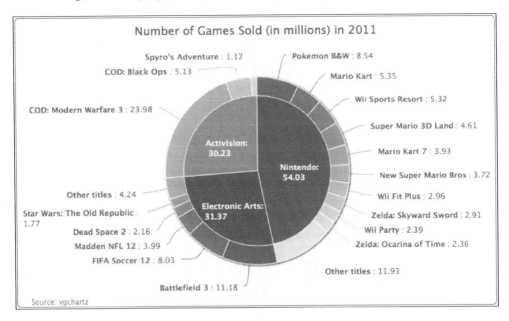

Note that it is not mandatory to put a pie chart in the center of a donut chart. It is just the presentation style of this example. We can have multiple concentric rings instead. The following chart is exactly the same example as mentioned earlier, with an addition of the `innerSize` option in the inner series of publishers:

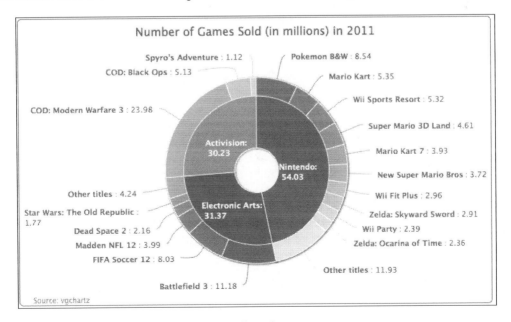

We can even further complicate the donut chart by introducing a third series. We plot the following chart with three layers. The code is simply extended from the example with another series and includes more data. The source code and the demo are available at http://joekuan.org/Learning_Highcharts/Chapter_5/. The two outer series use the innerSize option. As the inner pie will become even smaller and will not have enough space for the labels, we therefore enable the legend box for the most inner series with the showInLegend option.

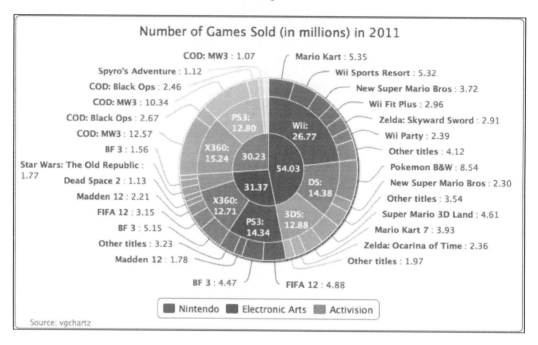

Building a chart with multiple series types

So far we have learned about the line, columns, and pie series types. It's time to bring all these different series presentations into a single chart. In this section, we use the annual data from 2008 through 2011 to plot three different kinds of series type—column, line, and pie. The column type represents the yearly number of games sold for each type of gaming console. The pie series shows the annual number of gaming consoles sold for each vendor. The last one is the spline series type that discloses how many new game titles there are in total for all the consoles released each year.

In order to enforce the whole graph to use the same color scheme for each type of gaming console, we have to manually assign a color code for each data point in the pie charts and the columns series:

```
var wiiColor = '#BBBBBB';
var x360Color = '#89A54E';
var ps3Color = '#4572A7';
var splineColor = '#FF66CC';
```

We then decorate the chart in a more funky way. First, we give the chart a dark background with a color gradient:

```
var chart = new Highcharts.Chart({
  chart: {
    renderTo: 'container',
    borderWidth: 1,
    spacingTop: 40,
    backgroundColor: {
      linearGradient: { x1: 0, y1: 0,
              x2: 0, y2: 1 },
      stops: [ [ 0, '#0A0A0A' ],
          [ 1, '#303030' ] ]
    }
  },
```

Then we need to shift the columns to the right-hand side, so that we have enough room for an image (described later) that we are going to put at the top left-hand side corner.

```
  xAxis: {
    minPadding: 0.2,
    tickInterval: 1,
    labels: {
      formatter: function() {
        return this.value;
        },
      style: {
       color: '#CFCFCF'
      }
    }
  }
```

The next task is to make enough space for the pie charts to locate them above the columns. This can be accomplished by introducing the maxPadding option on both y axes.

```
  yAxis: [{
    title: {
      text: 'Number of games sold',
```

```
        align: 'low',
        style: {
          color: '#CFCFCF'
        }
      },
      labels: {
        style: {
          color: '#CFCFCF'
        }
      },
      maxPadding: 0.5
    }, {
      title: {
        text: 'Number of games released',
        style: {
          color: splineColor
        }
      },
      labels: {
        style: {
          color: splineColor
        }
      },
      maxPadding: 0.5,
      opposite: true
    }],
```

Each pie series is displayed separately and aligned at the top of the columns, as well as in the year category. This is done by adjusting the pie chart's `center` option in the series array. We also want to reduce the display size for the pie series, as there are other types of series to share within the chart. We will use the `size` option and set the value in percentages. The percentage value is the diameter of the pie series comparing the size of plot area:

```
      series:[{
        type: 'pie',
        name: 'Hardware 2011',
        size: '25%',
        center: [ '88%', '20%' ],
        data: [{ name: 'PS3', y: 14128407,
            color: ps3Color },
          { name: 'X360', y: 13808365,
            color: x360Color },
          { name: 'Wii', y: 11567105,
            color: wiiColor } ],
      .....
```

The spline series is defined to correspond to the opposite y axis. To make the series clearly associated with the second axis, we apply the same color scheme for the line, axis title, and labels:

```
{   name: "Game released",
    type: 'spline',
    showInLegend: false,
    lineWidth: 3,
    yAxis: 1,
    color: splineColor,
    pointStart: 2008,
    pointInterval: 1,
    data: [ 1170, 2076, 1551, 1378 ]
},
```

We use the `renderer.image` method to insert the image to the chart and make sure that the image has a higher `zIndex`, so that the axis line does not lie at the top of the image. Instead of including a PNG image, we use an SVG image. This way the image stays sharp and avoids the pixelation effect when the chart is resized.

```
chart.renderer.image('./pacman.svg', 0,
        0, 200, 200).attr({
    'zIndex': 10
}).add();
```

The following is the final look of the graph with Pac-Man SVG image to give a gaming theme to the chart:

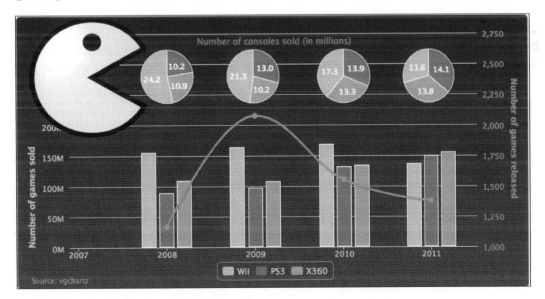

Summary

In this chapter, we have learned how to outline a pie chart and its variant, the donut chart. We also summarized this chapter by sketching a chart that includes all the series types we have learned so far.

In the next chapter, we will explore the newer series types in Highcharts such as gauge, radar, and range series. We will also learn how to apply radial gradient in Highcharts.

6
Gauge, Polar, and Range Charts

In this chapter we will learn how to create a gauge chart step by step. A gauge chart is very different from other Highcharts graphs. We will explore the new settings by plotting something similar to a twin-dials Fiat 500 speedometer. After that we will review the structure of the polar chart and its similarity with other charts. Then we will move on to examine how to create a range chart by using examples from the past chapter. Finally, we will use a gauge chart to tweak the radial gradient in stages to achieve the desired effect. In this chapter we will cover the following:

- Plotting a speedometer gauge chart
- Converting a spline chart to a polar/radar chart
- Plotting range charts with market index data
- Using a radial gradient on a gauge chart

Loading gauge, polar, and range charts

In order to use any gauge, polar, and range type charts, first we need to include an additional file, `highcharts-more.js`, provided in the package:

```
<script type="text/javascript"
    src="http://code.highcharts.com/highcharts.js"></script>
<script type="text/javascript"
    src="http://code.highcharts.com/highcharts-more.js"></script>
```

Plotting a speedometer gauge chart

Gauge charts have a very different structure compared to other Highcharts graphs. For instance, the backbone of gauge charts is made up of a "pane". A **pane** is a circular plot area for laying out chart content. We can adjust the size, position, and the backgrounds of the pane. Once a pane is laid out, we can then put the axis on top of it. Highcharts supports multiple panes within a chart, hence we can display multiple gauges (that is multiple gauge series) within a chart. A gauge series is composed of two specific components – a pivot and a dial.

Another distinct difference in gauge charts is that the series is actually one dimensional data, that is a single value. Hence there is one axis, the y axis, used in this type of chart. The `yAxis` properties are used the same way as other series type charts which can be on a `linear`, `datetime`, or `logarithmic` scale, and it also responds to the `tickInterval` option and so on.

Plotting a twin dials chart – a Fiat 500 speedometer

So far, we have mentioned all the parts and their relationships that make up a gauge chart. There are many selectable options that can be used with gauge charts. In order to fully utilize them, we are going to learn in stages how to construct a sophisticated gauge chart by following the design of a Fiat 500 speedometer, as follows:

The speedometer is assembled with two dials on top of each other. The outer dial has two axes—mph and km/h. The inner dial is the rpm meter, which has a different scale and style. Another uncommon feature is that the body parts of both dials are hidden underneath; only the top needle parts are displayed. In the center of the gauge is an LED screen showing journey information. Using all these unique appearances, Highcharts provides enough flexibility to assemble a chart that looks very similar.

Plotting a gauge chart pane

First, let's see what a pane does in Highcharts. In order to do that, we should start by building a single dial speedometer. The following is the chart configuration code for a gauge chart with a single pane and a single axis:

```
chart: {
        renderTo: 'container'
},
title: {  text: 'Fiat 500 Speedometer' },
pane: [{
        startAngle: -120,
        endAngle: 120,
        size: 300,
        backgroundColor: '#E4E3DF'
}],
yAxis: [{
        min: 0,
        max: 140,
        labels: {
                rotation: 'auto'
        }
}],
series: [{
        type: 'gauge',
        data: [ 0 ]
}]
```

The preceding code snippet produces the following gauge chart:

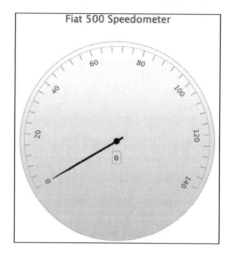

At the moment, this looks nothing like a Fiat 500 speedometer but we will see the chart evolving gradually. The configuration declares a pane with a circular plot area starting from -120 to 120 degrees, with the y axis laying horizontally, whereas degree zero is at the twelve o'clock position. The `rotation` option generally takes a numerical degree value; `'auto'` is the special keyword to enable the y-axis labels to automatically rotate so that they get aligned with the pane angle. The little box below the dial is the default data label showing the current value in the series.

Setting pane backgrounds

Gauge charts support more advanced background settings than just a single background color, as we saw in the last example. Instead we can specify another property, `background`, inside the `pane` option which accepts an array of different background settings. Each setting can be declared as an inner ring with both the `innerRadius` and `outerRadius` defined, or a circular background with only the `outerRadius` option. Both options are assigned with percentage values with respect to the size of the pane. Here we set multiple backgrounds to the pane, as follows:

```
chart: { .... },
title: { .... },
series: [{
    name: 'Speed',
    data: [ 0 ],
    dial: { backgroundColor: '#FA3421' }
}],
pane: [{
    startAngle: -120,
    endAngle: 120,
```

```
size: 300,
background: [{
    backgroundColor: {
        radialGradient: {
            cx: 0.5,
            cy: 0.6,
            r: 1.0
        },
        stops: [
            [0.3, '#A7A9A4'],
            [0.45, '#DDD'],
            [0.7, '#EBEDEA'],
        ]
    },
    innerRadius: '72%',
    outerRadius: '105%'
}, {
    // BG color in between speed and rpm
    backgroundColor: '#38392F',
    outerRadius: '72%',
    innerRadius: '67%'
}, {
    // BG color for rpm
    .....
}]
```

As we can see, several backgrounds are defined which include the backgrounds for the inner gauge, the rpm dial. Some of these backgrounds are rings and the last one is a circular background. Moreover, we have set the dial color to red initially, so that we can still see the needle with the black background. Later in this section, we will explore the details of shaping and coloring the dial and pivot. As for the backgrounds with the radialGradient feature, we will examine them later in this chapter.

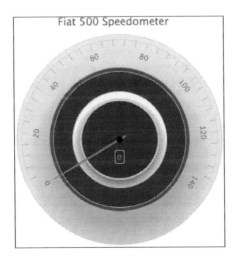

Managing axes with different scales

The next task is to lay a secondary y axis for the km/h scale and we will set the new axis below the current display axis. We insert the new axis configuration, as follows:

```
yAxis: [{
    min: 0,
    max: 140,
    labels: {
        rotation: 'auto'
    }
}, {
    min: 0,
    max: 220,
    tickPosition: 'outside',
    minorTickPosition: 'outside',
    offset: -40,
    labels: {
        distance: 5,
        rotation: 'auto'
    }
}],
```

The new axis has a scale from 0 to 220 and we use the offset option with a negative value, which pushes the axes' line towards the center of the pane. In addition, both tickPosition and minorTickPosition are set to 'outside'; this changes the interval ticks' direction opposite to the default settings. Both axes are now facing each other which is similar to the one in the following photo:

However, there is an issue arising in which the scale at the top axis has been disturbed; it is no longer between 0 and 140. This is because the default action for having a secondary axis is to align the intervals between multiple axes. To resolve this issue, we must set the `chart.alignTicks` option to `false`. After that, the issue is resolved and both axes are laid out as expected, as follows:

Extending to multiple panes

Since the gauge consists of two dials, we need to add an extra pane for the second dial. The following is the pane configuration:

```
pane: [{
    // First pane for speed dial
    startAngle: -120,
    endAngle: 120,
    size: 300,
    background: [{
        backgroundColor: {
            radialGradient: {
                .....
    }]
}, {
    // Second pane for rpm dial
    startAngle: -120,
    endAngle: 120,
    size: 200
}]
```

The second pane's plot area starts and ends at the same angles as the first pane with a smaller size. Since we haven't used the center option to position any panes within the chart, the inner pane is automatically placed at the center of the outer pane. The next step is to create another axis, rpm, which has a red region marked between the values of 4.5 and 6. Then we bind all the axes to their panes, as follows:

```
yAxis: [{
    // axis for mph - pane 0
    min: 0,
    max: 140,
    .....
    pane: 0
}, {
    // axis for km/h - pane 0
    min: 0,
    max: 220,
    ....
    pane: 0
}, {
    // axis for rpm - pane 1
    min: 0,
    max: 6,
    labels: {
        rotation: 'auto',
        formatter: function() {
            if (this.value >= 4.5) {
                return '<span style="color:' +
                '#A41E09">' + this.value +
                "</span>";
            }
            return this.value;
        }
    },
    plotBands: [{
        from: 4.5,
        to: 6,
        color: '#A41E09',
        innerRadius: '94%'
    }],
    pane: 1
}]
```

For the rpm axis, we use `labels.formatter` to mark up the font color in the high-revolution region and also create a plot band for the axis. The `innerRadius` option is to control how thick the red area appears to be. The next task is to create a new gauge series, that is, a second dial for the new pane. Since the chart contains two different dials, we need to make the dial movement relative to an axis; therefore we assign the `yAxis` option to bind the series to an axis. Also we set the initial value for the new series to 4, just for demonstrating how two dials are constructed, not superimposed on each other, as follows:

```
series: [{
    type: 'gauge',
    name: 'Speed',
    data: [ 0 ],
    yAxis: 0
}, {
    type: 'gauge',
    name: 'RPM',
    data: [ 4 ],
    yAxis: 2
}]
```

With all these additional changes, the following is the new look of the internal dial:

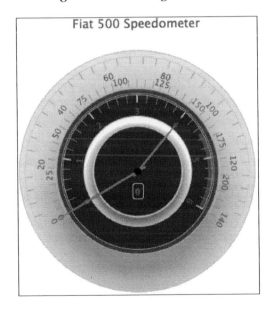

In the next part, we will address how to set up the look and feel of the dial needles.

Gauge series – dial and pivot

There are a couple of properties specific to the gauge series which are `plotOptions.gauge.dial` and `plotOptions.gauge.pivot`. The `dial` option controls the look and feel of the needle itself, whereas `pivot` is the tiny circle object at the center of the gauge attached to the dial.

First of all, we want to change the color and the thickness of the dials, as follows:

```
series: [{
    type: 'gauge',
    name: 'Speed',
    ....
    dial: {
        backgroundColor: '#FA3421',
        baseLength: '90%',
        baseWidth: 7,
        topWidth: 3,
        borderColor: '#B17964',
        borderWidth: 1
    }
}, {
    type: 'gauge',
    name: 'RPM',
    ....
    dial: {
        backgroundColor: '#FA3421',
        baseLength: '90%',
        baseWidth: 7,
        topWidth: 3,
        borderColor: '#631210',
        borderWidth: 1
    }
}]
```

The preceding code snippet results in the following:

First we widen the needle by setting the `baseWidth` option to 7 pixels across and 3 pixels at the end of the needle. Then instead of having the needle narrowing down gradually to the end of the tip, we set the `baseLength` option to `'90%'` which is the position on the dial where the needle starts to narrow down to a point.

As we can see, the dials are still not quite right in that they are not long enough to reach to their axis lines, as shown in the photo. Secondly, the rest of the dial bodies are not covered up. We can resolve this issue by fiddling with the `rearLength` option. The following is the amendment of series settings:

```
series: [{
    type: 'gauge',
    name: 'Speed',
    . . . . .
    dial: {
        . . . . .
        radius: '100%',
        rearLength: '-74%'
    },
    pivot: { radius: 0 }
}, {
```

```
    type: 'gauge',
    name: 'RPM',
    .....
    dial: {
        .....
        radius: '100%',
        rearLength: '-74%'
    },
    pivot: { radius: 0 }
}]
```

The trick is that instead of having a positive value like most of the gauge charts would have, we input a negative value that creates the covered-up effect. Finally, we remove the pivot by specifying `radius` as 0. The following is the final adjustment of the dials:

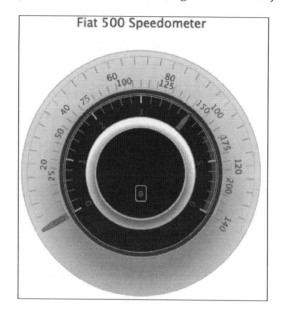

Polishing the chart with fonts and colors

The next step is to apply the axis options to tweak the tick intervals' color and size. The axis labels use fonts from the Google web fonts service (See `http://www.google.com/webfonts` for Google web fonts.). Then we adjust the font size and color similar to the one shown in the photo. There is a myriad of fonts to choose from with Google web fonts and they come with easy instructions to apply. The following is an example of embedding the "Squada One" font into the `<head>` section of an HTML file:

```
<link href='http://fonts.googleapis.com/css?family=Squada One'
  rel='stylesheet' type='text/css'>
```

This significantly improves the look of the gauge, as follows:

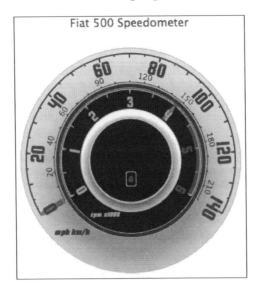

The final part is to transform the series data labels to resemble an LED screen. We will change the data labels' font size, style, and color and remove the border of the label box. The rpm data label has a smaller font size and moves above the mph data label. To make it look more realistic, we will also set the background for the data labels to a pale orange color. All the details of the tunings can be found in the online example at `http://joekuan.org/Learning_Highcharts/Chapter_6/`. The following is the final look of the polished gauge chart:

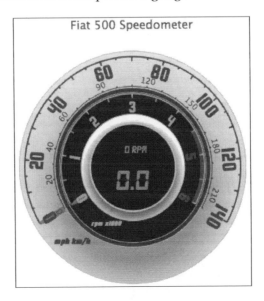

Converting a spline chart to a polar/radar chart

Polar (or radar) charts are generally used for spotting data trends. They have few differences to line and column type charts. Even though it may look like a pie chart, it has nothing in common with one. In fact, a polar chart is a round representation of the conventional two-dimensional charts. To visualize it another way, it is a folded line or a column chart placed in a circular way with both ends of x axis meeting together. The following screenshot illustrates the structure of a polar chart:

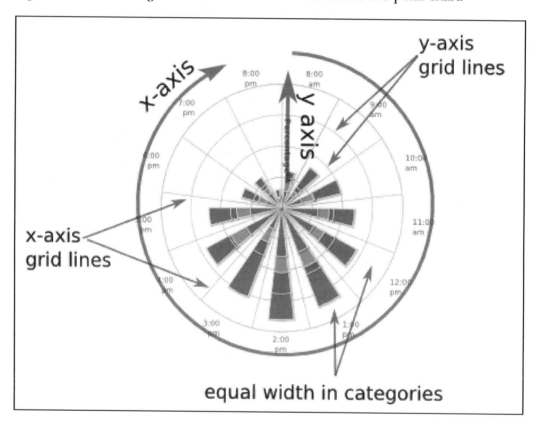

As there are very little differences in principle, the same also applies to the Highcharts configuration. Let's use our very first example browser's usage chart in *Chapter 1, Web Charts*, and turn it into a radar chart. Recalling the browser's line chart, we have the following:

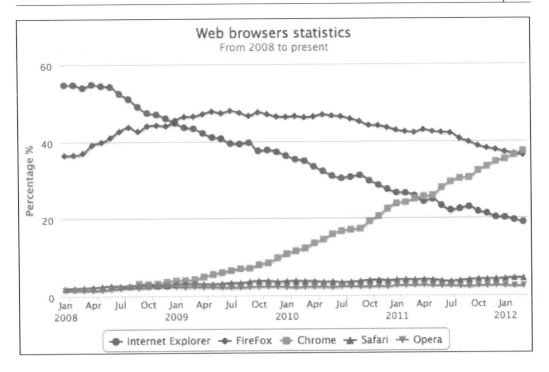

To turn the line chart into a polar chart, we only need to set the `chart.polar` option to `true` which transforms the orthogonal x and y coordinates into a polar coordinate system. To make the new polar chart easier to read, we set the x-axis labels' `rotation` to `'auto'`, as follows:

```
chart: {
    .....
    polar: true
},
.....,
xAxis: {
    ....,
    labels: { rotation:  'auto' }
},
```

The following is the polar version of the line chart:

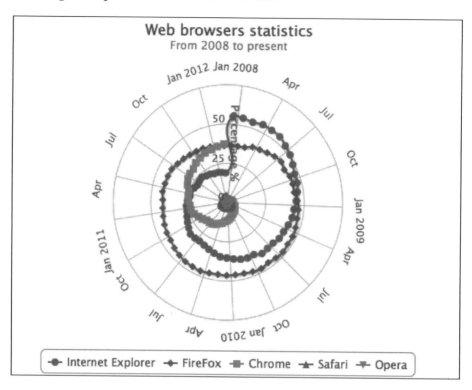

As we can see, a characteristic of a polar chart is that it reveals data trends differently compared to conventional charts. From a clockwise direction, we see the data line "spirals up" for an upward trend (Chrome) and "spirals down" for a downward trend (Internet Explorer), whereas the data line for Firefox reflects without much movement. As for Safari and Opera, essentially these series are lost as they are completely invisible. Another characteristic is that the last and first data points in the series are connected together. As a result, the Firefox series shows a closed loop and there is a sudden jump in the Internet Explorer series (the Chrome series is not connected because it already has null values in the beginning of the series; the Chrome browser was not released until late 2008.). To correct this behavior, we can simply add a null value at the end of each series data array to break the continuity, which is demonstrated in the following screenshot:

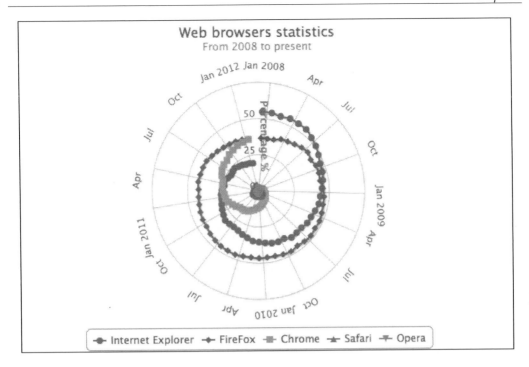

Instead of having a round polar chart, Highcharts supports polygon interpolation along the y-axis grid lines. This means the grid lines are straightened and the whole chart becomes like a spider web.

For the sake of illustration, we set the width of x- and y-axis lines to 0, which removes the round outline from the chart. Then we set a special option on the y axis—`gridLineInterpolation` to `'polygon'`. Finally, we change the `tickmarkPlacement` option of the x axis to `'on'` instead of the default value, `'between'`. This basically gets the interval ticks on the x axis to align with the start of each category. The following code snippet summarizes the changes that we need to make:

```
xAxis: {
    categories: [ ..... ],
    tickmarkPlacement: 'on',
    labels: {
        rotation: 'auto',
    },
    lineWidth: 0,
    plotBands: [{
        from: 10,
        to: 11,
        color: '#FF0000'
    }]
```

```
    },
    yAxis: {
        .....,
        gridLineInterpolation: 'polygon',
        lineWidth: 0,
        min: 0
    },
```

In order to demonstrate a spider web shape, we will remove most of the data samples from the previous chart. We will also add a couple of grid line decorations and an x-axis plot band (Nov – Dec) just to show that other axis options can still be applied to a polar chart:

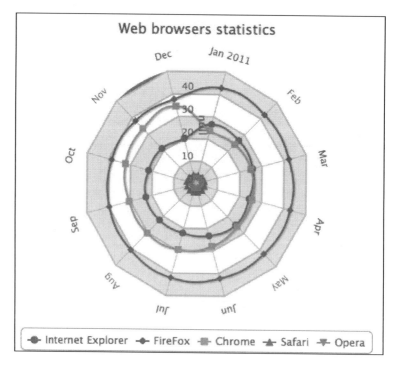

Plotting range charts with market index data

Range charts are really line and column type charts presenting a series of data in range. The set of range type series can be `arearange`, `areasplinerange`, and `columnrange`. These series expect an array of three data points, x, y min, y max, in the `data` option or array of y min, y max if `xAxis.cateogries` has already been specified.

Let's use our past examples to see whether we can make an improvement to the range charts. Back in *Chapter 2*, *Highcharts Configurations*, we have a five-series graph showing the monthly data of Nasdaq 100—open, close, high, low, and volume, as shown in the following screenshot:

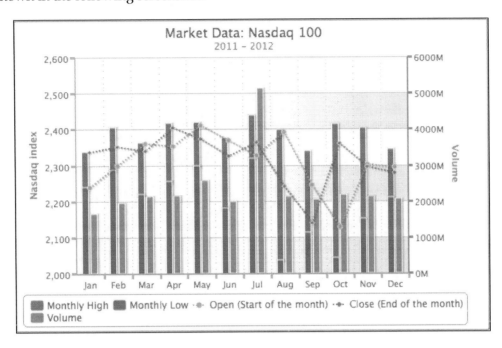

With the new range series, we sort the series data and merge the **Monthly High** and **Monthly Low** columns into a column range series and the **Open** and **Low** columns into an area spline range series, as follows:

```
series: [{
  type: 'columnrange',
  name: 'High & Low',
  data: [ [ 2237.73, 2336.04 ],
          [ 2285.44, 2403.52 ],
          [ 2217.43, 2359.98 ],  ...... ]
}, {
  type: 'areasplinerange',
  name: 'Open & Close',
  // This array of data are pre-sorted,
  // not in Open, Close order.
  data: [ [ 2238.66, 2336.04 ],
          [ 2298.37, 2350.99 ],
          [ 2338.99, 2359.78 ], ...... ]
}, {
  name: 'Volume',
  ......
```

The following screenshot shows the range chart version:

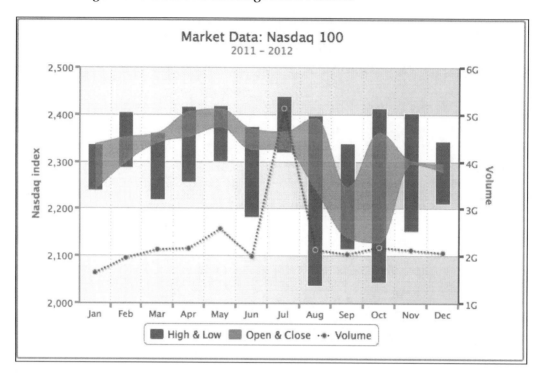

The new chart looks much simpler to read and the graph is less packed. It is worth noting that for the column range series, it is mandatory to keep the range as min to max order. As for the area spline and area range series type, we can still plot the range series even without sorting them beforehand.

For instance, the **High & Low** range series have to be in between min and max order, according to the natural meaning of the name of the series. However, this is not the same for the **Open & Close** range series; we wouldn't know which way is open or close. If we plot the **Open & Close** area range series by keeping the range as open to close order instead of y min to y max, the area range is displayed differently, as shown in the following screenshot:

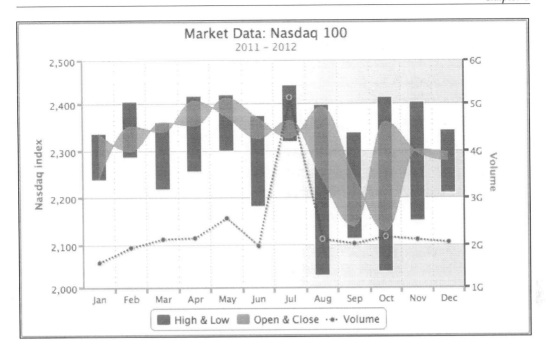

As we can see, there are twisted bits in the area range series; these crossovers are caused by the reverse order in the data pairs. Nonetheless, we won't know whether open is higher than close or vice versa. If we only want to know how wide the range between the **Open & Close** series is, then the preceding area range chart achieves the goal. By keeping them as separate series, there will be no such issue. In a nutshell, this is the subtle difference for plotting range series data with ambiguous meanings.

Using a radial gradient on a gauge chart

The radial gradient setting is based on SVG. As its name implies, a **radial gradient** is color shading radiating outwards in a circular direction. Therefore, it requires three properties to define the gradient circle—cx, cy, and r. The gradient circle is the outermost circle for shading, such that no shading can go outside of this. All the gradient positions are defined in ratio values between zero and one with respect to their containing elements. The cx and cy options are at the x, y center position of the outermost circle, whereas r is the radius of the outmost circle. If r is 0.5, it means the gradient radius is half the diameter of its element, that is, the same size as the containing pane. In other words, the gradient starts from the center and goes all the way to the edge of the gauge. The stop offsets option works the same way as the linear gradient; the first parameter is the ratio position in the gradient circle to stop the shading. These control the intensity of shading between the colors. The shorter the gap, the higher the contrast between the colors.

Let's explore how to set up the color gradient. The following is a mood swing detector without any color gradient:

We will apply a radial gradient to the preceding chart with the following settings:

```
background: [{
    backgroundColor: {
        radialGradient: {
            cx: 0.5,
            cy: 0.5,
             r: 0.5,
        },
        stops: [
            [ 0, '#CCD5DE' ],
            [ 1, '#002E59' ],
        ]
    }
}]
```

We have set cx, cy, and r to 0.5 for the gradient to start shading from the center position all the way towards the edge of the circle, as follows:

As we can see, the preceding chart shows white shading evenly radiating from the center. Let's change some of the parameters and see the effect:

```
backgroundColor: {
    radialGradient: {
        cx: 0.5,
        cy: 0.7,
        r: 0.25,
    },
    stops: [
        [ 0.15, '#CCD5DE' ],
        [ 0.85, '#002E59' ],
    ]
}
```

Here we have changed the size of the gradient circle to half the size of the gauge and moved the circle down. The bright color doesn't start shading until it reaches 15 percent of the size of the gradient circle, hence there is a distinct white blob in the middle, and the shading stops at 85 percent of the circle:

In the SVG radiant gradient, there are two other options, fx and fy, which are used for setting the focal point position for the shading; they are also referred to as the inner circle settings. Let's experiment with how the focal point can affect the shading:

```
backgroundColor: {
    radialGradient: {
        cx: 0.5,
        cy: 0.7,
        r: 0.25,
        fx: 0.6,
        fy: 1.0
    },
    stops: [
        [ 0.15, '#CCD5DE' ],
        [ 0.85, '#002E59' ],
    ]
}
```

The preceding code snippet produces the following:

We can observe that the `fx` and `fy` options move the bright color starting from the bottom of the gradient circle and slightly to the right-hand side. This makes the shading much more directional. Finally we can finish the chart by moving the bright side to where we want it to be, as follows:

 The `fx` and `fy` options are only for SVG, which older versions of Internet Explorer (8.0 or earlier) using VML won't support.

Summary

In this chapter we learned about gauge, polar, and range charts. An extensive step-by-step demonstration showed how to plot a complex speedometer by utilizing most of the gauge options. We also demonstrated the little difference between the polar, column, and line charts with respect to principle and configuration. We used range charts to improve past chapter examples and study the subtle differences they insert into the chart. Finally, we explored how to define radial gradients by tweaking the options in stages.

In the next chapter we will explore the Highcharts APIs, which are responsible for making a dynamic chart, such as using Ajax query to update the chart content, accessing components in Highcharts objects, and exporting charts to SVG.

7
Highcharts APIs

Highcharts offers a small set of APIs that are aimed for plotting charts with dynamic interactions. In order to understand how the APIs work, we must first familiarize ourselves with the chart's internal objects and how they are organized inside a chart. In this chapter, we will learn about the chart classes model and how to call the APIs by referencing the objects. Then a simple stock price application is built with PHP, jQuery, and jQuery UI to demonstrate the use of Highcharts APIs. After that, we turn our attention to four different ways of updating a series. We experiment with all the series update methods with a purpose to build an application to illustrate the variation in visual effects and CPU performance between them. Finally, we investigate the performance of updating a series in terms of different sizes of datasets with popular web browsers.

- Understanding the Highcharts class model
- Getting data in Ajax and displaying new series with `Chart.addSeries`
- Displaying multiple series with simultaneous Ajax calls
- Using `Chart.getSVG` to format SVG data into an image file
- Using `Chart.renderer` methods
- Exploring different methods to update series and their performances
- Experimenting Highcharts' performance on large datasets

Understanding the Highcharts class model

The relationship between Highcharts classes is very simple and obvious. A chart is composed of five different classes—Chart, Axis, Series, Point, and Renderer. Some of these classes contain an array of lower-level components and an object property to back reference to a higher level-owner component, for example, Point class has the series property pointing back to the owner Series class. Each class also has a set of methods for managing and displaying for its own layer. The following class diagram describes the association between these classes:

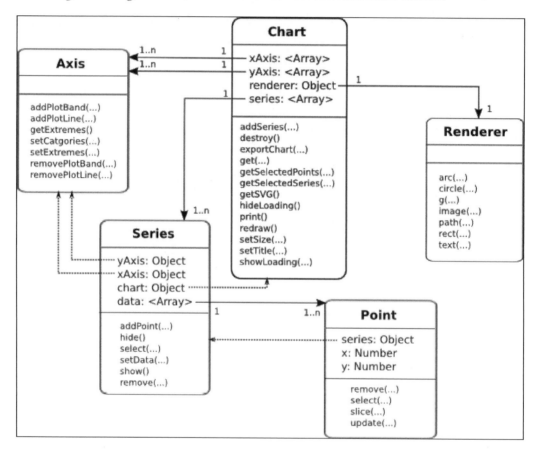

Chart is the top level class representing the whole chart object. It contains method calls to operate the chart as a whole, for example, exporting the chart into SVG or other image formats and setting the dimension of the chart, and so on. The class Chart has multiple arrays of Axis and Series objects, that is, a chart can have one or more x axis, y axis, and series. The Renderer class is a utility class that has a one-to-one relationship per chart and to provide a common interface for drawing in SVG and VML-based browsers.

The Series class has an array of Point objects. The class has back reference properties towards Chart and Axis objects (see the dotted lines in the previous diagram) and provides functions for managing its list of Point objects. The yAxis and xAxis properties in the Series class are necessary, as a chart can have multiple axes.

The Point class is just a simple object containing X and Y values and a back reference to its series object (see the dotted line). The APIs are for managing the data point in the chart.

Highcharts constructor – Highcharts.Chart

Needless to say, the most important method in the APIs is the Highcharts.Chart with which we have seen plenty of actions so far. However, there is more to this constructor call. Highcarts.Chart creates and returns a chart object but it also has a second optional parameter known as callback.

```
Chart(Object options, [ Function callback ])
```

The callback function is called when a chart is created and rendered. Inside the function, we can either call the components' methods or access the properties inside the chart object. The newly created chart object is passed via the only callback function parameter. We can also use the 'this' keyword inside the callback function, which also refers to the chart object. Instead of using the Highcharts. Chart callback parameter, we can achieve the same by declaring our code inside the chart.events.load handler, which will be explored in the next chapter.

For general use, it works fine to access the chart object after the Highcharts.Chart call. Strictly speaking, all the code referring to the chart object should be located inside the callback handler for two reasons as follows:

- There is an issue with IE that the $.ready method can be called before the scripts are loaded under a certain scenario (there is a bug in jQuery 1.8.0 in which the ready method is called before the scripts are loaded. See http://bugs.jquery.com/ticket/12018. This bug has been fixed in 1.8.1.). Putting the code inside the callback function can avoid such a problem.

- It can be beneficial if we want to run a concurrent JavaScript code on the chart object. For example, using the new HTML5 Worker object to split the heavy work into separate threads.

Navigating through Highcharts components

In order to use the Highcharts API, we must navigate to the right object inside the class hierarchy. There are several ways to traverse within the chart object—through the chart hierarchy model, retrieving the component directly with `Chart.get` method, or a mixture of both.

Using object hierarchy

Suppose that the chart object is created, as follows:

```
<script type="text/javascript">
  $(document).ready(function() {
    var chart = new Highcharts.Chart({
      ...
      xAxis: [{
        ....
      }, {
        ....
      }],
      series: [{
        data: [ ... ]
      }, {
        data: [ ... ]
      }],
      ...
    });
  }, function() {
    ...
  });
</script>
```

We can then get the first series object from the chart inside the callback handler as follows:

```
var series = this.series[0];
```

Suppose there are two x axes in the configuration. To retrieve the second x axis, we can do as follows:

```
var xAxis = this.xAxis[1];
```

To retrieve the third data point object from the second series of the chart, type the following :

```
var point = this.series[1].data[2];
```

Using the Chart.get method

Instead of cascading down the object hierarchy, we can directly retrieve the component using the `Chart.get` method (the `get` method is only available at the chart level, not in each component class). To do so, the component must be configured with the `id` option in the first place.

Suppose we have created a chart with the following configuration code:

```
xAxis: {
  id: 'xAxis',
  categories: [ ... ]
},
series: [{
  name: 'UK',
  id: 'uk',
  data: [ 4351, 4190,
      { y: 4028, id: 'thirdPoint' },
      ... ]
}]
```

We can retrieve the components as follows:

```
var series = this.get('uk');
var point = this.get('thirdPoint');
var xAxis = this.get('xAxis');
```

Using the object hierarchy and Chart.get method

It is cumbersome to define the `id` option for every component inside the chart. Alternatively, we can navigate through the components using both the approaches, as follows:

```
var point = this.get('uk').data[2];
```

Using Highcharts APIs

In this section, we will build an example using jQuery, jQuery UI, and Highcharts to explore each component's APIs. All the example code from here on will be using object hierarchy to access chart components, that is `chart.series[0].data[0]`. The user interface used here has a very minimal look and is far from perfect, as the main purpose of this exercise is to examine the Highcharts APIs.

First, let's see the usage of this user interface and then we will dissect the code to understand how the operations are performed. The following is the screenshot of the frontend:

This is a simple web front end for plotting the stock data chart for the past 30 days. The top part is a group of buttons for setting the stock symbols, getting the stock price, and retrieving the chart image by downloading it or via e-mail. The **Add to the list** button is for adding a stock symbol straight to the list without getting the stock prices and plotting the data. The **Plot All** button is for launching multiple stock price queries from the symbol list simultaneously and to plot the data when all the results arrive. Alternatively, **Add & Plot** is a quick option for plotting a single stock symbol.

The bottom half contains a chart that we have already created. The chart is displayed with empty data and axes with titles (setting the showAxes option to true). The whole idea is to re-use the existing chart rather than re-creating a new chart object every time new results arrive. Therefore there is no "flickering" effect when the chart is destroyed and created and it appears as a smooth update animation. Also this gives a better performance without running extra code to regenerate the chart object.

This example is also available online at http://joekuan.org/
Learning_Highcharts/Chapter_7/Example_1.html. Due to security
restrictions, the e-mail and download chart features are disabled in the
online demo.

Chart configurations

The following is the chart configuration used for the example. The x axis is
configured as a datetime type with intervals on a daily basis, as follows.

```
var chart = new Highcharts.Chart({
  chart: {
    renderTo: 'container',
    showAxes: true,
    borderWidth: 1
  },
  title: { text: 'Last 30 days stock price' },
  credits: { text: 'Learning Highcharts' },
  xAxis: {
    type: 'datetime',
    tickInterval: 24 * 3600 * 1000,
    dateTimeLabelFormats: { day: '%Y-%m-%d' },
    title: {
      text: 'Date',
      align: 'high'
    },
    labels: {
      rotation: -45,
      align : 'center',
      step: 2,
      y: 40,
      x: -20
    }
  },
  yAxis: {
    title: { text: 'Price ($)' }
  },
  plotOptions: {
    line: { allowPointSelect: true }
  }
});
```

Getting data in Ajax and displaying new series with Chart.addSeries

Let's examine the action behind the **Add & Plot** button, which is defined as the following HTML syntax:

```
<input type='button' value='Add & Plot' id='plotStock'>
```

The jQuery code for the button action is listed, as follows:

```
$('#plotStock').button().click(
  function(evt) {

    // Get the input stock symbol, empty the
    // list andinsert the new symbol into the list
    $('#stocklist').empty();
    var symbol = $('#symbol').val();
        $('#stocklist').append($("<li/>").append(symbol));

    // Kick off the loading screen
    chart.showLoading("Getting stock data ....");

    // Launch the stock query
    $.getJSON('./stockQuery.php?symbol=' +
                symbol.toLowerCase(),
        function(stockData) {
          // parse JSON response here
          .....
        }
    );
  }
);
```

The previous code defines the event handler for the **Add & Plot** button's click event. First, it empties all the entries in the stock symbol list box that have IDs as stocklist. Then it retrieves the stock symbol value from the input field symbol and appends the symbol into the list. The next step is to initiate a loading message screen on the chart by calling the chart.showLoading method. The following shows the loading message screen:

[180]

The next call is to launch a jQuery Ajax call, $.getJSON, to query the stock price. The server script stockQuery.php (of course any other server-side language can be used) does two tasks—resolves the symbol into full name of the organization and launches the symbol query from another website (http://ichart.finance.yahoo.com/) for the past stock price data, then packs the data into rows and encodes them into JSON format. The following is the code in the stockQuery.php file:

```php
<?php
  $ch = curl_init();
  curl_setopt($ch, CURLOPT_RETURNTRANSFER, true);

  // Get the stock symbol name
  curl_setopt($ch, CURLOPT_URL, "http://download.finance.yahoo.com/d/
quotes.csv?s={$symbol}&f=n");
  $result = curl_exec($ch);
  $name = trim(trim($result), '"');

  // Get from now to 30 days ago
  $now = time();
  $toDate = localtime($now, true);
  $toDate['tm_year'] += 1900;
  $fromDate = localtime($now - (86400 * 30), true);
  $fromDate['tm_year'] += 1900;
  $dateParams = "a={$fromDate['tm_mon']}&b={$fromDate['tm_
mday']}&c={$fromDate['tm_year']}" ."&d={$toDate['tm_
mday']}&e={$toDate['tm_mday']}&f={$toDate['tm_year']}";

  curl_setopt($ch, CURLOPT_URL, "http://ichart.finance.yahoo.com/
table.csv?s={$symbol}&{$dateParams}&g=d");
  $result = curl_exec($ch);
  curl_close($ch);

  // Remove the header row
  $lines = explode("\n", $result);
  array_shift($lines);

  $stockResult['rows'] = array();
  // Parse the result into dates and close value
  foreach((array) $lines as $ln) {
    if (!strlen(trim($ln))) {
      continue;
    }
```

```php
        list($date, $o, $h, $l, $c, $v, $ac) =
          explode(",", $ln, 7);
        list($year, $month, $day) = explode('-', $date, 3);
        $tm = mktime(12, 0, 0, $month, $day, $year);
        $stockResult['rows'][] =
          array('date' => $tm * 1000,
            'price' => floatval($c));
    }

    $stockResult['name'] = $name;
    echo json_encode($stockResult);
?>
```

The following is the result returned from the server side in JSON format:

```
{"rows":[ {"date":1348138800000,"price":698.7},
      {"date":1348225200000,"price":700.09},
      ... ],
  "name": "Apple Inc."
}
```

Once the JSON result arrives, the data is passed to the definition of the handler of getJSON and parsed into an array of rows. The following are the details of the handler code:

```javascript
$.getJSON('./stockQuery.php?symbol=' +
    symbol.toLowerCase(),
    function(stockData) {

        // Remove all the chart existing series
        while(chart.series.length) {
          chart.series[0].remove()
        }

        // Construct series data and add the series
        $.each(stockData.rows,
            function(idx, data) {
              $.histStock.push([ data.date,
                    data.price ]);
            }
        );

        var seriesOpts = {
          name: stockData.name + ' - (' + symbol +')',
          data: $.histStock,

          // This is to stop Highcharts rotating
          // the color and data point symbol for
          // the series
          color: chart.options.colors[0],
```

```
      marker: {
        symbol: chart.options.symbols[0]
      }
    };

    chart.hideLoading();
    chart.addSeries(seriesOpts);
  }
);
```

First of all, we remove all the existing series displayed in the chart by calling `Series.remove`. We then construct a series option with a data array of date (in UTC time) and price. We then remove the loading screen with `Chart.hideLoading` and display a new series with the `Chart.addSeries` methods. The only minor issue is that the default color and point marker for the series changes when the series is re-inserted, that is, the internal indices in `chart.options.colors` and `chart.options.symbols` are incremented when a series is removed and added back to the chart. We explicitly set the series color and point symbol to resolve this issue.

Alternatively, we can call `Series.setData` to achieve the same result but once the `name` (subject) of a series is assigned and the series is created, it is not allowed to change. Therefore, we stick to `Chart.addSeries` and `Series.remove` in this example.

The following is the screenshot of a single stock query:

Displaying multiple series with simultaneous Ajax calls

The next part is to explore how to launch multiple Ajax queries simultaneously and plot series together when all the results have been returned. The implementation is pretty much the same as plotting a single stock query except that we build up the series array option as we gather the result and plot them only when the last result arrives.

```
// Query all the stocks simultaneously and
// plot multipleseries in one go
$('#plotAll').button().click(

  function(evt) {

    // Kick off the loading screen
    chart.showLoading("Getting multiple stock data ....");

    // Get the list of stock symbols and launch
    // the query foreach symbol
    var total = $('#stocklist').children().length;

    // start Ajax request for each of the items separately
    $.each($('#stocklist').children(),
      function(idx, item) {
       var symbol = $(item).text();
       $.getJSON('./stockQuery.php?symbol=' +
         symbol.toLowerCase(),
            function(stockData) {

              // data arrives, buildup the series array
              $.each(stockData.rows,
                function(idx, data) {
                  $.histStock.push([ data.date,
                          data.price ]);
                }
              );
```

```
        seriesOpts.push({
         name: stockData.name + ' - (' +
             symbol +')',
         data: $.histStock,
         // This is to stop Highcharts
         // rotating the colorfor the series
         color: chart.options.colors[idx],
         marker: {
             symbol: chart.options.symbols[idx]
         }
        });

        // Plot the series if this result
        // is the last one
        if (seriesOpts.length == total) {

           // Remove all the chart existing series
           while (chart.series.length) {
              chart.series[0].remove()
           }

           chart.hideLoading();
           $.each(seriesOpts,
              function(idx, hcOption) {
               chart.addSeries(hcOption,
                      false);
              }
           );

           chart.redraw();
               } // else - do nothing,
         // not all results came yet
       } // function(stockData)
     ); // getJSON
  }); // $.each($('#stocklist')
}); // on('click'
```

The second Boolean parameter of `Chart.addSeries`, redraw, is passed as `false`. Instead, we finalize all the updates in one single call, `Chart.redraw`, to save CPU time. The following is the screenshot for the multiple stock queries:

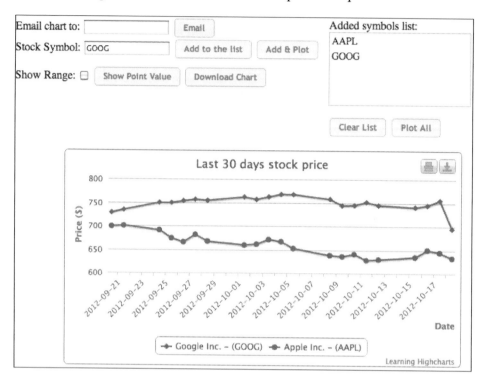

Extracting SVG data with Chart.getSVG

In this section, we will learn how to extract the chart output and deliver it via e-mail or file download. Although we can rely on the exporting module and call the `exportChart` method to export the chart into desired image format, it would be beneficial to see the whole process from formatting the original SVG content to an image file. After that, it is just a matter of calling different utilities to deliver the image file on the server side.

To extract the data underneath SVG from the displaying chart, the `getSVG` method is called, which is available when the exporting module is loaded. This method is similar to `exportChart`; it accepts the `chartOptions` parameter, which is for applying configurations towards the export chart output.

Here is the client-side jQuery code for handling both **Download** and **Email** buttons.

Here, we use the `protocol` variable to specify the action for the chart and both buttons call the defined common function, `deliverChart`:

```
// Export chart into SVG and deliver it to the server
function deliverChart(chart, protocol, target) {

  // First extracts the SVG markup content from the
  // displayed chart
  var svg = chart.getSVG();

  // Send the whole SVG to the server and url
  $.post('./deliverChart.php', {
    svg: svg,
    protocol: protocol,
    target: target
    },
    function(result) {
      var message = null;
      var title = null;

      switch (protocol) {

        // Create a dialog box to show the
        // sent status
        case 'mailto':
          message = result.success ?
            'The mail has been sent successfully' :
            result.message;
          title = 'Email Chart';
          break;

        // Uses hidden frame to download the
        // image file created on the server side
        case 'file':
          // Only popup a message if error occurs
          if (result.success) {
            $('#hidden_iframe').attr("src",
                    "dlChart.php");
          } else {
            message = result.message;
            title = 'Download Chart';
          }
          break;
      }

      if (message) {
        var msgDialog = $('#dialog');
```

```
        msgDialog.dialog({ autoOpen: false,
          modal: true, title: title});
        msgDialog.text(message);
        msgDialog.dialog('open');
      }
    }, 'json');
  }
```

The `deliverChart` method first calls the Highcharts API `getSVG` to extract the SVG content, then launches a POST call with both SVG data and action parameters. When $.post returns with a task status value, it shows a message dialog. As for the download chart, we create a hidden `<iframe>` to download the chart image file upon the success return.

The following is a simple server-side script for converting the SVG content and delivering the exported file:

```php
<?php
$svg = $_POST['svg'];
$protocol = $_POST['protocol'];
$target = $_POST['target'];

function returnError($output) {
  $result['success'] = false;
  $result['error'] = implode("<BR/>", $output);
  echo json_encode($result);
  exit(1);
}

// Format the svg into an image file
file_put_contents("/tmp/chart.svg", $svg);
$cmd = "convert /tmp/chart.svg /tmp/chart.png";
exec($cmd, $output, $rc);
if ($rc) {
  returnError($output);
}

// Deliver the chart image file according to the url
if ($protocol == 'mailto') {

  $cmd = "EMAIL='{$target}' mutt -s 'Here is the chart' -a /tmp/chart.
png -- {$protocol}:{$target} <<.
Hope you like the chart
.";
```

```
    exec($cmd, $output, $rc);
    if ($rc) {
     returnError($output);
    }
    $result['success'] = true;

} else if ($protocol == 'file') {
    $result['success'] = true;
}

echo json_encode($result);
?>
```

The web server is running on a Linux platform (Ubuntu 12.04). As for the e-mail action, we use two command line utilities to help us. First is a fast image conversion tool, **convert**, which is part of the **ImageMagick** package (see the package website for more details: http://www.imagemagick.org/script/index.php). Inside the script, we save the SVG data from the POST parameter into a file and then run the convert tool to format it into a PNG image. The convert tool supports many other image formats and comes with a myriad of advanced features. Alternatively, we can use Batik to do a straightforward conversion by issuing the following command:

```
java -jar batik-rasterizer.jar /tmp/chart.svg
```

The given command also converts an SVG file and outputs /tmp/chart.png automatically. For the sake of implementing the e-mail feature quickly, we will launch an e-mail tool, **mutt** (see the package website for more details: http://www.mutt.org), instead of using the PHP mail extension. Once the PNG image file is created, we use mutt to send it as an attachment and use a heredoc to specify the message body.

> A heredoc is a quick way of inputting string in a Unix command line with new lines and white spaces. See http://en.wikipedia.org/wiki/Here_document.

The following is the screenshot of the e-mail which is sent:

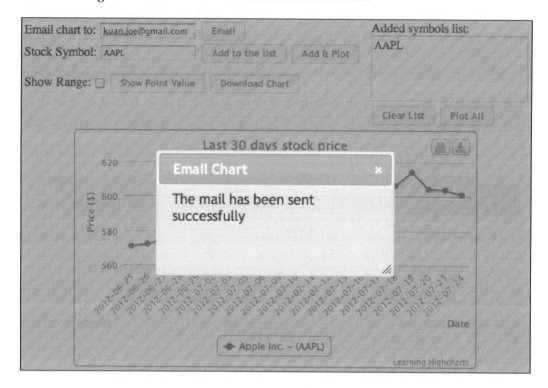

The following is the screenshot of the attachment e-mail which arrived in my e-mail account:

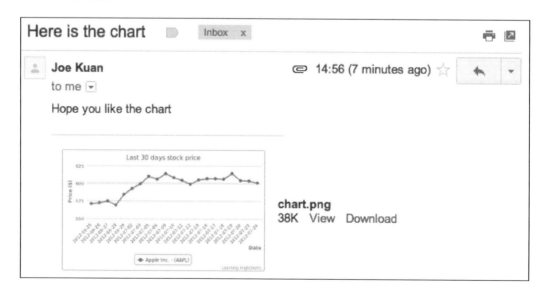

Selecting data points and adding plot lines

The next part is to implement the **Show Range** checkbox and the **Show Point Value** button. The **Show Range** option displays plot lines along the highest and lowest points in the chart, whereas **Show Point Value** displays a box with the value at the bottom left-hand side if a point is selected. The following screenshot demonstrates how both are enabled in the chart:

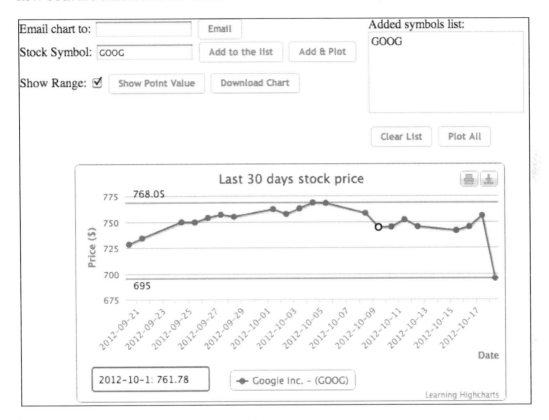

Although it is more natural for the **Show Point Value** checkbox to show the selected point display, this will become a callback implementation to every point select event. Instead, we use a button here, so that we can directly call the `Chart.getSelectedPoints` method.

Using Axis.getExtremes and Axis.addPlotLine

The `Axis.getExtremes` method not only returns the axis current minimum and maximum range in display, but also the highest and the lowest values for the data points. In here, we use the method to combine with `Axis.addPlotLine` function to add a pair of plot lines along the y axis. The `addPointLine` routine expects a plot line configuration. In this example we specify a data label as well as an `id` name, such that we can remove lines at both high and low ends when the **Show Range** is unchecked or plot lines need to be redisplayed with a new value. The following is the code for the **Show Range** action:

```
// Show the highest and lowest range in the plotlines.
var showRange = function(chart, checked) {
   if (!chart.series || !chart.series.length) {
   return;
   }

   // Checked or not checked, we still need to remove
   // any existing plot lines first
   chart.yAxis[0].removePlotLine('highest');
   chart.yAxis[0].removePlotLine('lowest');

   if (!checked) {
     return;
   }

   // Checked - get the highest & lowest points
   var extremes = chart.yAxis[0].getExtremes();

   // Create plot lines for the highest & lowest points
   chart.yAxis[0].addPlotLine({
     width: 2,
     label: {
       text: extremes.dataMax,
       enabled: true,
       y: -7
     },
     value: extremes.dataMax,
     id: 'highest',
     zIndex: 2,
     dashStyle: 'dashed',
     color: '#33D685'
   });

   chart.yAxis[0].addPlotLine({
     width: 2,
     label: {
```

```
        text: extremes.dataMin,
        enabled: true,
        y: 13
    },
    value: extremes.dataMin,
    zIndex: 2,
    id: 'lowest',
    dashStyle: 'dashed',
    color: '#FF7373'
  });
};
```

Using Chart.getSelectedPoints and Chart.renderer methods

The **Show Point Value** button makes use of the `Chart.getSelectedPoints` method to retrieve the data point that is currently selected. Note that this method requires the series option `allowPointSelect` to be enabled in the first place. Once a data point is selected and the **Show Point Value** button is clicked, we use functions provided by the `Chart.renderer` to draw a tooltip-like box showing the selected value. We can use the method `Renderer.path` or `Renderer.rect` to draw the rounded box, then `Renderer.text` for the data value.

 Highcharts also supports multiple data point selection which can be done by clicking on the left mouse button while holding the *Ctrl* key pressed.

Additionally, we use the `Renderer.g` routine to group the SVG box and value string together and add the resulting group element into the chart. The reason for that is that we can re-display the box with a new value by removing the old group object as a whole instead of each individual element.

```
$('#showPoint').button().click(function(evt) {
    // Remove the point info box if exists
    chart.infoBox && (chart.infoBox =
            chart.infoBox.destroy());

    // Display the point value box if a data point
    // is selected
    var selectedPoint = chart.getSelectedPoints();
    var r = chart.renderer;
    if (selectedPoint.length) {
        chart.infoBox = r.g();
        r.rect(20, 255, 150, 30, 3).attr({
```

```
       stroke: chart.options.colors[0],
       'stroke-width': 2
    }).add(chart.infoBox);

    // Convert selected point UTC value to date string
    var tm = new Date(selectedPoint[0].x);
    tm = tm.getFullYear() + '-' +
       (tm.getMonth() + 1) + '-' + tm.getDate();
    r.text(tm + ': ' + selectedPoint[0].y,
       28, 275).add(chart.infoBox);
    chart.infoBox.add();
  }
});
```

Highcharts' Renderer class also comes with other methods to draw simple SVG shapes on the chart, such as arc, circle, image, rect, text, g, and path. For more advanced shapes, we can use the path method, which accepts SVG path syntax and has limited support on VML path. Moreover, the Renderer class can be used independently from a chart, that is, we can call methods of the Renderer class without creating a chart beforehand and add SVG contents to an HTML element.

```
var renderer = new Highcharts.Renderer($('#container')[0],
            200, 100);
```

This creates a Renderer object that allows us to create SVG elements inside the container element with an area 200 pixels wide and 100 pixels high.

Exploring the series update

The series update is one of the most frequent tasks performed in charts. In this section, we investigate it in high definition. In Highcharts, there are several approaches to update a series. Generally, we can update a series from a series or data point level. Then the update method itself can be either an actual changing or re-inserting the value. We will discuss each approach and create a comprehensive example to experiment with all the techniques.

In order to compare each approach, we continue using stock market data but we will change the user interface this time to be able to replay through the historical stock price. The following is the screenshot of the example in action:

As we can see, there are multiple selection boxes to choose from: how many years of historical stock price to replay, how many data points to update in each iteration, and how long the wait is in between each update. Most importantly, we can choose which series update method to be used, and it is interesting to observe the behavioral difference between them, especially during the whole replay. This demo is also available on my website at `http://joekuan.org/Learning_Highcharts/ Chapter_7/Example_2.html`. I strongly recommend readers to give it a go. Before we look into each update approach, let's find out how to construct this continuous series update process.

Continuous series update

Once we enter a stock symbol and select the number of years of stock price to replay, we can click on the **Load Data** button to retrieve the price data. Once the data arrives, a confirm dialog is popped up with the **Start** button to kick-start the process. The following is the action code for the **Start** button:

```
// Create a named space to store the current user
// input field values and the timeout id
$.histStock = {};

$('#Start').button().click(function() {

  chart.showLoading("Loading stock price ... ");

  // Remove old timeout if exists
  $.histStock.timeoutID &&
    clearTimeout($.histStock.timeoutID);

  var symbol =
    encodeURIComponent($('#symbol').val().toLowerCase());
  var years = encodeURIComponent($('#years').val());

  // Remember current user settings and initialize values
  // for the run
  $.histStock = {
    // First loop start at the beginning
    offset: 0,
    // Number of data pts to display in each iteration
    numPoints: 30,
    // How long to wait in each iteration
    wait: parseInt($('#updateMs').val(), 10),
    // Which Highcharts method to update the series
    method: $('#update').val(),
    // How many data points to update in each iteration
    'update:' parseInt($('#updatePoints').val(), 10)
  };

  // Clean up old data points from the last run
  chart.series.length && chart.series[0].setData([]);

  // Start Ajax query to get the stock history
  $.getJSON('./histStock.php?symbol=' + symbol +
      '&years=' + years,
    function(stockData) {
```

```
        // Got the whole period of historical stock data
        $.histStock.name = stockData.name;
        $.histStock.data = stockData.rows;

        chart.hideLoading();
        // Start the chart refresh
        refreshSeries();
      }
    );
  })
```

We first create a variable histStock under the jQuery namespace, which is accessed by various parts within the demo. The histStock variable holds the current user's inputs and the reference to the refresh task. Any changes from the user interface updates the $.histStock, hence the series update responds accordingly.

Basically, when the **Start** button is clicked, we initialize the $.histStock variable and start an Ajax query with the stock symbol and number of years parameters. Then when the stock price data returns from the query, we store the result into the variable. We then call refreshSeries, which calls itself by the setting via a timer routine. The following code is the simplified version of the method:

```
var refreshSeries = function() {
  var i = 0, j;

  // Update the series data according to each approach
  switch ($.histStock.method) {
    case 'setData':
      ....
    break;
    case 'renewSeries':
      ....
    break;
    case 'update':
      ....
    break;
    case 'addPoint':
      ....
    break;
  }

  // Shift the offset for the next update
  $.histStock.offset += $.histStock.update;

  // Update the jQuery UI progress bar
  ....
```

```
  // Finished
  if (i == $.histStock.data.length) {
    return;
  }

  // Setup for the next loop
  $.histStock.timeoutID =
      setTimeout(refreshSeries, $.histStock.wait);
};
```

Inside the `refreshSeries`, it inspects the settings inside the `$.histStock` and updates the series depending on the user's choice. Once the update is done, we increment the `offset` value, which is at the start position for copying the stock result data into the chart. If the counter variable `i` hits the end of the stock data, then it simply exits the method. Otherwise, call the JavaScript timer function to set up the next loop. The next goal is to review how each update method is performed.

Running the experiment

There are four techniques for updating the series data: `Series.setData`, `Series.remove`/`Chart.addSeries`, `Point.update`, and `Series.addPoint`. We measure the performance for all four techniques in terms of CPU usage. A CPU measurement tool `typeperf` is running in the background in another window. Each method is timed for replaying the stock prices for past one year along with 0.5 seconds of wait between each update. We repeated the same run twice and took the average. The experiment is repeated on a selection of browsers: Firefox, Chrome, Internet Explorer 8 and 9, and Safari. Although IE 8 does not support SVG and only supports VML, it is important to bring into the experiment because Highcharts' implementation is compatible with IE 8. Also, IE8 still has a significant presence in the browser market. One thing that we instantly notice is the same chart on IE8 is not as appealing as in SVG.

> The whole experiment is running on a Windows 7 PC and the hardware is 2 GB RAM Core 2 Duo 2.66 GHz and ATI Radeon 4890 1 GB.
>
> The browser versions are Firefox 16.0.1, Chrome 22.0.1129, IE9 9.0.8112, Safari 5.1.7, and IE8 8.0.760.

In the following sections, each series update approach is explained and a performance comparison is presented between the browsers. Readers must not conclude the result as a guideline of the browser's general performance which is derived from running a myriad of tests in a number of areas. What we are experimenting here is only how Highcharts performs on each browser in terms of SVG animations.

Applying a new set of data with Series.setData

We can apply a new set of data to an existing series using the
`Series.setData` method.

```
setData (Array<Mixed> data, [Boolean redraw])
```

The data can be either an array of one dimensional data, an array of x and y value
pairs, or an array of data point objects. Note that this method is the simplest form of
all the approaches, which doesn't provide any animation effect at all. Here is how we
use the `setData` function in our example:

```
case 'setData':
  var data = [];

  // Building up the data array in the series option
  for (i = $.histStock.offset, j = 0;
       i < $.histStock.data.length &&
       j < $.histStock.numPoints; i++, j++) {
    data.push([
      $.histStock.data[i].date,
      $.histStock.data[i].price ]);
  }

  if (!chart.series.length) {

    // Insert the very first series
    chart.addSeries({
      name: $.histStock.name,
      data: data
    });
  } else {

    // Just update the series with
    // the new data array
    chart.series[0].setData(data, true);
  }
  break;
```

With no animations, the whole replay becomes choppy. The following graph shows the performance comparison on using the `setData` method across the browsers:

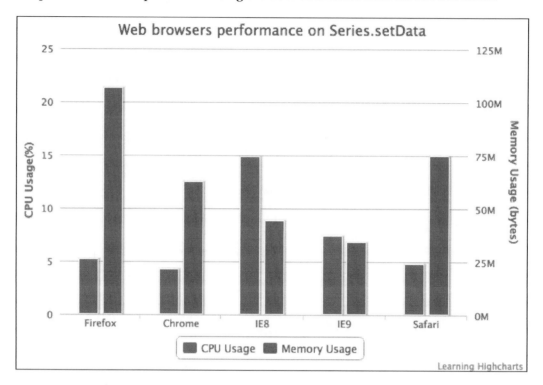

As `setData` has no animation effect, the method does not take as much CPU usage as expected, except for IE8, which does not support SVG. The VML technology runs rather slowly and that explains the higher CPU usage. Among the browsers, Chrome has the lowest CPU usage (4.25 percent), the next lowest is Safari (4.79 percent), and then Firefox. Out of the browsers, Firefox has the highest memory footprint, whereas IE 9 consumed the least. Perhaps a slight surprise is that Safari has a better performance than Firefox and is also very close to Chrome.

Using Series.remove and Chart.addSeries to reinsert series with new data

Alternatively, we can remove the whole series with the Series.remove method. Then rebuild the series options with the data and reinsert a new series using Chart.addSeries. The downside of this approach is that the internal index for the default colors and point symbols are incremented, like we came across in the earlier example. We can compensate for that by specifying the color and the marker options. Here is the code for the addSeries method:

```
case 'renewSeries':
  var data = [];
  for (i = $.histStock.offset, j = 0;
      i < $.histStock.data.length &&
      j < $.histStock.numPoints; i++, j++) {
    data.push([ $.histStock.data[i].date,
          $.histStock.data[i].price ]);
  }
  // Remove all the existing series
  if (chart.series.length) {
    chart.series[0].remove();
  }

  // Re-insert a new series with new data
  chart.addSeries({
    name: $.histStock.name,
    data: data,
    color: chart.options.colors[0],
    marker: {
      symbol: chart.options.symbols[0]
    }
  });
  break;
```

In this experiment, we use the refresh rate for every half a second, which is shorter than the time span of default animation. Hence, the series update appears choppy, like in setData. However, if we change the refresh rate to 3 seconds or more, then we can see the series being redrawn from the left-hand to the right-hand side in each update.

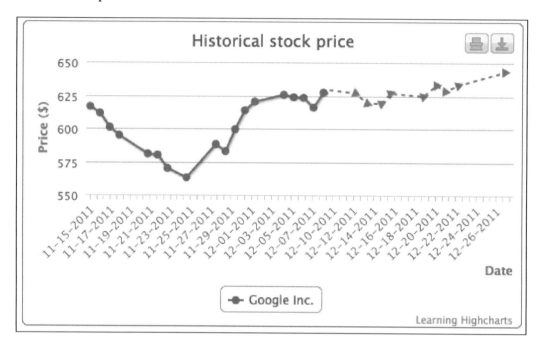

The following graph shows the performance comparison on using the addSeries method across the browsers:

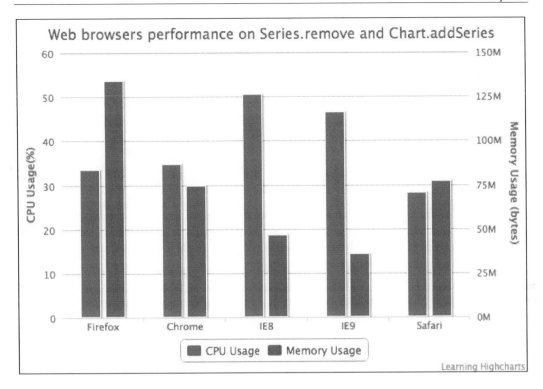

The memory consumption remains roughly the same as the previous test. Both IE8 and IE9 have higher CPU usages. The most unusual result is that Safari requires less CPU usage compared to both Chrome and Firefox. We will investigate this further in a later section.

Updating data points with Point.update

We can update individual data points with the `Point.update` method. The update method has a similar prototype as the `setData`, which accepts a single value, an array of x and y values, or a data point object. Each update call can be redrawn into the chart with or without animation.

```
update ([Mixed options], [Boolean redraw], [Mixed animation])
```

Here is how we use the `Point.update` method; we traverse through each point object and call its member function. In order to save CPU time, we set the `redraw` parameter to `false` and call `Chart.redraw` after the last data point is updated:

```
case 'update':
  // Note: Series can be already existed
  // at start if we click 'Stop' and 'Start'
  // again
  if (!chart.series.length ||
      !chart.series[0].points.length) {
    // Build up the first series
    var data = [];
    for (i = $.histStock.offset, j = 0;
         i < $.histStock.data.length &&
         j < $.histStock.numPoints; i++, j++) {
      data.push([
        $.histStock.data[i].date,
        $.histStock.data[i].price ]);
    }

    if (!chart.series.length) {
      chart.addSeries({
        name: $.histStock.name,
        data: data
      });
    } else {
      chart.series[0].setData(data);
    }

  } else {
    // Updating each point
    for (i = $.histStock.offset, j = 0;
         i < $.histStock.data.length &&
         j < $.histStock.numPoints; i++, j++) {
      chart.series[0].points[j].update([
        $.histStock.data[i].date,
        $.histStock.data[i].price ],
        false);
    }
    chart.redraw();
  }
  break;
```

`Point.update` animates each data point vertically; overall it gives a wavy effect as the graph is progressively updated. Another difference in animation is the x axis labels; the labels approach the axis line diagonally in `Chart.addSeries`, whereas labels just shift horizontally in `Point.update`.

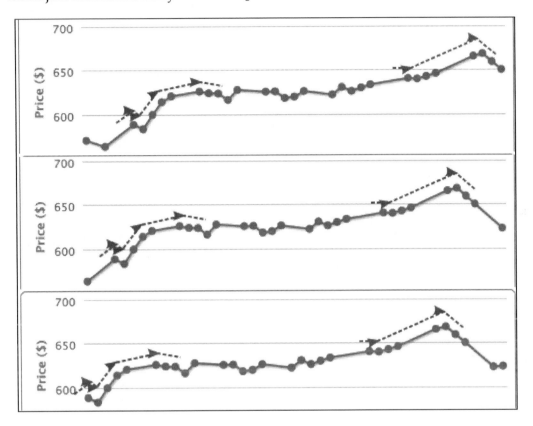

The following graph shows the performance comparison of the `Point.update` method across the browsers:

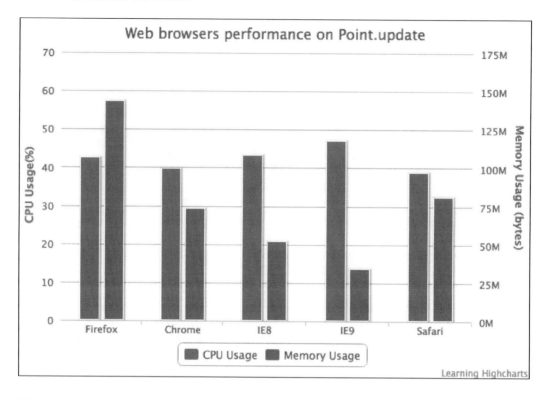

The memory footprint remains roughly static across all the browsers. The CPU usage in each browser is fractionally less than the last experiment, which indicates that there are fewer animations.

Removing and adding data points with Point. remove and Series.addPoint

Instead of updating each individual data point, we can use `Point.remove` to remove data points within the `series.data` array and use `Series.addPoint` to add new data points back into the series.

```
remove ([Boolean redraw], [Mixed animation])
addPoint (Object options, [Boolean redraw], [Boolean shift],
        [Mixed animation])
```

As for the time series data, we can use `addPoint` alone with `shift` parameter set to `true`, which will automatically shift the series point array:

```
case 'addPoint':
  // Note: Series can be already existed at
  // start if we click 'Stop' and 'Start' again
  if (!chart.series.length ||
    !chart.series[0].points.length) {

    // Build up the first series
    var data = [];
    for (i = $.histStock.offset, j = 0;
        i < $.histStock.data.length &&
      j < $.histStock.numPoints; i++, j++) {
      data.push([
        $.histStock.data[i].date,
        $.histStock.data[i].price ]);
    }

    if (!chart.series.length) {
      chart.addSeries({
        name: $.histStock.name,
        data: data
      });
    } else {
      chart.series[0].setData(data);
    }

    // This is different, we don't redraw
    // any old points
    $.histStock.offset = i;

  } else {

    // Only updating the new data point
    for (i = $.histStock.offset, j = 0;
      i < $.histStock.data.length &&
      j < $.histStock.update; i++, j++) {
      chart.series[0].addPoint([
        $.histStock.data[i].date,
        $.histStock.data[i].price ],
        false, true );
    }
    chart.redraw();
  }
  break;
```

The `addPoint` approach has a better overall display, in that all the data points smoothly slide from the right-hand to the left-hand side and the labels are also shifted horizontally.

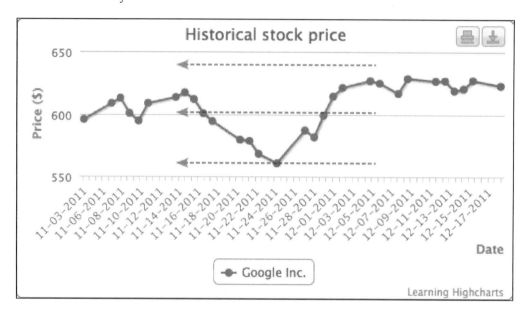

The following graph shows the performance comparison of the `Point.update` method across the browsers:

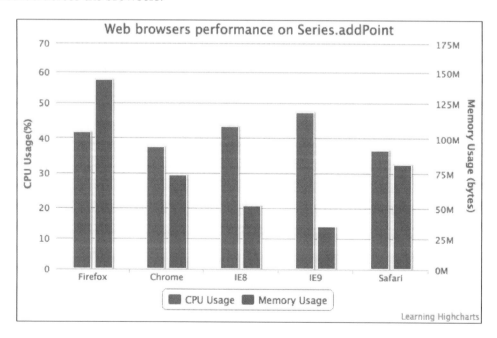

There is hardly any difference in the `Point.update` method in terms of both CPU and memory usage.

Exploring SVG animations performance on browsers

So far we have seen the CPU cost increased with animations. However, the question left unanswered is why Safari has lower CPU consumption than Chrome and Firefox. A number of browser benchmark suites have been run on the test machine to confirm the general consensus that Firefox and Chrome browsers have an overall better performance than Safari.

 All browsers were benchmarked with SunSpider – `http://www.webkit.org/perf/sunspider/sunspider.html`, Google's V8 Benchmark suite – `http://v8.googlecode.com/svn/data/benchmarks/v3/run.html`, and Peacekeeper – `http://peacekeeper.futuremark.com/`.

Nonetheless, there is one particular area where Safari has better performance than the other browsers, which is SVG animations, and this is reflected in our previous experiments. In here, we use a benchmark test written by Cameron Adams, which is designed to especially measure SVG animations with bouncing particles in frames per second. The test (HTML5 versus Flash: Animation Benchmarking `http://www.themaninblue.com/writing/perspective/2010/03/22/`) was originally written for comparing various HTML5 animation technologies against Flash. In here, we run the SVG test with Chrome and Safari browsers; the following is a Safari screenshot running with a 500 particles test:

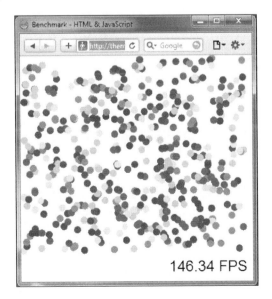

As for Chrome, the test is running at around 102 FPS. We repeat the assessment with various numbers of particles between both browsers. The following graph summarizes the performance difference in SVG animations:

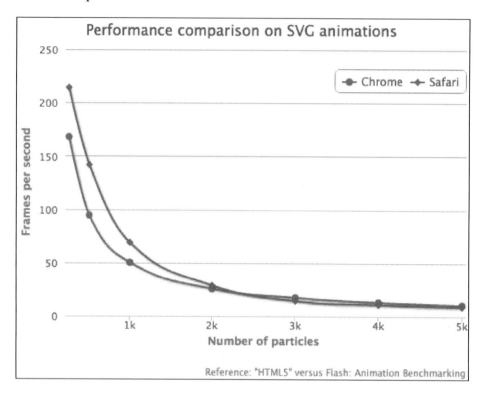

As we can see, Safari manages higher frame rates with particles less than 2,000. After that, the Safari performance starts to degrade in alignment with Chrome.

This leads to another inevitable question—why is there such a difference given that both browsers run with the same code base of webkit? It is difficult to pinpoint where the discrepancy is caused. However, one of the few differences in both products is the JavaScript engines, which may affect that area, or the minor difference in the webkit version. In addition, other specific SVG performance tests in http://jsperf.com are also run, in which Safari again has a higher score than Chrome.

In the next section, we will see how Highcharts' performance corresponds to data size.

Comparing Highcharts' performance on large datasets

Our final test is to observe how Highcharts performs in large datasets. In this experiment, we are going to plot scatter series across various data sizes and observe the time taken to display the data. We chose to use the scatter series because when there is a very large dataset in tens of thousands of samples, the user is likely to plot only data points in the chart.

In this analysis, a simple HTML page with a chart and **Stop Timing** button is constructed. The page is loaded with URL parameters to specify the dataset size. We repeat the experiment with the same dataset size on each browser used in previous benchmarks. Once the page is loaded on a browser, the dataset is randomly generated. Then timing begins right before the chart object is constructed, then when the chart is finally displayed onto the screen, the **Stop Timing** button is clicked to measure the time taken from chart creation to display, like the following screenshot timing the display of 3,000 data points on Firefox browser:

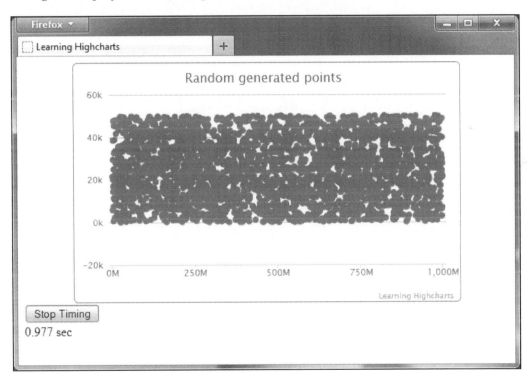

We don't measure the stop time when the chart is rendered through the `callback` parameter in `Highcharts.Chart` or `events.load handler`. This is because for large datasets, there is a large time gap from the rendered chart to the actual display, where this is negligible for the normal size dataset. Hence relying on the chart rendered property will result in a smaller time frame than the actual time taken.

The following graph illustrates Highcharts' performance on different browsers with various dataset sizes:

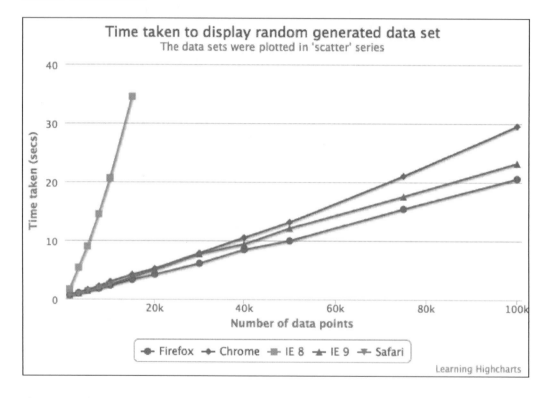

The most obvious part from the previous graph is the skewed line from IE8 performance. As IE8 uses the obsolete VML, it is around 2.5 times slower than IE9 at 1,000 data points, and approximately just under 10 times slower at 15,000 data points. Besides, it is difficult to time IE8 reliably after that point, as the long timing process has on-going interruptions by warning dialogs.

As we can see, the general performance of SVG is going in one direction whereas VML is almost heading north. To put it another way, this graph demonstrates the scalability difference between the VML and SVG technologies.

Among the SVG browsers, they all have very close performance ranges in the region of 1,000 - 10,000 data points, which takes from 0.56 seconds to 2.99 seconds. In terms of scalability, Safari on the Windows platform did not complete the whole experiment. Beyond 10,000 samples, the timing for the browser becomes erratic.

Apart from Safari, all the browsers pretty much have linear performance as the number of data points increases. Chrome performance starts to diverge at 50,000 data points. Firefox overall is more scalable in terms of running Highcharts. All the three browsers are capable of running further but this probably exceeds the users' needs. For general usage, it is unlikely to plot above 1,000 data points. However, the most important thing is that Highcharts runs pretty well across all the browsers for normal use and is capable of going beyond this, if required.

Summary

In this chapter, we studied the Highcharts APIs from the class model to applying them in applications. Then a comprehensive study was done on all the different techniques to update a chart series in Highcharts and an experiment was carried out analyzing the differences in their performances. Finally the chapter finished by analyzing the speed in rendering data points with regards to different sizes of large datasets and web browsers.

In the next chapter, we will look into Highcharts events handling, which is closely related to Highcharts APIs.

8
Highcharts Events

In the last chapter we learned about the Highcharts API. In this chapter we will go through Highcharts events handling. We will start the chapter by introducing the set of events that are supported by Highcharts. Then we will build two web applications to cover most of the events; each one explores a different set of events. Although the applications are far from perfect and there is plenty of room for improvement, the sole purpose is to aim at demonstrating how Highcharts events work. In this chapter we will cover the following:

- Launching an Ajax query with a chart load event
- Activating the user interface with a chart redraw event
- Selecting and unselecting a data point with point select and unselect event
- Zooming the selected area with the chart selection event
- Hovering over a data point with point mouseOver and mouseOut events
- Using the chart click event to create plot lines
- Launching a dialog with the series click event
- Launching a pie chart with the series checkboxClick event
- Editing the pie chart with the point click, update, and remove events

Introducing Highcharts events

So far, we have gone through most of the Highcharts configurations, however there is one area not yet covered, which is event handling. Highcharts offers a set of event options in several areas such as chart events, series events, and axis base events, and they are triggered by API calls and user interactions with the chart.

Highcharts events can be specified through object configuration while creating a chart or through APIs that accept object configurations, such as `Chart.addSeries`, `Axis.addPlotLine`, and `Axis.addPlotBand`.

An event object is passed by an event handler, which contains mouse information and specific action data related to the event action; for example, `event.xAxis[0]` and `event.yAxis[0]` are stored in the event parameter for the `chart.events.click` handler. Inside each event function, the `'this'` keyword can be used and refers to a Highcharts component where the event function is based. For example, the `'this'` keyword in `chart.events.click` refers to the `chart` object, and the `'this'` keyword in `plotOptions.series.events.click` refers to the `series` object being clicked.

The following is a list of Highcharts events:

- `chart.events`: `addSeries`, `click`, `load`, `redraw`, `selection`

- `plotOptions.<series-type>.events`: `click`, `checkboxClick`, `hide`, `mouseOver`, `mouseOut`, `show`

> Alternatively, we can specify event options specifically to a series in the series array, for example:
>
> `series[ { events: { click: function { ... }, .... } } ]`

- `plotOptions.<series-type>.point.events`: `click`, `mouseOver`, `mouseOut`, `remove`, `select`, `unselect`, `update`

> We can define point events for a specific series, as follows:
>
> `series[ { point : { events: { click: function() { ... } }, ... } ]`
>
> As for defining events for a particular data point in a series, we can specify them, as follows:
>
> `series[ { data: [ { events: { click: function() { ... } } ], ... } ]`

- `x/yAxis.events`: `setExtremes`

- `x/yAxis.plotBands[x].events` and `x/yAxis.plotLines[x].events`: `click`, `mouseover`, `mousemove`, `mouseout`

The Highcharts online documentation provides a comprehensive reference and plenty of mini examples; you are strongly recommended to refer to that. There is not much point in repeating the same exercise. Instead, we will build two slightly sizable examples to utilize most of the Highcharts events and demonstrate how these events can work together in an application. Since the complete example code can be too much to list in this chapter, only the relevant parts are edited and shown. The full demo and source code can be found at `http://joekuan.org/Learning_Highcharts/Chapter_8/Example_1.html`.

Portfolio history example

This application basically extends from the historical stock chart in the previous chapter with an additional investment portfolio feature. The frontend is implemented with jQuery and jQuery UI, and the following events are covered in this example:

- `chart.events`: `click, load, redraw, selection`
- `plotOptions.series.points.events`: `mouseOver, mouseOut, select, unselect`
- `xAxis/yAxis.plotLines.events`: `mouseover, click`

The following is the startup screen of the demo with the components labeled:

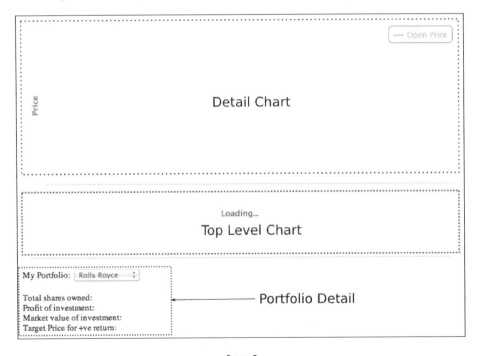

The application contains a pair of time series charts. The bottom chart is the top-level graph, which shows the entire historic price movement and points to when company shares are bought and sold. The top chart is the detail chart, which zooms in to the finer details when a selected area is made in the bottom graph.

As soon as the web application is loaded on to a browser, both charts are created. The top-level chart is configured with a load event, which automatically requests a stock historic price and portfolio history from the web server.

The following screenshot shows a graph after the top-level chart is autoloaded:

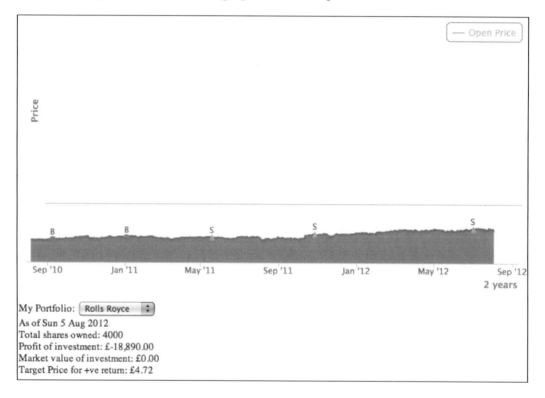

There are circular and triangular data points laid on top of the top-level chart; these denote the trade history. The **B** symbol indicates when the shares have been bought, whereas **S** signifies when they are sold. The information below the top-level chart is the portfolio detail for the stock as of the current date.

If we click on one of these trade history points, the portfolio detail section is updated to reflect the investment history as of the selected date. Moreover when we select an area, it zooms in and displays the stock price movement in the detail chart. There are other features involved in event handling and we will discuss them in the later sections.

Top-level chart

The following is the configuration code for the top-level chart (the bottom chart is showing the entire historic price movement) and we store the chart object inside the myApp namespace, as follows:

```
$.myApp.topChart = new Highcharts.Chart({
    chart: {
        zoomType: 'x',
        spacingRight: 15,
        renderTo: 'top-container',
        events: {
            // Load the default stock symbol of
            // the portfolio
            load: function() {  ....  },

            // The top level time series have
            // been redrawn, enable the portfolio
            // select box
            redraw: function() { .... },

            // Selection - get all the data points from
            // the selection and popluate into the
            // detail chart
            selection: function(evt) {  ....  },
        }
    },
    title: { text: null },
    yAxis: {
        title: { text: null },
        gridLineWidth: 0,
        labels: { enabled: false }
    },
    tooltip: { enabled: false },
    xAxis: {
        title: { text: null },
        type: 'datetime'
    },
    series: [ ... ],
    legend: { enabled: false },
    credits: { enabled: false }
});
```

There is a lot going on in this configuration. The chart is defined with most of the features disabled, such as tooltip, title, legend, and y-axis label. More importantly, the chart is configured with a zoomType option, which enables the chart to be zoomable along the x-axis direction, hence we can use the select event. The series array is composed of multiple series that also contain event configurations.

Constructing the series configuration for a top-level chart

In the series array, multiple series are defined with close and open price, bought and sold trade dates, and a hidden series for tracking mouse movement in the detail chart:

```
series: [{
    // Past closed price series
    type: 'areaspline',
    marker: { enabled: false },
    enableMouseTracking: false
}, {
    // This is the open price series and never shown
    // in the bottom chart. We use it to copy this
    // to the detail chart
    visible: false
}, {
    // Series for date and price when shares
    // are bought
    type: 'scatter',
    allowPointSelect: true,
    color: $.myApp.boughtColor,
    dataLabels: {
        enabled: true,
        formatter: function() { return 'B'; }
    },
    point: {
        events: { .... }
        }
}, {
    // Series for date and price when shares are sold
    type: 'scatter',
    allowPointSelect: true,
    color: $.myApp.soldColor,
    dataLabels: {
        enabled: true,
        formatter: function() { return 'S'; }
    },
    point: {
        events: { .... }
        }
}, {
    // This is the tracker series to show a single
    // data point of where the mouse is hovered on
    // the detail chart
    type: 'scatter',
    color: '#AA4643'
}]
```

The first series is the historic stock price series and is configured without data point markers. The second series is hidden and acts as a placeholder for historic open price data in the detail chart. The third (bought) and fourth (sold) series are the scatter series revealing the dates when shares have been traded. Both series are set with the `allowPointSelect` option, so that we can define the `select` and `unselect` events in the `point.events` option. The final series is also a scatter series to reflect the mouse movement in the detail chart using the `mouseOver` and `mouseOut` events, and we will see how all these are implemented later on.

Launching an Ajax query with the chart load event

As mentioned before, once the top-level chart is created and loaded on to the browser, it is ready to fetch the data from the server. The following is the chart's `load` event handler definition:

```
chart: {
    events: {
        load: function() {
            // Load the default stock symbol of
            // the portfolio
            var symbol = $('#symbol').val();
            $('#symbol').attr('disabled', true);
            loadPortfolio(symbol);
        },
```

We first retrieve the value from the **My Portfolio** selection box and disable the selection box during the query time. Then we call a pre-defined function, `loadPortfolio`. The method performs several tasks, as follows:

1. Launch an Ajax call, `$.getJSON`, to load the past stock price and portfolio data.

2. Set up a handler for the returned Ajax result which further executes the following steps:

    1. Hide the chart loading mask.

    2. Unpack the returned data and populate it into series data using the `Series.setData` method.

    3. Update the data inside the **Portfolio Detail** section to show how much the investment is worth as of the current date.

Activating the user interface with the chart redraw event

Once the top-level chart is populated with data, we can then enable the **My Portfolio** selection box in the page. To do that we can rely on the redraw event, which is triggered by the Series.setData call in sub-step 2 inside step 2.

```
redraw: function() {
    $('#symbol').attr('disabled', false);
},
```

Selecting and unselecting a data point with the point select and unselect events

The bought and sold series share the same events handling, the only differences between them are just the color and the point marker shape. The idea is that when the user clicks on a data point in these series, the **Portfolio Detail** section is updated to show the investment detail for the stock as of the trade date. The following screenshot shows the effect after the first bought trade point is selected:

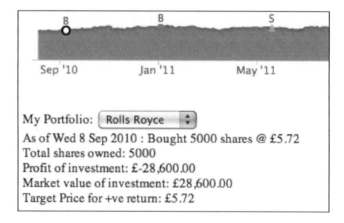

In order to keep the data point selected, we will use the allowPointSelect option, which allows us to define the select and unselect events. The following is the events configuration for the bought and sold series:

```
point: {
    events: {
        select: function() {
            updatePortfolio(this.x);
        },
        unselect: function() {
            // Only default back to current time
```

```
            // portfolio detail when unselecting
            // itself
            var selectPt =
                $.myApp.topChart.getSelectedPoints();
            if (selectPt[0].x == this.x) {
                updatePortfolio(new Date().getTime());
            }
        }
    }
}
```

Basically, the `select` event handler calls a pre-defined function, `updatePortfolio`, which updates the **Portfolio Detail** section based on the selected data point time — `this.x`. The `'this'` keyword in the handler refers to the selected point object, where x is the time value.

Unselecting the data point will call the `unselect` event handler. The preceding implementation means that if the unselected data point (`this.x`) is the same as the previously selected point, then it indicates the user has unselected the same point, hence we want to show the portfolio detail as of the current date. Otherwise do nothing because it means the user has selected another trade data point, hence another `select` event call is made with a different date.

Zooming the selected area with the chart selection event

The `selection` event forms the bridge between the top-level chart and the detail chart. When we select an area in the top-level chart, the selected area is highlighted and the data is zoomed in the detail chart. This action triggers the `selection` event and the following is the cut-down code of the event handler:

```
selection: function(evt) {
    // Get the xAxis selection
    var selectStart = Math.round(evt.xAxis[0].min);
    var selectEnd   = Math.round(evt.xAxis[0].max);

    // We use plotBand to paint the selected area
    // to simulate a selected area
    this.xAxis[0].removePlotBand('selected');
    this.xAxis[0].addPlotBand({
        color: 'rgba(69, 114, 167, 0.25)',
        id: 'selected',
        from: selectStart,
        to: selectEnd
    });
```

```
for (var i = 0;
     i < this.series[0].data.length; i++) {
    var pt = this.series[0].data[i];
    if (pt.x >= selectStart &&
        pt.x <= selectEnd) {
        selectedData.push([pt.x, pt.y]);
    }

    if (pt.x > selectEnd) {
        break;
    }
}

// Update the detail serie
var dSeries = $.myApp.detailChart.series[0];
dSeries.setData(selectedData, false);
....

// Update the detail chart title & subtitle
$.myApp.detailChart.setTitle({
    text: $.myApp.stockName + " (" +
        $.myApp.stockSymbol + ")",
    style: { fontFamily: 'palatino, serif',
            fontWeight: 'bold' }
    }, {
    text: Highcharts.dateFormat('%e %b %y',
        selectStart) + ' -- ' +
        Highcharts.dateFormat('%e %b %y',
        selectEnd),
    style: { fontFamily: 'palatino, serif' }
});

$.myApp.detailChart.redraw();
return false;
}
```

There are several steps taken in the handler code. First, we extract the selected range values from the handler parameters — evt.xAxis[0].min and evt.xAxis[0].max. The next step is to make the selected area stay highlighted in the top-level chart. To do that we create a plot band using this.xAxis[0].addPlotBand over the same area to simulate the selection. The 'this' keyword refers to the top-level chart object. The next task is to give a fixed id, so that we can remove the previous old selection and highlight a new selection. Additionally, the plot band should have the same color as the selection being dragged on the chart. All we need to do is to assign the plot band color as the same as the default value of the chart. selectionMarkerFill option.

After that we copy the data within the selected range into an array and pass it to the detail chart using `Series.setData`. Since we called the `setData` method a couple of times, it is worth setting the `redraw` option to `false` to save resources and then call the `redraw` method afterwards.

Finally, the most important step is to return `false` at the end of the function. This tells Highcharts not to take the default action after the selection has been made. Otherwise the whole top-level chart is redrawn and stretched (alternatively, we can call `event.preventDefault()`).

The following is the screenshot of zooming and displaying the detail in another chart:

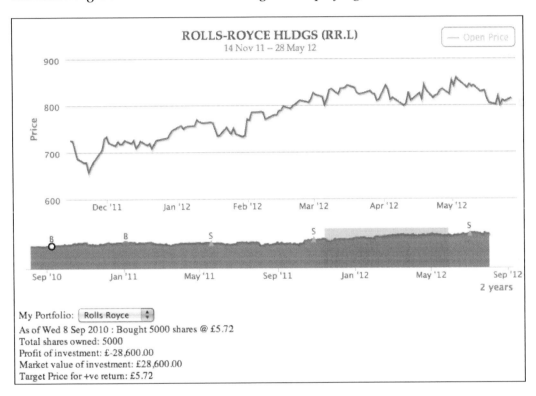

Detail chart

The detail chart is simply a line chart showing the selected region from the top-level chart. The chart is configured with a tooltip fixed at the upper-left corner and a number of events that we will discuss later.

```javascript
$.myApp.detailChart = new Highcharts.Chart({
    chart: {
        showAxes: true,
        renderTo: 'detail-container',
        events: {
            click: function(evt) {
                // Only allow to prompt stop order
                // dialog if the chart contains future
                // time
                ....
            }
        },
    },
    title: {
        margin: 10,
        text: null
    },
    credits: { enabled: false },
    legend: {
        enabled: true,
        floating: true,
        verticalAlign: 'top',
        align: 'right'
    },
    series: [ ... ],
    // Fixed location tooltip in the top left
    tooltip: {
        shared: true,
        positioner: function() {
            return { x: 10, y: 10 }
        },
        // Include 52 week high and low
        formatter: function() {  .... }
    },
    yAxis: {
        title: { text: 'Price' }
    },
    xAxis: { type: 'datetime' }
});
```

The following is a screenshot showing a data point being hovered over and the tooltip being shown at the upper-left corner:

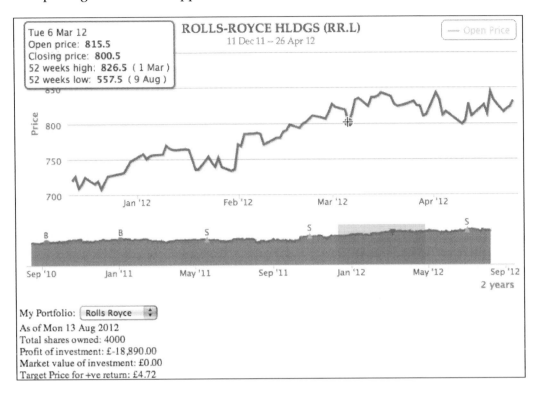

Constructing the series configuration for the detail chart

There are two series configured in the detail chart. The main focus is the first series which is the stock closed price. The series is defined without data point markers and has `'crosshair'` as the `cursor` option, as we can see in the preceding screenshot. In addition, the `mouseOut` and `mouseOver` events are defined for the data points that create a marker to the tracker series in the top-level chart. We will go through these events in the next section. The series array is defined, as follows:

```
series: [{
    marker: {
        enabled: false,
        states: {
            hover: { enabled: true }
        }
    },
    cursor: 'crosshair',
```

```
        point: {
            events: {
                mouseOver: function() { ... },
                mouseOut: function() { ... }
            }
        },
        stickyTracking: false,
        showInLegend: false
    }, {
        name: 'Open Price',
        marker: { enabled: false },
        visible: false
    }],
```

Hovering over a data point with the mouseOver and mouseOut point events

When we move the mouse pointer along the series in the detail chart, the movement is also reflected in the top-level chart within the selected area. The following screenshot shows the tracker point (inverted triangle) in the top-level chart:

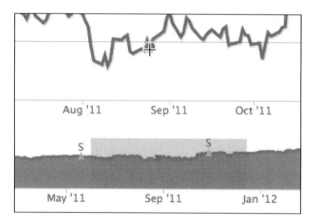

The inverted triangle indicates where we are browsing in the top-level chart. To do that we will set up the mouseOut and mouseOver point events options in the detail chart series, as follows:

```
    point: {
        events: {
            mouseOver: function() {
                var series = $.myApp.topChart.series[4];
                series.setData([]);
                series.addPoint([this.x, this.y]);
            },
```

```
                    mouseOut: function() {
                        var series = $.myApp.topChart.series[4];
                        series.setData([]);
                    }
                }
            },
```

Inside the `mouseOver` handler, the `'this'` keyword refers to the hovered data point object that the x and y properties which refer to the time and price values. Since both top-level and detail charts share the same data type along both x and y axes, we can simply add a data point into the tracker series in the top-level chart. As for the `mouseOut` event, we reset the series by emptying the data array.

Applying the chart click event

In this section we are going to apply the chart click event to create a "stop order" for investment portfolios. **Stop order** is an investment term for selling or buying a stock when it reaches the price threshold within a specified date/time range in the future. It is generally used to limit a loss or protect a profit.

Notice that there is an empty space at the right-hand side of the top-level chart. In fact, this is deliberately created for the next 30 days' range from the current date. Let's highlight that area, so that the future date appears in the detail chart:

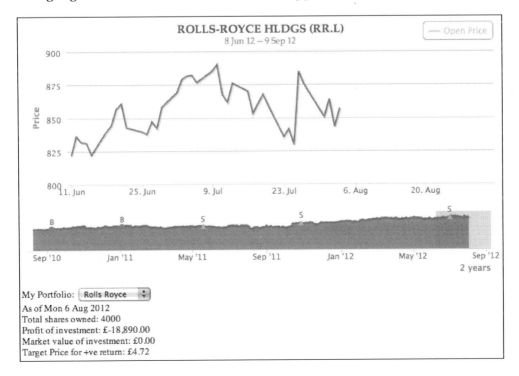

As we can see, the line series in the detail chart stops as soon as it hits the current date. If we click on the future dates zone in the detail chart, a **Create Stop Order** dialog box appears. The x, y position of the click in the chart is then converted into date and price, which then populates the values into the dialog box. The following is the screenshot of the dialog box:

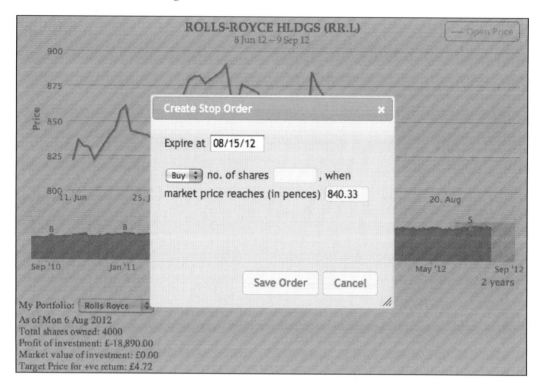

The expiry date and price fields can be further adjusted if necessary. Once the **Save Order** button is clicked, a stop order is created and a pair of x and y plot lines are generated to mark in the chart. The following is a screenshot showing two stop orders in the chart:

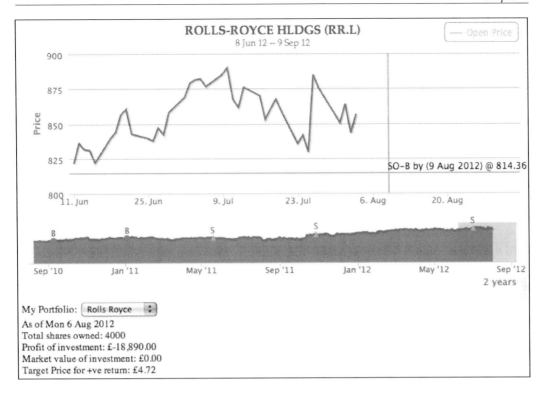

Let's see how all these actions can be derived from the code. First the jQuery UI dialog is created based on an HTML form declared in the page:

```
<div id='dialog'>
   <form>
      <fieldset>
         <label for="expire">Expire at</label>
         <input type=text name="expire" id="expire" size=9
><br/><br/>
         <select name='stopOrder' id='stopOrder'>
            <option value='buy' selected>Buy</option>
            <option value='sell'>Sell</option>
         </select>
         <label for="shares">no. of shares</label>
         <input type="text" name="shares" id="shares" value=""
size=7 class="text ui-widget-content ui-corner-all" />,
         <label for="price">when market price reaches (in pences)</
label>
         <input type="text" name="price" id="price" value="" size=7
class="text ui-widget-content ui-corner-all" />
      </fieldset>
   </form>
</div>
```

The `click` event handler for the detail chart is then defined, as follows:

```
click: function(evt) {

    // Only allow to prompt stop order dialog
    // if the chart contains future time
    if (!$.myApp.detailChart.futureDate) {
        return;
    }

    // Based on what we click on the time, set
    // input field inside the dialog
    $('#expire').val(
        Highcharts.dateFormat("%m/%d/%y",
        evt.xAxis[0].value));
    $('#price').val(
        Highcharts.numberFormat(
        evt.yAxis[0].value, 2));

    // Display the form to setup stop order
    $('#dialog').dialog("open");
}
```

The first guard condition is to see whether the detail chart contains any future date. If a future date exists, then it extracts the x and y values from the `click` event and assigns them into the form input fields. After that it calls the jQuery UI dialog method to lay out the HTML form into a dialog box and displays it.

The following code snippet shows how we define the jQuery UI dialog box and its action buttons. The code is edited for readability:

```
// Initiate stop order dialog
$( "#dialog" ).dialog({
    // Dialog startup configuration -
    // dimension, modal, title, etc
    .... ,
    buttons: [{
        text: "Save Order",
        click: function() {
            // Check whether this dialog is called
            // with a stop order id. If not, then
            // assign a new stop order id
            // Assign the dialog fields into an
            // object - 'order'
            ....
            // Store the stop order
            $.myApp.stopOrders[id] = order;
```

```
// Remove plotlines if already exist.
// This can happen if we modify a stop
// order point
var xAxis = $.myApp.detailChart.xAxis[0];
xAxis.removePlotLine(id);
var yAxis = $.myApp.detailChart.yAxis[0];
yAxis.removePlotLine(id);

// Setup events handling for both
// x & y axis plotlines
var events = {
    // Change the mouse cursor to pointer
    // when the mouse is hovered above
    // the plotlines
    mouseover: function() { ... },

    // Launch modify dialog when
    // click on a plotline
    click: function(evt) { ... }
};

// Create the plot lines for the stop
// order
xAxis.addPlotLine({
    value: order.expire,
    width: 2,
    events: events,
    color: (order.stopOrder == 'buy') ? $.myApp.
boughtColor : $.myApp.soldColor,
        id: id,
        // Over both line series and
        // plot line
        zIndex: 3
    });

    yAxis.addPlotLine({
        value: order.price,
        width: 2,
        color: (order.stopOrder == 'buy') ? $.myApp.
boughtColor : $.myApp.soldColor,
            id: id,
            zIndex: 3,
            events: events,
            label: {
```

```
                         text: ((order.stopOrder == 'buy') ?
    'SO-B by (' : 'SO-S by (')   + Highcharts.dateFormat("%e %b %Y",
    parseInt(order.expire)) + ') @ ' + order.price,
                         align: 'right'
                    }
                });

                $('#dialog').dialog("close");
            }
        }, {
            text: "Cancel",
            click: function() {
                $('#dialog').dialog("close");
            }
        }]
    });
```

The dialog box setup code is slightly more complicated. In the **Save Order** button's button handler, it performs several tasks, as follows:

1. It extracts the input values from the dialog box.

2. It checks whether the dialog box is opened with a specific stop order id. If not, then it assigns a new stop order id and stores the values with id into `$.myApp.stopOrders`.

3. It removes any existing plot lines that match with id, in case we modify an existing stop order.

4. It sets up the `click` and `mouseover` events handling for both x- and y-axis plot lines.

5. It creates x and y plot lines into the detail chart with the events definitions constructed in step 4.

One scenario with stop orders is that users may want to change or delete a stop order before the condition is fulfilled. Therefore in step 4, the purpose of the `click` event on plot lines is for bringing up a modify dialog box. Additionally, we want to change the mouse cursor to a pointer when hovering over the plot lines to show that it is clickable.

Changing the mouse cursor over plot lines with mouseover event

To change the mouse cursor over the plot lines, we define the mouseover event handler, as follows:

```
mouseover: function() {
    $.each(this.axis.plotLinesAndBands,
        function(idx, plot) {
            if (plot.id == id) {
                plot.svgElem.element.style.cursor =
                    'pointer';
                return false;
            }
        }
    );
},
```

The 'this' keyword contains an axis object where the hovered plot line belongs to. Since there can be multiple plot lines in each axis, we need to loop through the array of plot lines and plot bands that can be found in the plotLinesAndBands property inside the axis object. Once we have found the target plot line by matching id, we will dig inside the internal element and set the cursor style to 'pointer'. The following shows a screenshot of a mouse cursor hovered over the plot line:

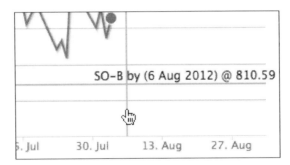

Setting up a plot line action with the click event

The click event for plot lines is to launch the **Modify Stop Order** dialog box for a stop order:

```
// Click on the prompt line
click: function(evt) {
    // Retrieves the stop order object stored in
    // $.myApp.stopOrders
```

```
$('#dialog').dialog("option",
                        "stopOrderId", id);
var stopOrder = $.myApp.stopOrders[id];

// Put the settings into the stop order form
$('#dialog').dialog("option", "title",
                        "Modify Stop Order");
$('#price').val(
    Highcharts.numberFormat(
            stopOrder.price, 2));

$('#stopOrder').val(stopOrder.stopOrder);
$('#shares').val(stopOrder.shares);
$('#expire').val(
    Highcharts.dateFormat("%m/%d/%y",
            stopOrder.expire));

// Add a remove button inside the dialog
var buttons =
    $('#dialog').dialog("option", "buttons");
buttons.push({
    text: 'Remove Order',
    click: function() {
        // Remove plot line and stop order
        // settings
        delete $.myApp.stopOrders[id];
        var xAxis =
            $.myApp.detailChart.xAxis[0];
        xAxis.removePlotLine(id);
        var yAxis =
            $.myApp.detailChart.yAxis[0];
        yAxis.removePlotLine(id);

        // Set the dialog to original state
        resetDialog();
        $('#dialog').dialog("close");
    }
});

$('#dialog').dialog("option",
                        "buttons", buttons);

$('#dialog').dialog("open");
}
```

The `click` event handler simply retrieves the stop order settings and puts the values inside the **Modify Stop Order** dialog box. Before launching the dialog box, add a **Remove Order** button into the dialog box which the button handler calls `removePlotLine` with the plot line's `id`. The following is a screenshot of the **Modify Stop Order** dialog box:

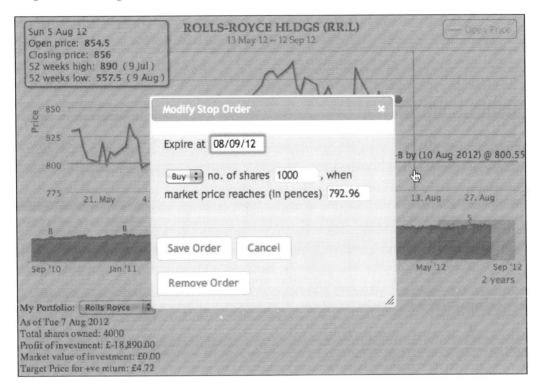

Stocks' growth chart example

Our next example is to demonstrate the following events:

- `chart.events: addSeries`
- `plotOptions.series.events: click, checkboxClick, legendItemClick`
- `plotOptions.series.point.events: update, remove`

Suppose we want to draft a long term investment portfolio based on the stocks' past growth performance as a reference. The demo contains a chart started with two series, Portfolio and Average growths, and a form to input stock symbols. Basically, we enter a stock symbol in this demo and then a line series of stock growth is inserted into the chart. So we can plot multiple stock yield trends and tweak their proportion in our portfolio to observe how **Average** and **Portfolio** lines perform. The following screenshot shows the initial screen:

Plot averaging series from displayed stocks series

Let's query for two stocks and click on the **Average** legend to enable the series:

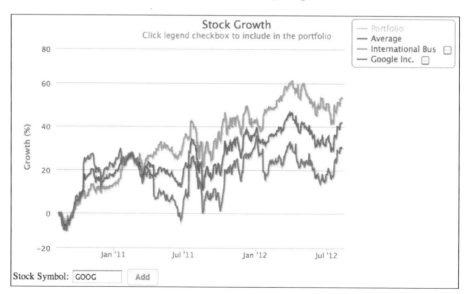

As expected, the **Average** line is plotted in between the two stock lines. Assuming the future growth is similar to the past, this **Average** line projects the future growth if we invest both stocks equally in our portfolio. Let's add another stock symbol into the chart:

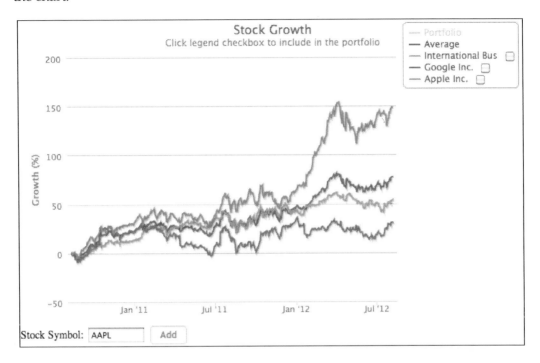

The new growth line generates a higher yield so that the **Average** line automatically re-adjusts itself and shifts to the second line from the top. Let's see how it is implemented. The following is the chart configuration code:

```
$.myChart = new Highcharts.Chart({
    chart: {
        renderTo: 'container',
        showAxes: true,
        events: {
            addSeries: function() { ... }
        }
    },
    series: [{
        visible: false,
        name: 'Portfolio',
        color: $.colorRange.shift(),
        marker: { enabled: false },
        events: {
```

```
                        legendItemClick: function(evt) { ... }
                }
        }, {
            name: 'Average',
            events: {
                legendItemClick: function(evt) { ... }
            },
            color: $.colorRange.shift(),
            visible: false,
            marker: { enabled: false }
        }, {
            visible: false,
            type: 'pie',
            point: {
                events: {
                    click: function(evt) { ... },
                        update: function(evt) { ... },
                        remove: function(evt) { ... }
                }
            },
            center: [ '13%', '5%' ],
            size: '30%',
            dataLabels: { enabled: false }
        }],
        title: { text: 'Stocks Growth' },
        credits: { enabled: false },
        legend: {
            enabled: true,
            align: 'right',
            layout: 'vertical',
            verticalAlign: 'top'
        },
        yAxis: {
            title: { text: 'Growth (%)' }
        },
        xAxis: { type: 'datetime' }
    });
```

The chart contains three series, Portfolio, Average, and a pie chart series, which is for editing the portfolio distribution.

When we hit the **Add** button with a stock symbol, the `showLoading` method is called to put a loading mask in front of the chart, and then an Ajax connection is established with the server to query the stock yield data. We implement the Ajax handler by calling the `addSeries` function to insert a new series into the chart. Once the `addSeries` event is triggered, it means that the data has returned and is ready to plot. In this case we can disable the chart loading mask, as follows:

```
chart: {
    .... ,
    events: {
        addSeries: function() {
            this.hideLoading();
        }
    },
    .... ,
```

The following is the implementation of the **Add** button action:

```
$('#add').button().on('click',
    function() {
        var symbol = $('#symbol').val().toLowerCase();
        $.myChart.showLoading();
        $.getJSON('./stockGrowth.php?symbol=' + symbol +
                '&years=' + $.numOfYears,
            function(stockData) {
                // Build up the series data array
                var seriesData = [];

                if (!stockData.rows.length) {
                    return;
                }

                $.symbols.push({
                    symbol: symbol,
                    name: stockData.name
                });

                $.each(stockData.rows,
                    function(idx, data) {
                        seriesData.push([
                            data.date * 1000,
                            data.growth ]);
                });

                $.myChart.addSeries({
                    events: {
                        // Remove the stock series
                        click: { ... },
                        // Include the stock into portfolio
```

```
                                checkboxClick: { ... }
                            },
                            data: seriesData,
                            name: stockData.name,
                            marker: { enabled: false },
                            stickyTracking: false,
                            showCheckbox: true,

                            // Because we can add/remove series,
                            // we need to make sure the chosen
                            // color used in the visible series
                            color: $.colorRange.shift()
                        }, false);

                        updateAvg(false);
                        $.myChart.redraw();
                }   // function (stockData)
            );   //getJSON
        });
```

We build a series configuration object from the Ajax returned data. Within this new series configuration, we set the showCheckbox option to true for a checkbox next to the legend item. A couple of events are also added into the configuration, click and checkboxClick, which are discussed later.

After the addSeries method call, we then call a pre-defined routine, updateAvg, which only recomputes and redraws the **Average** line if it is on display.

Recalling from the preceding Average series events' definition, we use the legendItemClick event to capture when the Average series is clicked in the legend box:

```
            series: [{
                ...
                }, {
                name: 'Average',
                events: {
                    legendItemClick: function(evt) {
                        if (!this.visible) {
                            updateAvg();
                        }
                    }
                },
                .....
```

The preceding code means that if the Average series is currently not in a visible state, then the series is going to be visible after this handler returns. Hence it calculates the average values and shows the series.

Launching a dialog with the series click event

Instead of enabling or disabling a stock yield line by clicking on the legend item, we may want to completely remove the series line. In this scenario we use the `click` event to do that, as follows:

```
$.myChart.addSeries({
    events: {
        // Launch a confirm dialog box to delete
        // the series
        click: function() {
            // Save the clicked series into the dialog
            $("#dialog-confirm").dialog("option",
                "seriesIdx", this.index);
            $("#dialog-confirm").dialog("option",
                "seriesName", this.name);
            $("#removeName").text(this.name);

            $("#dialog-confirm").dialog("open");
        },
        // Include the stock into portfolio
        checkboxClick: function(evt) { ... }
    },
    ....
});
```

The click action launches a confirmation dialog box for removing the series from the chart. We store the clicked series (the `'this'` keyword) information inside the dialog box; the **Remove** button's button handler uses that data to remove the series and recalculate the average series if it is shown. The following is the screenshot:

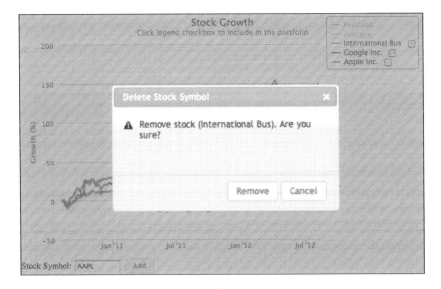

Launching a pie chart with the series checkboxClick event

Inside the legend box, each checkbox is for including the stock into the portfolio. As soon as the checkbox is checked, a pie chart appears in the upper-left corner showing the distribution of the stock within the portfolio. Each slice in the pie chart shares the same color with the corresponding stock line. The following screenshot shows three growth lines and a portfolio pie chart equally distributed for each stock:

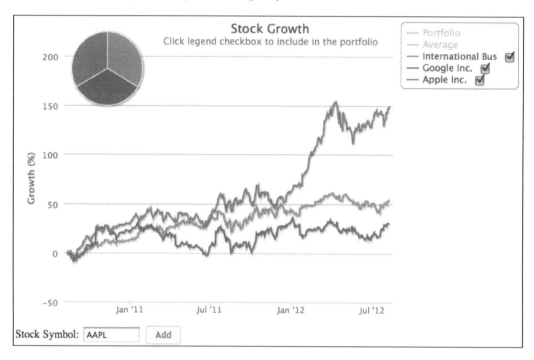

Since the growth line series is configured with the `showCheckbox` option, we can define the `checkboxClick` event to launch a pie chart when the checkbox is checked:

```
checkboxClick: function(evt) {
    updatePie(this, evt.checked);
}
```

The `updatePie` function is called at several places in this demo, such as for removing a series, when the legend checkbox is checked, and so on. The following is the shortened version of the code:

```
var updatePie = function(seriesObj, checked) {
    // Loop through the stock series. If checkbox
    // checked, then compute the equal distribution
    // percentage for the pie series data
    for (i = $.pfloIdx + 1;
          i < $.myChart.series.length; i++) {
        var insert = (i == index) ? checked : $.myChart.
series[i].selected;
        if (insert) {
            data.push({
                name: $.myChart.series[i].name,
                y: parseFloat((100 / count).toFixed(2)),
                color: $.myChart.series[i].color
            });
        }
    }

    // Update the pie chart series
    $.myChart.series[$.pfloIdx].setData(data, false);
    $.myChart.series[$.pfloIdx].show();
};
```

The preceding code snippet basically loops through the stock series array and checks whether it is selected. If so, then it includes stock into the pie series in an equally distributed manner. Then the pie chart is displayed if there are one or more entries.

Editing the pie chart's slice with the point click, update, and remove events

It is unlikely for an investment portfolio to have an equal distribution on all the stocks. Therefore we enhance the example to modify portions within the pie chart. When a slice in the pie chart is clicked, a dialog box pops up. This allows us to adjust or remove the portion within the portfolio. The following screenshot shows this::

The **Update** button in the **Update Portfolio** dialog box updates the pie chart slice with the Point.update method, whereas the **Remove** button calls the Point.remove method. Both calls trigger the update and remove events respectively. Here we define the data point's click, update, and remove events inside the pie chart.

```
series: [ {
    ....
    },
    visible: false,
    type: 'pie',
    point: {
        events: {
            // Bring up the modify dialog box
            click: function(evt) {
                // Store the clicked pie slice
                // detail into the dialog box
                $('#updateName').text(evt.point.name);
                $('#percentage').val(evt.point.y);
                $('#dialog-form').dialog("option",
                    "pieSlice", evt.point);

                $('#dialog-form').dialog("open");
            },
            // Once the Update button is clicked,
            // the pie slice portion is updated
            // Hence, this event is triggered and the
            // portfolio series is updated
            update: function(evt) {
                updatePortfolio();
            },
            // Pie slice is removed, unselect the series
            // in the legend checkbox and update the
            // portfolio series
            remove: function(evt) {
                var series = nameToSeries(this.name);
                series && series.select(false);
                updatePortfolio();
            }
        }
    }
```

The click event function stores the clicked slice (point object) inside the modify dialog box and launches it. Inside the dialog box the **Update** and **Remove** buttons' button handlers then extract these stored point objects and call the pie chart. Use the objects' update or remove method to reflect the change in the displayed pie chart. This subsequently triggers point update or remove event handlers and calls the pre-defined function, updatePortfolio, which recalculates the Portfolio series with the new distribution among the included stocks. So let's update the distribution for the best past performance stock to 80 percent ratio and the rest of the two stocks to 10 percent each. The Portfolio series automatically re-adjusts itself from the update event, as shown in the following screenshot:

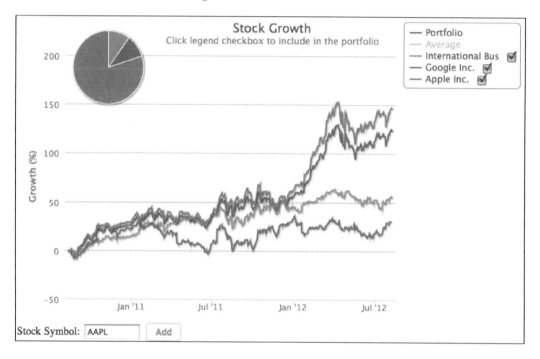

As we can see, the Portfolio series (second line from the top) has been weighted towards the higher growth trend rather than in the middle of all the stock's pie chart, like the Average series.

Summary

In this chapter we covered the last part of Highcharts configuration—events handling. We built two shares' portfolio applications using jQuery and jQuery UI to demonstrate most of the Highcharts events.

In the next chapter we will take Highcharts into mobile devices with jQuery Mobile.

Highcharts and jQuery Mobile

9

Highcharts does not only work in desktop browsers but also supports mobile platforms. In this chapter, we will explore how to deploy Highcharts into mobile platforms with a web mobile framework, jQuery Mobile, which is built on top of jQuery. A very brief introduction of jQuery Mobile is given. We will look into a couple of areas that are crucial to understanding the basics of the mobile framework. Then we will integrate Highcharts and jQuery Mobile by building a mobile application using an Olympic 2012 medals table. We will demonstrate how to apply mobile events such as swipe, rotation, and pinch to navigate through the charts.

- Introducing jQuery Mobile
- Understanding mobile page structure
- Understanding page initialization
- Linking between mobile pages
- Integrating Highcharts and jQuery Mobile
- Drilling down for data from one chart to another
- Changing chart displays with touch actions—swipe, rotate, and pinch

A short introduction of jQuery Mobile

This chapter by all means is not a full tutorial for jQuery Mobile (or jQM), but it is a quick-start guide for using it with Highcharts. JQuery Mobile is a web development framework for mobile devices built on top of jQuery. It is designed to be compatible across all mobile platforms and the UI look and feel emulate native mobile applications. The benefit of that is low cost development in a single source code without the need for testing across all the mobile platforms and browsers.

At the time of writing, Version 1.2.0 is used in this book. Before we drill down on how Highcharts can be integrated with jQM, a few important concepts need to be understood.

Understanding a mobile page structure

The most important concept of jQM is to understand the structure of a mobile page, which is not the same as a normal HTML page. A mobile page is constructed inside an HTML <div> box with a jQM specific attribute, data-role='page', marked as a boundary. In fact, the data-* syntax is **Customer Data Attributes** defined in HTML5 standard. This allows web developers to store custom data specific to the page or application, which can easily access the data attribute values. For more information on APIs for HTML visit http://dev.w3.org/html5/spec/single-page. html#custom-data-attribute. Within a mobile page, normal HTML tags, such as input, hyperlinks, select, and so on are used.

An HTML document can contain multiple mobile pages and links through anchor and the id attribute. An anchor is the same as a normal HTML anchor (for example, #chart). The framework resolves the anchor reference and retrieves a mobile page with matching id attribute, which has the following syntax:

```
<div data-role="page" id="chart">
```

The following is an example of a single mobile page in an HTML document:

```
<html>
<head>
  <title>My Page</title>
  <meta name="viewport"
        content="width=device-width, initial-scale=1,
                 maximum-scale=1, user-scalable=0">
  <!-- CDN loading of jQuery and jQM -->
  <link rel="stylesheet"
   href="http://.../jquery.mobile-1.2.0.min.css" />
  <script
   src="http://.../1.7.1/jquery.min.js"></script>
  <script
   src="http://.../jquery.mobile-1.2.0.min.js"></script>
</head>
<body>
    <div data-role="page">
    <div data-role="header">
        <h1>jQuery Mobile</h1>
```

```
        </div><!-- /header -->
      <div data-role="content">
            ....
      </div>
   </div><!-- /page -->
</body>
</html>
```

Depending on the purpose of the mobile application, all the pages can be built into a single HTML document, or they can exist in separate documents. One important aspect is that if multiple mobile pages are defined within a document, the first page in the <body> tag is always loaded on the screen. In jQM, a page is generally composed of head and content, optionally a footer and navigation bar. Each component also has a <div> box with data-role to indicate the type of component within a mobile page. The following code shows how multiple mobile pages in a document are loaded:

```
<div data-role="page" >
   <div data-role="header">
       <h1>jQuery Mobile</h1>
       <a href="#config" data-rel='dialog'
          data-icon="gear">Options</a>
   </div><!-- /header -->
   <div data-role="content">
       ....
   </div>
</div><!-- /page -->

<!-- Page for the option dialog -->
<div data-role="page" id='config'>
   <div data-role="header">
       <h1>Config</h1>
   </div><!-- /header -->

   <div data-role="content">
       <a href="#" data-role="button"
          data-rel="back" >Cancel</a>
   </div>
</div><!-- /page -->
```

As we can see, there are two `<div>` boxes with the `data-role='page'` attribute. The first `<div>` box is the same as the previous example with an additional `Options` link button, which redirects to the second mobile page, `id='config'`. The attribute `data-icon="gear"` decorates the button with a gear icon provided by the framework. For the list of icons visit `http://jquerymobile.com/demos/1.2.0/docs/buttons/buttons-icons.html`. When the button is pressed, it will open the second page as a modal dialog box because of the `data-rel='dialog'` attribute. The following screenshot shows the view of the first mobile page appearing on an iPhone:

Understanding page initialization

In this section, we will learn the concept of why we don't use the traditional DOM ready method to run initialization code for mobile pages. Suppose a page content requires some sort of initialization, using the traditional DOM ready method, `$.ready`, that can have an undesired effect. This is because the `$.ready` method runs as soon as all the DOMs inside the document are loaded. In other words, we have no control over when to run the page initialization code, if it is inside the DOM ready handler.

However, jQM provides a specific event, `pageinit`, catered for this scenario. All we need to do is to assign an `id` value inside the `<div data-role='page'>` markup, then define the `pageinit` event handler for that `id` value. Whenever a page is going to be initialized for the display, this event is triggered. Note that the `$.ready` method is still going to be called, but we just don't use it in jQM. To demonstrate this concept, let us use the previous multi-page example with an additional `$.ready` call:

```
<script type="text/javascript">
    $('#main_page').live('pageinit', function() {
        alert('jQuery Mobile: pageinit for Main page');
    });

    $('#config').live('pageinit', function() {
        alert('jQuery Mobile: pageinit for Config page');
    });

    $(document).ready(function() {
        alert('jQuery ready');
    });
</script>
</head>
<body>
  <!--   MAIN PAGE -->
  <div data-role="page" id='main_page'>
     <div data-role="header">
        <h1>jQuery Mobile</h1>
           <a href="#config" data-rel='dialog'
              data-icon="gear"
              class='ui-btn-right'>Options</a>
     </div><!-- /header -->

     <div data-role="content" id=''>
     </div>
  </div><!-- /page -->

  <!-- CONFIG PAGE -->
  <div data-role="page" id='config' >
     <div data-role="header">
        <h1>Config</h1>
     </div><!-- /header -->

     <div data-role="content">
        <a href="" data-role="button"
           data-rel="back" >Cancel</a>
     </div>
  </div><!-- /page -->
```

There are two mobile pages defined in this example: `main_page` and `config`. Each mobile page is tied to its `pageinit` event handler. With the `$.ready` method, we can observe the call sequence with other `pageinit` events. When we first load the document to the browser, we see the following screenshot:

Remember that jQM always displays the first page in the HTML body. That means the `pageinit` event for `main_page` is fired as soon as the DOM for the `main_page` is fully loaded and initialized for the display. It is also important to understand that at this point of execution, the DOM for the subsequent `config` page is not loaded yet. When we touch the **OK** button, the execution resumes and the DOM for the `config` page is then loaded. Hence all the DOMs in the document are loaded and the `$.ready` method is then called, which shows the second alert message as shown in the following screenshot:

When we touch the **OK** button, the alert box disappears and the control resumes back to the browser. Now if we touch the **Options** button at the top right-hand corner, the `config` dialog page is initialized and displayed on the screen. Hence the `pageinit` handler for the `config` page is called.

Linking between mobile pages

The second important concept in jQM is how the mobile pages are being linked together. Understanding this concept can help us to design a web mobile application with a fluid user experience. In jQM, there are two ways to load an external mobile page: HTTP and Ajax. Depending on how we set the `data-` attribute, it interprets the `href` value and decides which way to load a mobile page. By default, apart from the first document load which is a normal HTTP transfer, the mobile page is loaded through Ajax. The following block diagram explains how multiple mobile page blocks are managed within a document:

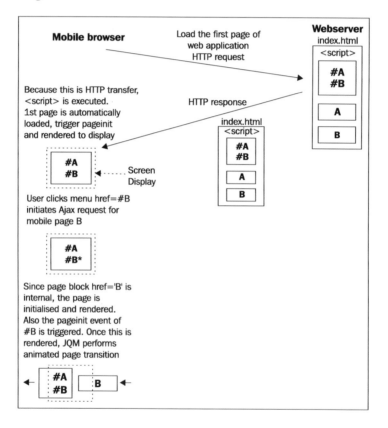

When a mobile page invokes another mobile page, the jQM framework basically parses the `href` value. Since this is an anchor reference, it indicates that this is an internal mobile page block. The framework locates the page block from the current DOM by matching the `id` value. It then initializes and renders the page which also triggers the `pageinit` event for page B as shown in the previous block diagram.

Suppose we have two separate HTML documents, a button in one page is referring to another document. The following block diagram describes the scenario:

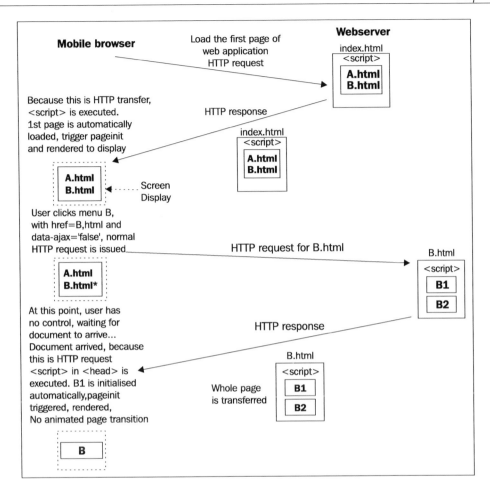

In this case, we add an attribute, `data-ajax="false"` (for the sake of a simpler approach on managing JavaScript code), to tell jQM that this button requires a document load instead of a background Ajax load. This is important because otherwise the `pageinit` handler code (or any JavaScript file) inside the `<script>` tag will not be loaded for the new mobile page, B.html.

 JavaScript code can be embedded inside a `<script>` tag within a mobile page block and get executed. The downside of this approach is that it requires more code management, as each page block has its own `pageinit` handler code.

There is an alternative way to load external mobile page in Ajax, but we will leave it here. This is more than sufficient to implement a simple mobile web application. Readers can learn more from the jQuery Mobile documentation.

Highcharts in touch screen environments

The good thing with Highcharts is that it works perfectly well on both desktop browsers and web mobile environments without requiring any change of code. The only part that needs slight consideration is the events handling because mobile devices are all touch screen based and that means the mouse cursor is invisible.

In Highcharts, all the mouse hover events can still be triggered in touch devices, even though the mouse cursor is not shown. For instance, suppose we define a series with the mouseOut, mouseOver, and click events handling. If we touch the series, both the mouseOver and click events are triggered. However, if we touch another series causing the previous selected series to be unselected, a mouseOut event for the first series is fired. Needless to say, the sequence of events would be different with a real pointing device. In general, we should refrain from using any mouse hover events in touch screen based devices.

In the next section we will learn how to integrate jQM with Highcharts, such as applying touch events to charts, using the chart click events to launch another chart and mobile page, and so on.

Integrating Highcharts and jQuery Mobile using an Olympic medals table application

In this section we will build a mobile application for browsing the results of the Olympic 2012 medals table. This application is only tested on iPhone and iPad. The startup screen provides four menus for looking up the results as shown in the following screenshot:

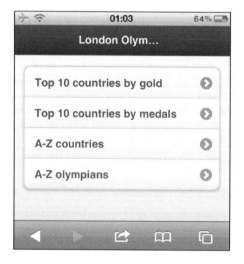

```
<head>
    <!-- CDN load of Highcharts, jQuery and jQM -->
    ....
</head>
<body>
<div data-role="page">
   <div data-role="header">
      <h1>London Olympic 2012 </h1>
   </div><!-- /header -->

   <div data-role="content">
       <ul data-role="listview" data-inset="true">
          <li><a href="./gold.html"
             data-ajax="false" >Top 10 countries by gold</a></li>
          <li><a href="./medals.html"
             data-ajax="false" >Top 10 countries by medals</a></
li>
          <li><a href="#">A-Z countries</a></li>
          <li><a href="#">A-Z olympians</a></li>
       </ul>
   </div>
</div><!-- /page -->
</body>
```

So when the **Top 10 countries by gold** button is clicked, the gold.html file is HTTP loaded (not Ajax) because we define data-ajax="false". Since it is an HTTP load, the whole page, gold.html, is loaded onto the browser as well as everything within the <script> tags that are being executed.

Loading up the gold medals page

The following is the content of the gold.html file:

```
<head>
   <!-- CDN load of Highcharts, jQuery and jQM -->
   ....
   <script type="text/javascript" src="common.js"></script>
   <script type="text/javascript" src="gold.js"></script>
</head>
<body>
<div data-role="page" id='gold_chart'>
 <div data-role="header">
```

```
      <a href="olympic.html" data-icon="home"
         data-iconpos="notext">Home</a>
      <h1>London Olympic 2012 - Top 10 countries by gold</h1>
      <a href="#options" data-rel='dialog'
         data-icon="gear" id='options'>Options</a>
    </div><!-- /header -->

    <div data-role="content">
        <div id='chart_container'></div>
    </div>
  </div><!-- /page -->

  <!-- options dialog -->
  <div data-role="page" id='options' >
      ....
  </div>
  </body>
```

Since this whole HTML document is HTTP loaded onto the browser, the `common.`
`js` and `gold.js` files are also loaded. The file `common.js` contains common routine
code shared in the demo such as device detection, orientation detection, chart
creation, and so on. The `gold.js` file contains the `pageinit` handler code for all the
mobile pages in the `gold.html` file. As the mobile page block, `gold_chart`, is the
first defined block in the document, it is automatically loaded and rendered to the
display, hence the `pageinit` event for the `gold_chart` page block is triggered.

Detecting device properties

For detecting mobile devices, the technique ranges from string matching of the
`navigator.userAgent` option, `jQuery.support`, `jQuery.browser` (deprecated), CSS
media queries, to a third-party plugin such as Modernizr; see `http://modernizr.`
`com/` for details. However, there is no standard way of doing so. Perhaps it is due
to the diverse requirements for compatibility checks. It is beyond the scope of this
book to debate the merits of each technique. For this demo, all we are interested in is
the difference in screen size, that is if there is more space in the display (that is tablet
devices) then we display the full country name in the charts instead of the country
code for smaller devices (touch phones). We assume the following technique is
sufficient to differentiate between phone and tablet devices:

```
function getDevice() {
    return ($(window).width() > 320)  ? "tablet" : "phone";
}
```

The $(window).width property returns the width of the device in pixels regardless of the device orientation. As for getting the current device orientation, we have the following method:

```
function getOrientation() {
    return (window.innerHeight/window.innerWidth) > 1 ?
           'portrait' : 'landscape';
}
```

Plotting a Highcharts chart on mobile device

The following is the pageinit handler code for the gold_chart mobile page:

```
$('#gold_chart').live('pageinit',
    function() {
        var device = getDevice();

        // current orientation
        var orientation = getOrientation();

        // Setup the point click events for all the
        // country medal charts - used by plotGoldChart method
        var pointEvt = {
            events: {
                click: function(evt) { ... }
            }
        };

        // Switch between column and pie chart
        $('#chart_container').on('swipeleft',
            function(evt) { ... } );

        $('#chart_container').on('swiperight',
            function(evt) { ... } );

        // Switch between column and bar chart on
        // smaller display
        $(document).on('orientationchange',
            function(evt) { ... } );

        // General method for plotting gold medal chart
        // Used by dialog box also to toggle chart options
        // such as column stacking, labels etc
        $.olympicApp.plotGoldChart = function(chart, options) {
            .....
        };
```

```
        // Create and display Highcharts for gold medal chart
        $.olympicApp.goldChart = createChart({
                device: device,
                orientation: orientation,
                load: $.olympicApp.plotGoldChart,
                type: (orientation == 'landscape') ?
                        'bar' : 'column',
                // legend and title settings specific
                ....

        });
    }
);
```

The touch events such as `swipeleft`, `swiperight`, and `orientationchange` will be discussed later on. The event handler, `pointEvt`, drills down further to another chart when the user taps on a country bar in the gold medal chart. We will also explore this interaction later on. Let's first focus on the last part of the code, which creates the chart. The `createChart` method is a general routine to create a Highcharts graph, which has the common options shared by all the chart mobile pages, for example the `renderTo` option is always set to `chart_container`, which is inside the `data-role='content'` attribute. The following code shows the `createChart` implementation:

```
    // Main routine for creating chart
    function createChart(options) {

        // Based on the device display and current orientation
        // Work out the spacing options, labels orientation
        return new Highcarts.Chart({
            chart: {
                renderTo: 'chart_container',
                type: options.type,
                events: {
                    load: function(chart) {
                        // Execute the page general plot routine
                        options.load &&
                        options.load(chart, options);
                    }
                },
                spacingLeft: ....,
                ....
            },
            title: { text: options.title },
            xAxis: {
                labels: ....
            },
            ....
        });
    }
```

Note that there is no series defined in the `options` parameter and the `options.load` property is set up to call the `plotGoldChart` function once the chart is created and loaded into the browser. The following code snippet is the part of the `plotGoldChart` function:

```
// chart is the target chart object to apply new settings,
// options is an object containing the new settings
$.olympicApp.plotGoldChart =
    function(chart, options) {

        // Get the top 10 countries with the
        // most gold medals
        $.getJSON('./olympic.php',
                { order: 'gold', num: 10 },

            function(result) {

                var device = getDevice();

                // Remove any series in the chart if exists
                ....

                // If display pie chart,
                // then we only plot the gold medals series
                if (options && options.type == 'pie') {
                    var goldOpt = {
                        data: [],
                        point: pointEvt,
                        type: 'pie',
                        dataLabels: { ... }
                    };
                    $.each(result.rows,
                        function(idx, data) {
                            goldOpt.data.push({

                                // If device is phone,
                                // set short country labels
                                // otherwise full names
                                name: (device === 'phone') ?
                                    data.code : data.country,
                                y: data.gold,
                                color: pieGoldColors[idx]
                            });
                        });
                    chart.addSeries(goldOpt, false);
```

```
                    // Disable option button for pie chart
                    $('#options').addClass('ui-disabled');

            } else {
                    // Sorting out chart option - stacking,
                    // dataLabels if specified in the option
                    // parameters
                    var dataLabel = ... ;
                    var stacking = ... ;
                    var bronzeOpt = {
                        data: [], name: 'Bronze',
                        color: '#BE9275',
                        stacking: stacking,
                        dataLabels: dataLabel,
                        point: pointEvt
                    };
                    var silverOpt = {
                        data: [], name: 'Silver',
                        color: '#B5B5B5',
                        stacking: stacking,
                        dataLabels: dataLabel,
                        point: pointEvt
                    };
                    var goldOpt = {
                        data: [],
                        name: 'Gold',
                        color: '#FFB400',
                        point: pointEvt,
                        stacking: stacking,
                        dataLabels: dataLabel
                    };
                    var category = [];

                    $.each(result.rows,
                        function(idx, data) {
                            // Display country code on phone
                            // otherwise name
                            category.push((device === 'phone') ?
                                    data.code : data.country);
                            goldOpt.data.push(data.gold);
                            silverOpt.data.push(data.silver);
                            bronzeOpt.data.push(data.bronze);
                    });

                    chart.xAxis[0].setCategories(category);
                    chart.addSeries(bronzeOpt, false);
                    chart.addSeries(silverOpt, false);
                    chart.addSeries(goldOpt, false);
```

```
                    // Enable the option button for the
                    // column chart
                    $('#options').removeClass('ui-disabled');
                }
            chart.redraw();
        });    // function(result)
    };   // function(chart, …
```

The `plotGoldChart` method is a general routine to plot a series into an existing chart. The `options` parameter is a configuration object with new settings to be applied to the chart. First, the function invokes an Ajax call, `olympic.php`, to get the list of countries with the most gold medals. Upon the returned results, the handler function examines the `options` parameter for series type, device orientation, and other fields (stacking and data labels from the `config` dialog, which we will discuss later). Then it creates the chart based on the settings. If `type` property is `column`, then we create three column series as `Gold`, `Silver`, and `Bronze` with the point `click` event configured. If the `type` value is `pie` then it creates a single pie series of gold medals with a gradual change of colors and data labels.

So when the `gold_chart` page is first loaded, a column chart is created and displayed. The following screenshot shows the initial column chart in portrait mode:

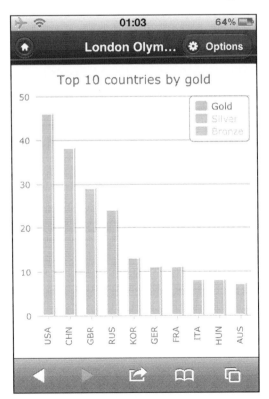

If we touch the legend items to display number of silver and bronze medals, the chart looks like the following screenshot:

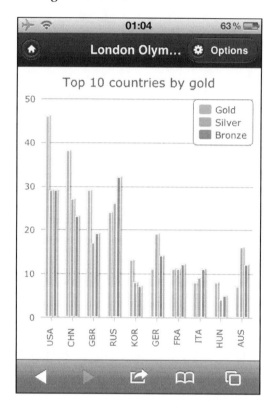

Switching graph options with the jQuery Mobile dialog box

The **Options** button in the top right-hand corner is only enabled if the current display chart is a column chart. It launches an option dialog box for switching stack column and data labels. The following code is for the mobile page for the dialog box:

```
<div data-role="page" id='options' >
    <div data-role="header">
        <h1>Config</h1>
    </div><!-- /header -->

    <div data-role="content">
        <label for="stacking">Stacking:</label>
        <select name="stacking" id="stacking"
                data-role="slider">
```

```
            <option selected="selected">Off</option>
            <option>On</option>
        </select>

        <label for="dataLabel">Show Values:</label>
        <select name="dataLabel" id="dataLabel"
                data-role="slider">
            <option selected="selected">Off</option>
            <option>On</option>
        </select>

        <a href="#" data-role="button"
            data-rel="back" id='updateChart' >Update</a>
        <a href="#" data-role="button"
            data-rel="back" >Cancel</a>
    </div>
</div><!-- /page -->
```

The `<select>` markups in jQM are rendered into slider switches with the `data-role='slider'` attribute and the hyperlinks are rendered as dialog buttons with the `data-role='button'` attribute. The following screenshot shows the dialog page:

Likewise, we program the `pageinit` handler for the dialog page to initialize the **Update** button action.

```
$('#options').live('pageinit',
    function() {
        var myApp = $.olympicApp;

    $('#updateChart').click(function() {

        var stacking =
            ($('#stacking').val() === 'Off') ?
                null: 'normal';
        var dataLabel =
            !($('#dataLabel').val() == 'off');

        myApp.plotGoldChart(myApp.goldChart, {
            stacking: stacking,
            dataLabel: dataLabel
        });
    });
});
```

Actually the action code for the button is very simple. Since we define the **Update** button with the `data-rel='back'` attribute, as soon as we tap the button, the dialog box is closed and goes back to the previous page. The option values from the `<select>` inputs are passed to the `plotGoldChart` routine to redraw the current chart. The following is a screenshot with only **Show Values** switched on:

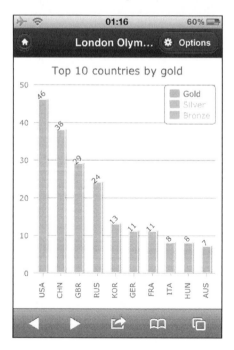

The following screenshot shows a column chart with both stacking and data labeling switched on:

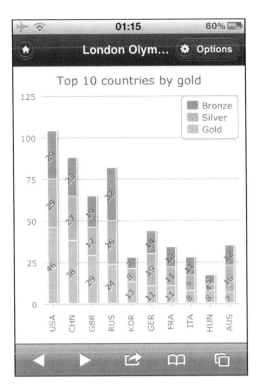

Changing the graph presentation with a swipeleft motion event

Here we enhance the experience by adding a `swipeleft` event to a chart. What we try to achieve is applying a swipe motion from the right-hand side to the left-hand side to an existing column chart; this action switches the column chart to a pie chart with the same dataset and vice versa with the swipe right-hand side motion.

```
// Switch to pie chart
$('#chart_container').on('swipeleft',
    function(evt) {
        var myApp = $.olympicApp;
        if (myApp.goldChart.series[0].type == 'column') {
            myApp.plotGoldChart(myApp.goldChart, {
                type: 'pie'
            });
        }
```

```
        });
    // Switch back to default column chart
    $('#chart_container').on('swiperight',
        function(evt) {
            var myApp = $.olympicApp;
            if (myApp.goldChart.series[0].type == 'pie') {
                myApp.plotGoldChart(myApp.goldChart);
            }
    });
```

The guard condition inside the handler is to stop redrawing the chart with the same presentation. The following is the view after the swipeleft action:

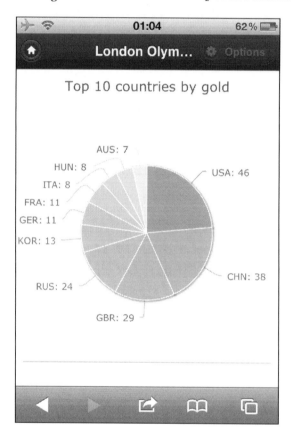

Switching graph orientation with the orientationchange event

Assume we are viewing the column chart on a touch phone device in portrait position. If we rotate the device, the chart will resize itself, but the scale along the y axis is squashed. As a result, it is less obvious in comparing how well each country did. To overcome that, we use another jQuery Mobile event, `orientationchange`, which triggers when the mobile device is rotated. The following is the implementation for the handler:

```
// Switch between vertical and horizontal bar
$(document).on('orientationchange',
    function(evt) {

        // We only do this for phone device because
        // the display is narrow
        // Tablet device have enough space, the
        // chart will look fine in both orientations
        if (device == 'phone') {

            var myApp = $.olympicApp;
            var orientation = getOrientation();

            // I have to destroy the chart and recreate
            // to get the inverted axes and legend box
            // relocated
            myApp.goldChart.destroy();

            // create the chart optimized for horizontal
            // view and invert the axis.
            myApp.goldChart = createChart({
                device: device,
                orientation: orientation,
                inverted: (orientation === 'landscape'),
                load: myApp.plotGoldChart,
                legend: ....,
            });

            // Hide the address bar
            window.scrollTo(0,1);
        }
    }
);
```

We recreate the chart with the `inverted` option set to `true` to swap both x and y axes, as well as positioning the legend in the lower-right corner instead. A method for the chart `load` event is also set up in the configuration. In the end, an inverted chart is produced, as shown in the following screenshot:

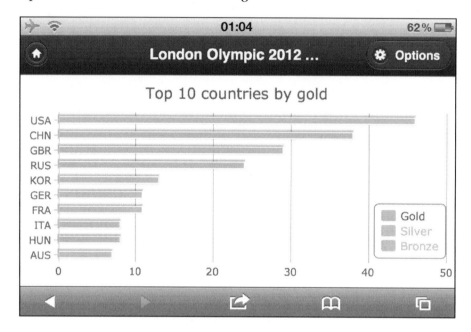

The following is a screenshot from a tablet device showing the gold and silver medals' chart:

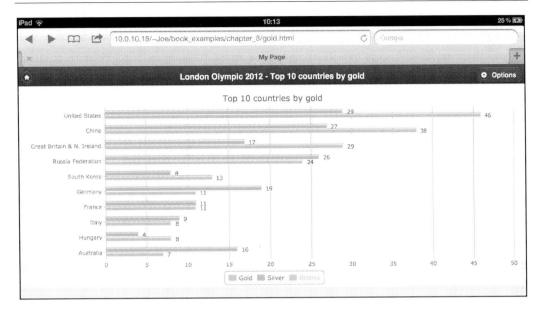

The `plotGoldChart` method detects a larger display and renders the chart with full country names.

Drilling down for data with the point click event

So far we have only fiddled with the top countries ordered by gold medals. Let's see how we can use a Highcharts event to navigate other charts in jQuery Mobile. Back to the `pageinit` handler code for `chart_page`, we declared the variable `pointEvt`, which is a `click` event handler shared by all the series in gold medal charts. The following code is for the event:

```
var pointEvt = {
    events: {
        click: function(evt) {
            document.location.href = './sport.html?country='
            // Country code or name
            + encodeURIComponent(this.category) +
            // Medal color
            '&color=' + this.series.name;
        }
    }
};
```

This event is triggered by touching a bar in a column chart or a slice in a pie chart. As a result, it loads a new document page with a bar chart. The URL for the document page is built inside the handler with the selected country code and the medal color as parameters. The `this` keyword refers to the data point (that is the country bar) being clicked. The bar chart displays the list of sports winning the medals from the selected country and medal color. The following screenshot shows a chart for a list of sports that won the gold medals for Great Britain and Northern Ireland:

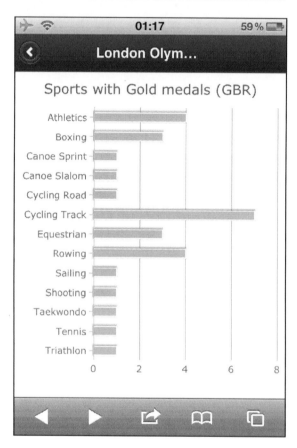

Inside the new page, it uses similar code from the gold medal countries chart to produce the graph shown in the preceding screenshot. The only difference is that it is embedded with the point `click` callbacks. We will see that in the next section.

Building a dynamic content dialog with the point click event

Now we know which sports have achieved gold medals in the Olympics, but we want to further find out who are medalists. Let's touch the **Athletics** bar in the chart; a dialog appears and presents a list of athletes in thumbnails along with their names, photos, and their event information, as shown in the following screenshot:

Notice that the dialog box shown in the preceding screenshot is not a static HTML page. This is constructed via a point `click` event and builds the dialog box content dynamically from the result. The problem is that in order to launch a dialog page in jQM, we need to have a button somewhere in the page to start from. The trick is to create a jQM hidden button and call a method to invoke the click action from inside the event handler. The following code is the HTML for both the hidden button and dialog page:

```
<!-- hidden dialog -->
<a id='hiddenDialog' href="#atheletes_dialog"
   data-rel="dialog" data-transition="pop"
   style='display:none;'></a>
```

```
<!-- medalists page -->
<div data-role="page" id='atheletes_dialog' >
   <div data-role="header">
       <h1></h1>
   </div><!-- /header -->

   <div data-role="content">
      <ul data-role="listview" data-inset="true"
          id='atheletes_list' >
      </ul>
   </div>

   <a href="" data-role="button" data-rel="back">Cancel</a>
</div><!-- /page -->
```

The following is the implementation of the `click` handler for the sports chart:

```
point: {
    events: {
        click: function(evt) {
            var params = {
                country : urlParams.country,
                color : urlParams.color.toLowerCase(),
                sport : this.category
            };

            // Set the title for dialog
            $('#atheletes_dialog h1').text(this.category +
                " (" + urlParams.country + ") - " +
                urlParams.color + " medalists");

            // Simulate a button click to launch the
            // list view dialog
            $('#hiddenDialog').click();

            // Launch ajax query, append the result into
            // a list and launch the dialog
            $.getJSON('./olympic.php', params,
                function(result) {

                    $("#atheletes_list").empty();
                    $.each(result.rows,
                        function(idx, athelete) {
                            // Formatting the image, name, and
                            // the sport event
                            var content = "<li><img src='" +
                                athelete.image + "' />" + "<h3>" +
```

```
                            athelete.name + "</h3><p><strong>"
                            + athelete.event +
                            "</strong></p><p>" +
                            athelete.desc + "</p></li>";

                        $("#atheletes_list").append(content);
                    });
                    // Need this to apply the format to
                    // the new entry
                    $('#atheletes_list').listview('refresh');
                });   // getJSON
            }
        }
```

First we assemble the title for the dialog page ready to launch. Then we trigger an action click to the hidden button with the call as follows:

```
$('#hiddenDialog').click();
```

This in turn generates a click event to launch the dialog page. Then we issue an Ajax query for the list of medalists with the current selected country, medal color, and sport as the filters. Upon return, we format each item from the result and insert them into the `<ul>` list, `atheletes_list`.

Applying the gesturechange (pinch actions) event to a pie chart

So far we have only explored actions involving a single touch point. Our next goal is to learn how to apply more advanced action events with multi-touch. One of the common actions is the pinch-in/out for zooming out/in respectively. The Safari browser for iOS supports this motion with `gesturestart`, `gesturechange`, `gestureend` events. Whenever there are two or more fingers touching the screen, the `gesturestart` event is fired. Then the `gesturechange` event is triggered when the fingers are moved on the screen. When the fingers leave the screen, the `gestureend` event is generated. In returning control to the event handler, if the action is recognized, a certain property in the event object is updated. For instance, the `scale` property in the event object is set to larger than 1.0 for pinch-out and less than 1.0 for pinch-in. For the `GestureEvent` class reference, please see `http://developer.apple.com/library/safari/#documentation/UserExperience/Reference/GestureEventClassReference/GestureEvent/GestureEvent.html`.

In this section we are going to apply the pinch motions to a pie chart. For the pinch-out action, we turn the pie chart into a doughnut chart with extra information on the outer ring, and vice versa for pinch-in, turning the doughnut chart back to a pie chart. First of all, let's launch a new chart, **Top 10 countries by medals**, the second item from the front menu. The following screenshot is the output of the chart:

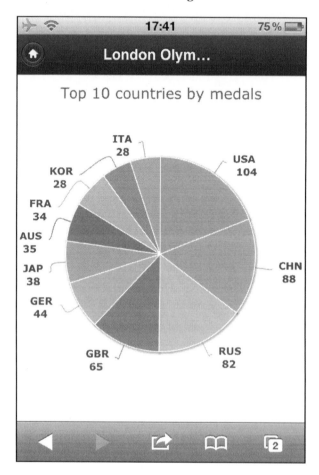

When we perform a pinch-out action, and the chart is redrawn, as shown in the following screenshot:

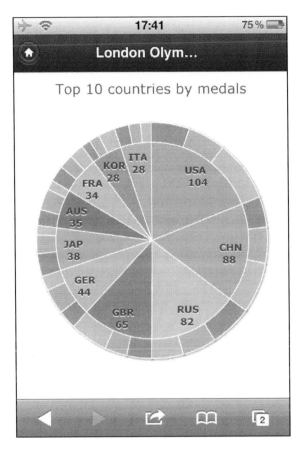

The outer ring shows the ratio of each color medal for each country. Moreover, the original pie chart data labels move inwards to make space for the outer ring. Let's see how the `gesturechange` event is implemented. The following is the code inside the `pageinit` handler:

```
$('#chart_container').on('gesturechange',
    function(evt) {
        evt = evt.originalEvent || evt;
        var myApp = $.olympicApp;

        if (evt.scale > 1) {
            // Pinch open - from pie chart to
            // donut chart
            if (!myApp.medalChart.series[1].visible) {
```

```
                myApp.medalChart.destroy();
                myApp.medalChart = createChart({
                    orientation: getOrientation(),
                    device: device
                    outerRing: true,
                    load: myApp.plotMedalChart
                });
            }
        } else if (myApp.medalChart.series[1].visible) {
            // Pinch close
            myApp.medalChart.destroy();
            myApp.medalChart = createChart({
                orientation: getOrientation(),
                device: device:
                load: myApp.plotMedalChart
            });
        }
    });
});
```

We bind the gesture event to the chart container. This event handler is called whenever there is a multi-touch gesture made on the screen, like a pinch or rotate motion. In order to make sure this is a pinch action, we need to look into the original event generated by the browser which is wrapped by the jQuery layer. We will examine whether the scale property has been set and decide whether it is pinch-in or out, then we will recreate the pie or doughnut chart if necessary.

Summary

The goal of this chapter was to deploy Highcharts graphs into mobile touch devices. To do that, we used a mobile web development framework, jQuery Mobile. A very brief introduction and the concepts of the framework was given; we illustrated how to integrate between Highcharts and jQuery Mobile.

Then we demonstrated a mobile application showing the results of Olympic 2012 medals table. A menu of charts was built using the jQuery Mobile dialog page, and then we showed how to use the single touch, multi-touch, and orientation events to navigate between charts. We also show how to use the Highcharts click event to build a dialog page dynamically.

In the next chapter we will learn how to apply Highcharts with ExtJs, a very powerful and popular **Rich Internet Application (RIA)** framework for building a desktop style application.

10
Highcharts and Ext JS

This chapter starts with an introduction of Sencha's Ext JS. Since the Ext JS framework covers a broad range of features, it comprises of a large collection of classes. Therefore a quick start guide on a small set will be given, especially on the user interface components likely to be used with Highcharts. Then we will learn which Highcharts extension we have for Ext JS and how to create a Highcharts graph within Ext JS. We will also learn about a small set of APIs provided by the extension. After that we will use network data to build a simple application to demonstrate how the Ext JS components can interact with Highcharts. Finally, we will have a brief look at a commercial Ext JS application working together with Highcharts. In this chapter we will cover the following:

- Introducing and giving a quick tutorial on Sencha Ext JS classes
- Introducing the Highcharts extension for Ext JS
- Demonstrating how to convert a working Highcharts configuration for the extension
- Preparing Ext JS JsonStore object for the extension
- Describing APIs provided by the extension module
- Illustrating how to create an Ext JS application with the Highcharts extension

Short introduction to Sencha Ext JS

Sencha's Ext JS is one of the most comprehensive **Rich Internet Application (RIA)** frameworks on the market. An RIA framework can produce web frontend that behaves like a desktop application. Ext JS supports many features such as proxy storage, charting, managing SVG, tabs, toolbars, a myriad of different form inputs and many, many others. There are other popular RIA frameworks, such as Java-based **Google Web Toolkit (GWT)** and Python-based Dojo. Both frameworks can be integrated with Highcharts via third-party contributed software.

See http://www.highcharts.com/download for the full list of software contributed by other developers.

The Highcharts extension was originally written by Daniel Kloosterman for Ext JS 2+ as an adapter, as it wasn't supporting any charts. In Ext JS 3, it started adopting the YUI charting library as the charting solution. However the charts lack features and style, and the main drawback is that they require Flash to run. Since Ext JS 3.1, I have been maintaining the extension and added features such as supporting Donut charts and enhancing some of the APIs.

Although Ext JS 4 comes with its own charts library, some users still prefer Highcharts over Ext JS 4 charts for style and flexibility. Moreover Ext JS 4 can run along with Version 3 codes, so it is desirable to enhance extension to natively support Ext JS 4, which I have done. The extension implementation has always been following the original approach which is to preserve using Highcharts configurations as much as possible.

There are demos online at joe.org/demos/Highcharts_Sencha/desktop/ and the extension can be downloaded from http://github.com/JoeKuan/ Highcharts_Sencha/.

Unlike jQuery UI, an Ext JS application is programmed in pure JavaScript, without the need to collaborate with HTML markups nor fiddle with particular CSS classes (strictly speaking, there are times when it is necessary to interface with HTML and CSS, but it is not common and is only in small doses). This empowers programmers to focus on developing the entire web application in a single language and to concentrate on application logic. That also pushes the server-side development to reside in data operations only, unlike some approaches using server-side language with HTML and CSS to serve client pages.

Technically, JavaScript does not have classes; function itself is an object. The Ext JS framework provides access to its components through classes approach organized in a hierarchical manner. In this chapter we will use the word "class" to refer to the Ext JS classes.

A quick tour of Ext JS components

There are myriads of classes in Ext JS and it is beyond the scope of this book to introduce them. Sencha provides three types of online documentation in both quality and quantity — a reference manual, tutorials (written and video), and working demos. Readers are strongly recommended to spend ample time reviewing these materials. In this section a very brief introduction is given about some components, especially those that are likely to interface with Highcharts. This chapter is by no means enough to get readers to start programming in Ext JS but should be enough to give you an idea.

Implementing and loading Ext JS code

An Ext JS application can always be divided into multiple JavaScript files, but they should always start from one HTML file. The following code snippet demonstrates how to start up Ext JS from an HTML file:

```
<html>
  <head>
    <meta http-equiv="Content-Type"
          content="text/html; charset=UTF-8">
    <title>HighChart for Ext JS 4</title>
    <link rel="stylesheet" type="text/css"
          href="../extjs/resources/css/ext-all.css" />
  </head>
  <body></body>
  <script type="text/javascript"
          src="../extjs/ext-all.js"></script>
  <script type='text/javascript'>
          Ext.onReady(function() {
                // application startup code goes here
                ....
          });
  </script>
</html>
```

The script file, `ext-all.js`, contains all the Ext JS classes in a compressed format.

 Ext JS has the facility to build a custom class file to cut downloading for production deployment. We are leaving that for the readers to explore.

`Ext.onReady` is the DOM ready method, same as the `$.ready` jQuery that the application startup code starts running inside this function.

Creating and accessing Ext JS components

Out of all the classes in Ext JS, we should start discussing Ext.Component, which is the base class for Ext JS user interface components. Depending on the characteristic of the component, some of them such as Panel, Window, FieldSet, and RadioGroup, can contain multiple components, because they are inherited through another class— Container. We will look into Container in more detail later.

To create an Ext JS object, we use the Ext.create method, which takes two parameters. The first parameter is the string presentation of a class path, for example 'Ext.window.Window', or an alias name such as 'widget.window'. The second parameter is the object specifier containing the initial values to instantiate a class.

```
var win = Ext.create('Ext.window.Window', {
        title: 'Ext JS Window',
        layout: 'fit',
        items: [{
            xtype: 'textarea',
            id: 'textbox',
            value: 'Lorem ipsum dolor sit amet, ... '
        }]
});

win.show();
```

The preceding code snippet is used to create a window widget and its content is defined through the items option. Window is a class derived from the Container class which inherits the items option for containing other components. When the window is finally created and ready to render, it goes through each object specifier in the items array and creates each component.

The xtype option is the Ext-specific type, which has a short unique name to symbolize the component's class path. In Ext JS all interface components have their own xtype names (this refers to the Ext.Component manual). The xtype option is commonly used for convenience to create components within the container, as opposed to Ext.create with a full path name.

The id field is to give a unique ID name to a component. The purpose is to gain direct access to a component at any point inside a program. To retrieve the component with an ID value, we can execute the following line of code:

```
var tb = Ext.getCmp('textbox');
```

Alternatively, we can use the `itemId` option to assign a unique name. The difference is that the `id` option field has to be uniquely global to the application whereas `itemId` only has to be unique within the parent container to avoid name conflict elsewhere in the application. To access a component with the `itemId` value, we need to call `getComponent` from the immediate parent container, as follows:

```
var tb = win.getComponent('textbox');
```

Moreover we can chain the call all the way from the top level to the desired component, as follows:

```
var val =
win.getComponent('panel').getComponent('textbox').getValue();
```

The `'textbox'` (with `itemId` defined) component is constructed inside the parent container, `'panel'`, which resides inside the window object. Although the `getCmp` method provides a direct easy access to a component, it should generally be avoided because of slower performance and undesired effects if a duplicated `id` option field is accidentally used.

 For the sake of avoiding long sample code, we use the `getCmp` call in some of the demos.

Using layout and viewport

As we mentioned before, some types of components have the ability to contain other components because they are extended from the `Container` class. Another feature of the `Container` class is to arrange the layout between the contained components; the layout policy is specified via the `layout` option. There are about a dozen layout policies; among them `'anchor'`, `'border'`, and `'fit'` are most commonly used (the `card` layout is also used often but through the tab panel). Border layout is widely used within GUI programming. The layout is finely divided into the `'north'`, `'east'`, `'south'`, `'west'`, and `'center'` regions.

When developing an application that requires utilizing the whole browser space, we generally use a `Viewport` class coupled with border layout. `Viewport` is a special type of container whose size automatically binds to the browser. The following is a simple example for using a viewport:

```
var viewport = Ext.create('Ext.container.Viewport', {
    layout: 'border',
    defaults: {
        frame: true
    },
```

```
items: [{
    region: 'north',
    html: '<h1>North</h1>'
}, {
    region: 'east',
    html: '<h1>East</h1>',
    width: '15%'
}, {
    region: 'south',
    html: '<h1>South</h1>'
}, {
    region: 'west',
    html: '<h1>West</h1>',
    width: '20%'
}, {
    region: 'center',
    html: '<h1>Center</h1>'
}]
});
```

The following screenshot shows the border layout:

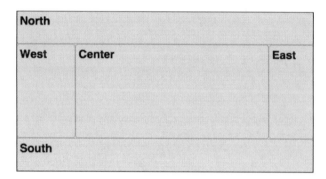

Panel

Panel is a basic container component and is generally used as a building block with layout format and then combined with more panels or components. Another general use is to extend the Panel class to a special purpose type of panel for example, PortalPanel in the online portal demo. The most widely used panel; types are GridPanel, FormPanel, and TabPanel.

GridPanel

GridPanel is used for displaying data in table format and it comes with lots of fruitful features, such as drag-and-drop column order, column sorting, flexible data rendering, enable or disable column display, and many others. GridPanel can also be used with different plugins such as row editor, allowing a user to edit field values on the fly. The class comes with a large set of events settings that can establish smooth coordination with other components. Nonetheless, the most tightly coupled component is with store object which we will demonstrate in a later section.

FormPanel

FormPanel is a panel for accommodating field input components in form style, that is, labels on the left-hand side, inputs on the right-hand side, and buttons array. Ext JS provides a great selection of form inputs, such as date time field, combobox, number field, slider, and many others. Underneath the FormPanel layer, there is a BasicForm component, which contributes to field validations, form submission, and loading services with the store's Record class for adding and editing entries. The following is a screenshot of FormPanel with various inputs:

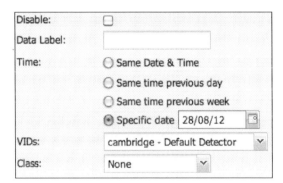

TabPanel

TabPanel, as its name implies, is a panel associated with tabs. It supports creating and removing tabs on the fly and scrolling between tabs. The following code snippet shows how to create a tab panel:

```
items:[{
    xtype: 'tabpanel',
    items: [{
        title: 'Tab 1',
        xtype: 'form',
        items: [{
            .....
```

```
            }]
        }, {
            title: 'Tab 2',
            ....
        }]
    }]
```

The following is a screenshot of tabs within the tab panel with a scrolling feature:

Window

`Window` is a special type of panel that is not bound to any parent container and it is free floating within the application. It offers many features found in normal desktop windows such as resize and maximize/minimize, and also comes with options for adding a toolbar, footer bar, and buttons. Later, we will see the `Window` panel in action in an example.

Ajax

The Ext JS framework provides its own method, `Ajax.request`, for issuing Ajax queries. This is used when the returned JSON data is not required to be converted into table rows and field columns. The method is generally coupled with `Ext.decode` to convert the returned JSON format string into a JavaScript object and directly access individual fields inside the object. The following code snippet shows a sample of issuing an Ajax query:

```
Ext.Ajax.request({
    url: 'getData.php ',
    params: { id: 1 },
    success: function(response) {
        // Decode JSON response from the server
        var result = Ext.decode(response.responseText);
        if (result && result.success) {
            ....
        } else {
            ....
        }
    }
});
```

Store and JsonStore

Store is a general purpose storage class for modeled data. There are several classes derived from Store but the most important one for Highcharts is JsonStore. It is a proxy-cached storage class responsible for issuing an Ajax query and unpacks the returned JSON data into modeled data. The JsonStore class is often used for accessing database data residing on the server side. A store object can bind with more than one component, for example a JsonStore object can bind to a grid panel and a column chart. Clicking on a column order direction in the grid panel can change the rows' sequence in JsonStore, hence affecting the order of the columns displayed in the chart. In other words the Store class acts as a skeleton to hold several components working together effortlessly and systematically.

It is important to note that the load method in the Store class is asynchronous. An event handler should be assigned to the load event if we want to tie an action after the data is loaded. The action can be specified either through listeners.click via the config or store.on method.

Example of using JsonStore and GridPanel

So far a number of Ext JS components have been introduced; we should see how they work together. Let's build a simple window application that contains a table (GridPanel) showing a list of hosts with their download usages, which are returned from the server. Assume we have rows of data returned in JSON format from the server:

```
{ "data": [
        { "host" : "192.168.200.145", "download" : 126633683 },
        { "host" : "192.168.200.99" , "download" : 55840235 },
        { "host" : "192.168.200.148", "download" : 54382673 },
        ...
] }
```

First we define the data model to correspond with the JSON data. For the sake of simple demonstration, we would put all our demo code inside Ext.onReady rather than in a separate JavaScript file.

```
Ext.onReady(function() {
    Ext.define('NetworkData', {
        extend: 'Ext.data.Model',
        fields: [
            {name: 'host',  type: 'string'},
            {name: 'download', type: 'int'}
        ]
    });
```

It is not mandatory to accept field names returned by the server. Ext.data.Model offers the mapping option to map for an alternative field name to use on the client side.

The next step is to define a JsonStore object with the URL, connection type, and the data format type. We will bind the JsonStore object with the NetworkData data model, defined in the preceding code snippet.

```
var netStore = Ext.create('Ext.data.JsonStore', {
        autoLoad: true,
        model: 'NetworkData',
        proxy: {
          type: 'ajax',
          url: './getNetTraffic.php',
          reader: {
              type: 'json',
              idProperty: 'host',
              root: 'data'
          }
        }
});
```

idProperty is to define which field is regarded as an ID if the default 'id' field name is not provided, so that methods such as Store.getById can function properly. The root option tells the reader (JsonReader) which property name holds the array of row data in the JSON response from the server. The next task is to build a Window panel with a GridPanel content, as follows:

```
var win = Ext.create('Ext.window.Window', {
        title: 'Network Traffic',
        layout: 'fit',
        items: [{
              xtype: 'grid',
              height: 170,
              width: 270,
              store: netStore,
              columns: [{
                  header: 'IP Address',
                  dataIndex: 'host',
                  width: 150
              }, {
                  header: 'Download',
                  dataIndex: 'download'
              }]
        }]
}).show();
```

We instruct the grid panel to bind with the `netStore` object, and define a list of columns to display and match each column to the store's data field through the `dataIndex` option. The following is a screenshot showing part of a window with a grid panel inside it:

The Highcharts extension

In this section we are going to examine how simple it is to create a Highcharts component in Ext JS. We do this by importing from an existing Highcharts configuration. Let's continue from the previous JsonStore example and incorporate it with the extension.

Step 1 – removing some of the Highcharts options

Assume we already have a working independent Highcharts configuration, as follows:

```
var myConfig = {
    chart: {
        renderTo: 'container',
        width: 350,
        height: 300,
        ....
    },
    series: [{
        type: 'column',
        data: [ 126633683, 55840235, .... ]
    }],
    xAxis: {
        categories: [ "192.168.200.145",
                      "192.168.200.99", ... ],
        ....
```

```
      },
      yAxis: { .... },
      title: { .... },
      ....
  };
```

The first step is to remove all the fields that the extension will internally handle and pass them to Highcharts. For that reason we need to remove `chart.renderTo` and the dimension options (`width` and `height`). We also need to remove the `chart.series` array, because eventually `JsonStore` will be the source of graph data. We also want to remove `chart.xAxis.categories` as it contains graph data.

Step 2 – converting to Highcharts extension configuration

The next step is to construct a new configuration for the extension deriving from the old Highcharts configuration. Let's start a new configuration object, `myNewConfig`, with the size properties:

```
var myNewConfig = {
        width: 350,
        height: 300
};
```

The next step is to create a new option, `chartConfig`, which is required by the extension. We put the rest of the properties left in the `myConfig` object towards `chartConfig`. The following code snippet shows what the new config should look like:

```
var myNewConfig = {
        width: 450,
        height: 350,
        chartConfig: {
                chart: { .... },
                xAxis: { .... },
                yAxis: { .... },
                title: { .... },
                ....
        }
};
```

Step 3 – constructing a series option by mapping the JsonStore data model

Recalling the data model of the store object, we have the following code snippet:

```
fields: [
    { name: 'host', type: 'string' },
    { name: 'download', type: 'int' }
]
```

The next task is to build a series array with options matching with the data model of JsonStore. The new series array has a similar structure to the one in Highcharts options. We also need to link the store object inside the object configuration. Eventually, the options object should become like the following code snippet:

```
var myNewConfig = {
    width: 450,
    height: 350,
    store: netStore,
    series: [{
        name: 'Network Traffic',
        type: 'column',
        dataIndex: 'download'
    }],
    xField: 'host',
    chartConfig: {
        ....
    }
};
```

The dataIndex option is used for mapping the y value from JsonStore into the series data array. As the 'host' field is a string type data, it is used as categories. Therefore we specify the xField option outside the series array shared by the series.

Step 4 – creating the Highcharts extension

The final step is to put everything together to display a chart in Ext JS. We can create a Highcharts component first and put it inside a Ext JS container object, as follows:

```
var hcChart = Ext.create('Chart.ux.Highcharts', myNewConfig);
var win = Ext.create('widget.window', {
    title: 'Network Traffic',
    layout: 'fit',
    items: [ hcChart ]
}).show();
```

Or alternatively, we can create the whole thing through one configuration using `xtype`, as follows:

```
var win = Ext.create('widget.window', {
    title: 'Network Traffic',
    layout: 'fit',
    items: [{
        xtype: 'highchart',
        itemId: 'highchart',
        height: 350,
        width: 450,
        store: netStore,
        series: [{ .... }],
        xField: 'host',
        chartConfig: {
            chart: { .... },
            xAxis: { .... },
            yAxis: { .... },
            ....
    }]
}).show();
```

The following screenshot shows a Highcharts graph inside an Ext JS window:

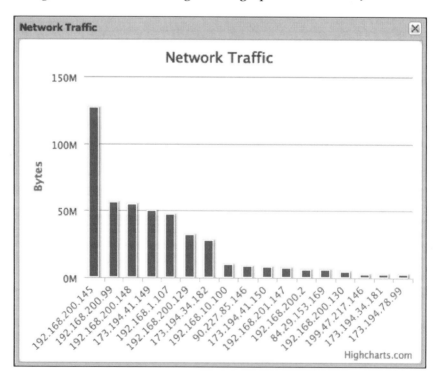

In order to display data at startup, the JsonStore must be instantiated by setting the `autoLoad` option to `true` or calling the `Store.load` method manually at the start of the program.

Passing series specific options in the Highcharts extension

If we need to pass specific series options, for example color, data point decorations, and so on, then we simply put it into the series configuration in the same way we normally do in Highcharts.

```
.....
store: netStore,
    series: [{
    name: 'Network Traffic',
    type: 'column',
    dataIndex: 'download',
    color: '#A47D7C'
    }],
```

The extension will copy these options across at the same time as creating the series.

Converting a data model into a Highcharts series

In the previous example we learned how to map a simple data model from the Ext JS store into Highcharts. However there are several ways to declare the data mapping and each way has different implications depending on the scenarios, especially in multiple series.

X-axis category data and y-axis numerical values

This is the simplest and probably the most common scenario. Each series has numerical values along the y axis and shares data between the categories. For historical reasons the `dataIndex` option can also be replaced with another option name, `yField`, which has a higher priority, and both behave in exactly the same way.

```
series: [{
    name: 'Upload',
    type: 'column',
    yField: 'upload'
}, {
```

```
        name: 'Download',
        type: 'column',
        yField: 'download'
}],
// 'Monday', 'Tuesday', 'Wednesday' ....
xField: 'day'
```

Numerical values for both x and y axes

Another scenario is where both x and y axes are made up of numerical values. There are two different ways to specify the data mapping. First each series holds the y-axis values and shares common x-axis values. In this case the series are specified in the same way as the previous example:

```
series: [{
        name: 'Upload',
        type: 'line',
        yField: 'upload'
}, {
        name: 'Download',
        type: 'line',
        yField: 'download'
}],
// Time in UTC
xField: 'time'
```

Another situation is each series holding its own pairs of x and y values, as follows:

```
series: [{
        name: 'Upload',
        type: 'line',
        yField: 'upload',
        xField: 'upload_time'
}, {
        name: 'Download',
        type: 'line',
        yField: 'download',
        xField: 'download_time'
}]
```

The difference between the two settings is that the first configuration ends up with two line series in the graph with data points aligning along the x axis, whereas the latter one doesn't, and the store data model is different as well.

Performing pre-processing from store data

Suppose we need to perform a pre-processing task on the server data before we can plot the chart. We can do this by overriding a template method in the series configuration.

Inside the extension code each series is actually instantiated from a `Serie` class. This class has a standard method defined, `getData`, which is for retrieving data from the store. Let's visit the original implementation of `getData`:

```
getData : function(record, index) {
    var yField = this.yField || this.dataIndex,
        xField = this.xField,
        point = {
            data : record.data,
            y : record.data[yField]
        };
    if (xField)
        point.x = record.data[xField];
    return point;
},
```

 The classes and methods in this extension are named that way with the word "`Serie`" by the original author.

Basically, `getData` is called for every row returned from `JsonStore`. The method is passed with two parameters. The first one is an Ext JS `Record` object, which is an object representation of a row of data. The second parameter is the index value of the record inside the store. Inside the `Record` object, the `data` option holds the values according to the model definition when the store object is created.

As we can see, the simple implementation of `getData` is to access `record.data` based on the values of `xField`, `yField`, and `dataIndex` and formats it into a Highcharts `Point` configuration. We can override this method as we declare a series to suit our need for data conversion. Let's continue the example; suppose the server is returning the data in a JSON string:

```
{"data":[
     {"host":"192.168.200.145","download":126633683,
      "upload":104069233},
     {"host":"192.168.200.99","download":55840235,
      "upload":104069233},
     {"host":"192.168.200.148","download":54382673,
      "upload":19565468},
     . . . .
```

`JsonStore` interprets the preceding data into rows with the following model definition:

```
fields: [
    {name: 'host',   type: 'string'},
    {name: 'download', type: 'int'},
    {name: 'upload', type: 'int'}
]
```

We need to plot a column chart with each bar as the total of upload and download fields, so we define the `getData` method for the series as shown next. Note that we don't need to declare `yField` or `dataIndex` anymore, because the `getData` method for this particular series has already taken care of the field mappings.

```
series: [{
    name: 'Total Usage',
    type: 'column',
    getData: function(record, index) {
        return {
            data: record.data,
            y: record.data.upload +
                record.data.download
        };
    }
}],
xField: 'host',
....
```

Plotting pie charts

Plotting pie charts is slightly different to line, column, and scatter charts. A pie series is composed of data values where each value is from a category. Therefore the module has two specific option names, `categorieField` and `dataField`, for category and data, respectively. To plot a pie chart the series is needed to specify the following:

```
series: [{
    type: 'pie',
    categorieField: 'host',
    dataField: 'upload',
}]
```

The `getData` method of the `PieSerie` class subsequently converts the mapped data from the store into the `Point` object with values assigned to the `name` and `y` fields.

Plotting donut charts

Let's remind ourselves that a donut chart is actually a two-series pie chart in which the data in the inner pie is a subcategory to its outside pie. In other words each slice in the inner series is always the total of its outer portions. Therefore data returned from JsonStore has to be designed in such a way that these can be grouped into subcategories by a field name. In this case the JSON data should be returned, as follows:

```
{ "data": [
      { "host" : "192.168.200.145", "bytes" : 126633683,
        "direction" : "download"},
      { "host" : "192.168.200.145", "bytes" : 104069233,
        "direction" : "upload"},
      { "host" : "192.168.200.99", "bytes" : 55840235,
        "direction" : "download"},
      { "host" : "192.168.200.99", "bytes" : 104069233,
        "direction" : "upload"},
      ....

] }
```

Then we use an extra boolean option, totalDataField, for the inner pie series to indicate that we want to use dataField to scan for the total value for each "host" category. As for the outer series we just define it as a normal pie series, but with "direction" and "bytes" as categorieField and dataField, respectively. The following is the series definition for the donut chart:

```
series: [{
        // Inner pie
        type: 'pie',
        categorieField: 'host',
        dataField: 'bytes',
        totalDataField: true,
        size: '60%',
        ....
}, {
        // Outer pie
        type: 'pie',
        categorieField: 'direction',
        dataField: 'bytes',
        innerSize: '60%',
        ....
}]
```

The following screenshot shows what a donut chart looks like in Ext JS:

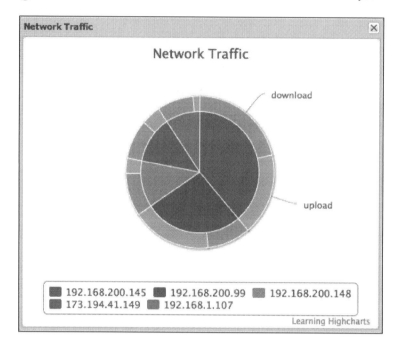

Inside the extension the implementation of the `getData` method for the `PieSerie` class is significantly different from other series types in order to handle both pie and donut series data. Therefore it is not advisable to overwrite this method. Later on we will see how the pie and donut charts are plotted with this module.

Module APIs

The Highcharts extension comes with a small set of APIs; most of them are helper functions to modify series in the Ext JS layer. As for the Highcharts native APIs, they can be invoked through the `chart` property inside the extension component, for example:

```
Ext.getComponent('highchart').chart.getSVG({ ... });
```

In the preceding line of code, `'highchart'` is the `id` value when the chart component is created.

As mentioned before, the `chartConfig` option contains all the Highcharts configurations. Once the chart component is created, it internally saves `chartConfig` inside the component. Hence the `chartConfig` property possesses all the initial configurations that have created the chart. Later we will see how this `chartConfig` property plays a role with the API calls.

addSeries

The `addSeries` method adds one or more series into the chart. The added series is/are also stored inside the `chartConfig.series` array, as follows:

```
addSeries : function(Array series, [Boolean append])
```

The series parameter is an array of series configuration objects. `addSeries` not only allows series configuration with the `xField`, `yField`, and `dataIndex` options but also supports series configuration with data array; hence it won't go via the store object to extract the data. The following are examples of using `addSeries` in different ways:

```
Ext.getComponent('highchart').addSeries([{
        name: 'Upload',
        yField: 'upload'
}], true);

Ext.getComponent('highchart').addSeries([{
        name: 'Random',
        type: 'column',
        data: [ 524524435, 434324423, 43436454, 47376432 ]
}], true);
```

The optional `append` parameter sets the series parameter to either replace the current displayed series or append the series to the chart. The default is `false`.

removeSerie and removeAllSeries

The `removeSerie` method removes a single series in the chart and the `removeAllSeries` method removes all the series defined for the chart. Both methods also remove the series configuration in `chartConfig.series`, as follows:

```
removeSerie : function(Number idx, [Boolean redraw])
removeAllSeries : function()
```

The `idx` parameter is the index value in the series array.

The optional `redraw` parameter sets whether redrawing the chart after the series is removed. The default is `true`.

setTitle and setSubTitle

Both `setTitle` and `setSubTitle` change the current chart title as well as the title settings in `chartConfig`, as follows:

```
setSubTitle : function(String title)
setTitle: function(String title)
```

draw

So far we have been mentioning `chartConfig` but haven't really explained what it does in the module. The `draw` method actually destroys the internal Highcharts object and recreates the chart based on the settings inside the current `chartConfig`. Suppose we have already created a chart component, but we want to change some of the display properties. We modify properties inside `chartConfig` (Highcharts configurations) and call this method to recreate the internal Highcharts object.

```
draw: function()
```

Although we can call Highcharts' native APIs via the internal `chart` option without destroying and recreating the chart, not all Highcharts elements can be changed with API calls, for example series color, legend layout, columns stacking option, invert chart axes, and so on.

As a result this method enables the extension component to refresh the internal chart with any configuration change without the need to recreate the component itself. Hence this empowers the Ext JS application by avoiding removing itself from the parent's container and reinserting a new one. Also the layout in the parent container is not disrupted.

Event handling and export modules

Specifying chart event handlers for the extension is exactly the same as how we normally declare in Highcharts. Since this is now under Ext JS as well as jQuery environments, the implementation can use both the Ext JS and jQuery methods.

The Highcharts exporting chart module is unaffected by the extension. The export settings simply bypass this extension and work straightaway.

Extending the example with Highcharts

In this section we are building a larger example that includes other types of panels and charts. The application is built with a viewport showing two regions—the `'center'` region is a tab panel containing three tabs for each different type of network data graphs and the `'west'` region shows the table of data of the current graph on display. The graph in the first tab is **Bandwidth Utilisation**, which indicates the data rate passing through the network. The following screenshot shows the front screen of the application:

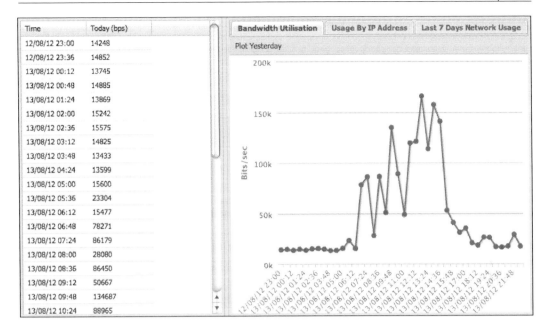

Time	Today (bps)	
12/08/12 23:00	14248	
12/08/12 23:36	14852	
13/08/12 00:12	13745	
13/08/12 00:48	14885	
13/08/12 01:24	13869	
13/08/12 02:00	15242	
13/08/12 02:36	15575	
13/08/12 03:12	14825	
13/08/12 03:48	13433	
13/08/12 04:24	13599	
13/08/12 05:00	15600	
13/08/12 05:36	23304	
13/08/12 06:12	15477	
13/08/12 06:48	78271	
13/08/12 07:24	86179	
13/08/12 08:00	28080	
13/08/12 08:36	86450	
13/08/12 09:12	50667	
13/08/12 09:48	134687	
13/08/12 10:24	88965	

Plot Yesterday in the toolbar is a toggle button which triggers an additional series, **Yesterday**, to be plotted on the same chart. An extra column of data called **Yesterday** is also displayed in the left-hand side table, as shown in the following screenshot:

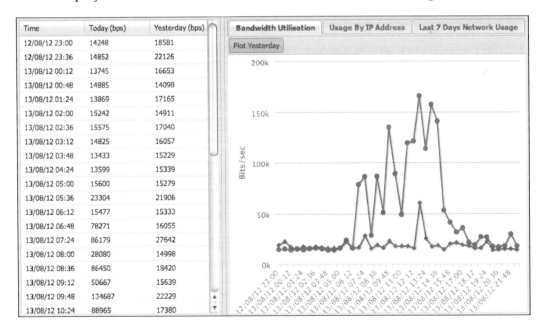

Time	Today (bps)	Yesterday (bps)
12/08/12 23:00	14248	18581
12/08/12 23:36	14852	22126
13/08/12 00:12	13745	16653
13/08/12 00:48	14885	14098
13/08/12 01:24	13869	17165
13/08/12 02:00	15242	14911
13/08/12 02:36	15575	17040
13/08/12 03:12	14825	16057
13/08/12 03:48	13433	15229
13/08/12 04:24	13599	15339
13/08/12 05:00	15600	15279
13/08/12 05:36	23304	21906
13/08/12 06:12	15477	15333
13/08/12 06:48	78271	16055
13/08/12 07:24	86179	27642
13/08/12 08:00	28080	14998
13/08/12 08:36	86450	18420
13/08/12 09:12	50667	15639
13/08/12 09:48	134687	22229
13/08/12 10:24	88965	17380

Inside the **Plot Yesterday** button's button handler it uses the `addSeries` and `removeSerie` methods to toggle the **Yesterday** series. The following is the implementation:

```
toggleHandler: function(item, pressed) {
    // Retrieve the chart extension component
    var chart = Ext.getCmp('chart1').chart;
    if (pressed && chart.series.length == 1) {
        Ext.getCmp('chart1').addSeries([{
            name: 'Yesterday',
            yField: 'yesterday'
        }], true);
        // Display yesterday column in the grid panel
        ....
    } else if (!pressed && chart.series.length == 2) {
        Ext.getCmp('chart1').removeSerie(1);
        // Hide yesterday column in the grid panel
        ....
    }
}
```

Let's move on to the second tab which is a column chart showing a list of hosts with their network usages in uplink and downlink directions, as follows:

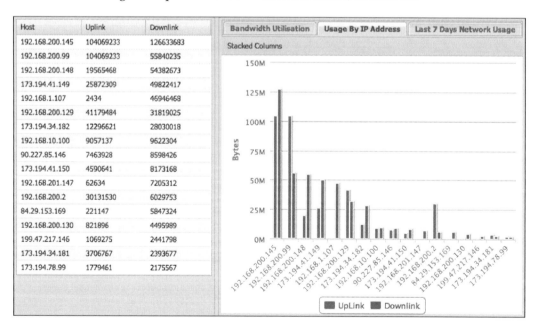

When we click on the **Stacked Columns** button, the bars of both series are stacked together instead of aligning adjacent to each other, as follows:

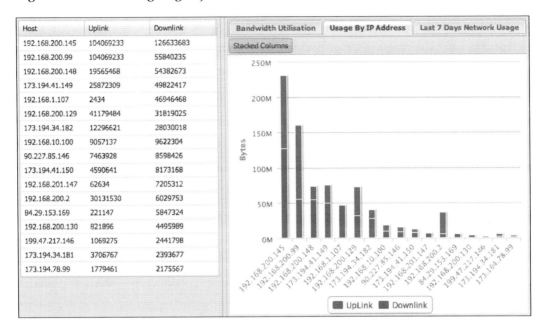

This is achieved by modifying the column `stacking` option inside the extension `chartConfig` property and recreating the whole chart with the module's `draw` method:

```
toggleHandler: function(item, pressed) {
    var chart2 = Ext.getCmp('chart2');
        chart2.chartConfig.plotOptions.column.stacking =
            (pressed) ? 'normal' : null;
        chart2.draw();
}
```

Note that we declare the default `stacking` option inside `chartConfig` when we create the chart, so that we can directly modify the property in the handler code later:

```
chartConfig: {

                .... ,

    plotOptions: {
        column: { stacking: null }
    },
    ......
```

The final tab is **Last 7 Days Network Usage**, which has a pie chart showing the network usage for each of the last seven days, as shown in the following screenshot:

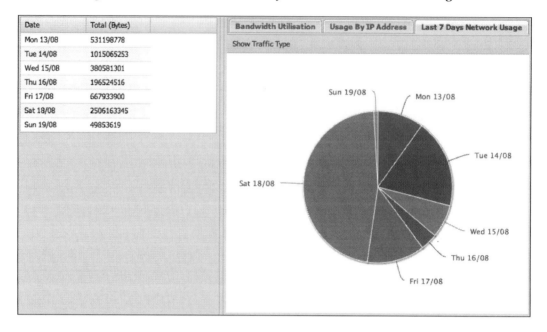

Date	Total (Bytes)
Mon 13/08	531198778
Tue 14/08	1015065253
Wed 15/08	380581301
Thu 16/08	196524516
Fri 17/08	667933900
Sat 18/08	2506163345
Sun 19/08	49853619

Let's see how this pie chart is implemented in detail. `JsonStore` is adjusted to return data in the following format:

```
{"data": [
      {"date": "Mon 13/08", "type": "wan",
       "bytes": 92959786, "color": "#8187ff" },
      {"date": "Mon 13/08", "type": "lan",
       "bytes": 438238992, "color": "#E066A3" },
      {"date": "Tue 14/08", "type": "wan",
       "bytes": 241585530, "color": "#8187ff" },
      {"date":"Tue 14/08", "type": "lan",
       "bytes": 773479723, "color": "#E066A3" },
      .....
```

Then we define the tab panel content, as follows:

```
            items:[{
                  xtype: 'highchart',
                  id: 'chart3',
                  store: summStore,
                  series: [{
                        type: 'pie',
```

```
                    name: 'Total',
                    categorieField: 'date',
                    dataField: 'bytes',
                    totalDataField: true,
                    size: '60%',
                    showInLegend: true,
                    dataLabels: { enabled: true }
                }],
                chartConfig: {
                    chart: { },
                    title: {  text: null },
                    legend: { enabled: false }
                }
            }]
```

The series is set up as an inner series, hence the use of the `totalDataField` and `dataField` options to get the total bytes of "lan" and "wan" as the slice value for each 'host'. If we click on the **Show Traffic Type** button, then the pie chart is changed to a donut chart, as shown in the following screenshot:

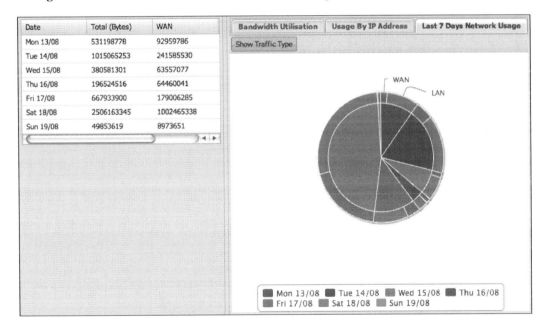

The original data labels in the first pie chart are replaced with items inside the legend box. An outer series is displayed with a fixed color scheme to show the **LAN** and **WAN** portion of traffic. The following is the **Show Traffic Type** button's button handler code:

```
toggleHandler: function(item, pressed) {
    var config = Ext.getCmp('chart3').chartConfig;
    if (pressed) {
        Ext.getCmp('chart3').addSeries([{
            type: 'pie',
            center: [ '50%', '45%' ],
            categorieField: 'type',
            dataField: 'bytes',
            colorField: 'color',
            innerSize: '50%',
            dataLabels: {
                distance: 20,
                formatter: function() {
                    if (this.point.x <= 1) {
                        return this.point.name.toUpperCase();
                    }
                    return null;
                }
            },
            size: '60%'
        }], true);

        config.legend.enabled = true;
        config.series[0].dataLabels.enabled = false;
        config.series[0].size = '50%';
        config.series[0].center = [ '50%', '45%' ];
    } else {
        Ext.getCmp('chart3').removeSerie(1);
        config.legend.enabled = false;
        config.series[0].dataLabels.enabled = true;
        config.series[0].size = '60%';
        config.series[0].center = [ '50%', '50%' ];
    }
    Ext.getCmp('chart3').draw();
}
```

If the toggle button is enabled, then we add an outer pie series (with `innerSize` option) via the `addSeries` method. Moreover, we align the outer series accordingly with the traffic `'type'`, hence `categorieField` and `dataField` are assigned to `'type'` and `'bytes'`. Since more information is needed to display the second series, we set the inner series to a smaller size for more space. In order to only show the first two data labels in the outer series, we implement `dataLabels.formatter` to print the label when `this.point.x` is 0 and 1. After that, we disable the data labels by returning null in the `formatter` function. Finally, the `draw` method is used to reflect all the changes.

Displaying a context menu by clicking on a data point

For interactive applications it would be handy to allow users to launch specific actions by clicking on a data point. To do that we need to handle Highcharts' click events. Here, we create a simple menu for showing the difference between the selected point and the average value of the series. The following is the sample code:

```
point: {
  events: {
    click: function(evt) {
      var menu =
        Ext.create('Ext.menu.Menu', {
          items: [{
            text: 'Compare to Average Usage',
            scope: this,
            handler: function() {
              var series = this.series,
                  yVal = this, avg = 0, msg = '';

              Ext.each(this.series.data, function(point) {
                avg += point.y;
              });
              avg /= this.series.data.length;

              if (yVal > avg) {
                msg =
                  Highcharts.numberFormat(yVal - avg) +
                  " above average (" +
                  Highcharts.numberFormat(avg) + ")";
              } else {
                msg =
                  Highcharts.numberFormat(avg - yVal) +
                  " below average (" +
                  Highcharts.numberFormat(avg) + ")";
              }
```

```
                    Ext.Msg.alert('Info', msg);
                }
            }]  // items:
        });

        menu.showAt(evt.point.pageX, evt.point.pageY);
        }
    }
}
```

First we create a simple Ext JS `Menu` object with the menu item **Compare to Average Usage**. The click handler is called with the mouse event parameter, `evt`, and then we obtain the mouse pointer location, `pageX` and `pageY`, and pass to the menu object. As a result the Ext JS menu appears next to the pointer after clicking on a data point.

The `'this'` keyword in the `click` event handler refers to the selected point object. We then use the `scope` option to pass the Highcharts point object to the menu handler layer. Inside the handler the `'this'` keyword becomes the data point object instead of the Ext JS menu item. We extract the series data to calculate the average and compute the difference with the selected point value. Then we display the message with the value. The following is the screenshot of the menu:

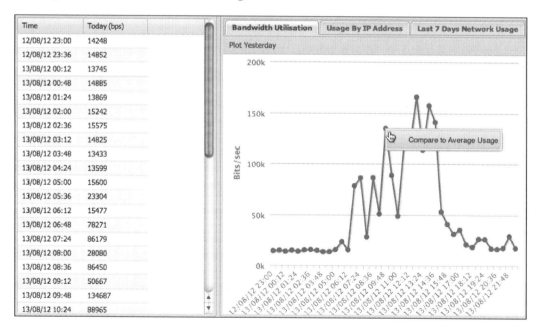

A commercially Rich Internet Application with Highcharts – AppQoS

So far we have demonstrated how Highcharts can be applied within the Ext JS framework. However the demo itself seems rather shrinkwrapped for an RIA product. In this section we will have a quick glance at a commercial application, AppQoS, a tool for monitoring networked applications' performance developed by iTrinegy. Due to the nature of its business, a stack of diagnostic graphs are required for this type of application. The whole application is designed as a collection of portals for monitoring network traffic from multiple sites. Users can drill down from utilization graph to top downlink usage by IP address graph and modify filter properties to display relative data in multiple series, and so on.

In order to fine-tune the monitoring parameters and provide a portal interface, a framework offering dynamic and calibrated user interfaces is needed. For that reason Ext JS is a suitable candidate, which offers a rich set of professional looking widget components and its cross-browsers' support makes building complicated RIA software manageable. The following is the interface for launching a bandwidth utilization graph with specific parameters:

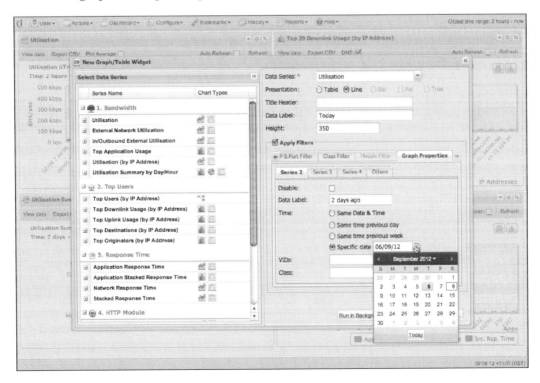

The Highcharts events are easily bound with Ext JS components, such that a fully interactive navigation style becomes possible. For instance, if a peak appears in the **Utilisation** graph, the users can either click on the peak data point or highlight a region for a specific time range, then a context menu with a selection of network graphs pops up. This action means that we can append the selected time region to be part of the accumulated filters and navigate towards a specific graph. The following is a screenshot of the context menu which shows up in one of the graphs:

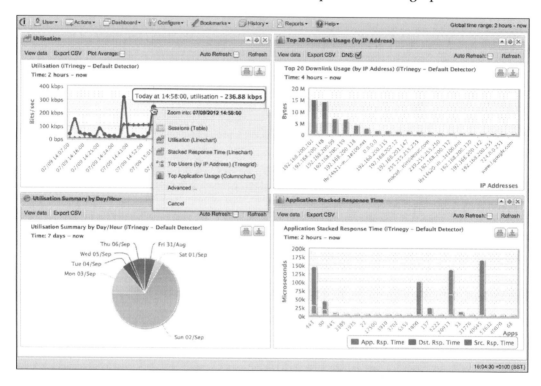

If we proceed by selecting the same graph again, that is **Utilisation**, it means we want to zoom into higher details within the selected time region. This doesn't use the Highcharts default zoom action, which just stretches the graph series and redraws the axes. In fact it launches another Ajax query with the selected time and returns graph data in finer granularity, hence the peak in the graph can be diagnosed further. In other words the application enables the users to visually filter through a sequence of different graphs. At the same time the users refine the filters gradually in different dimensions. This process makes the dissection of the problem into the root cause in a prompt, intuitive, and effective fashion.

Summary

In this chapter we learned the very basics of Ext JS, which is a framework for building **Rich Internet Applications (RIAs)**. A quick introduction was given on a dozen Ext JS components that are likely to be used with the Highcharts extension for Ext JS. Then we explored how to create a Highcharts component from an existing Highcharts configuration in a step-by-step approach. We looked into the small set of APIs, which provided the extension module, and built a simple application with network usage data. Finally, we took a brief look at Highcharts and Ext JS applied on a commercial network monitoring application.

In the next chapter we will explore how to run Highcharts on the server side.

11
Running Highcharts on the Server Side

In this chapter, we will learn why it is desirable to run Highcharts on the server side and which techniques are available for use. We learn each of the techniques and demonstrate some of them from installation to producing a chart on the server side. Finally, a review of pros and cons of each approach is given.

- Running Highcharts on the server side
- Using Xvfb and web browsers (Unix solution)
- Rhino and Batik (Java solution)
- `Node.js`/Node and Node-Highcharts (JavaScript solution)
- PhantomJS (headless webkit)
- Comparison between the approaches

Running Highcharts on the server side

The main reason for running Highcharts on the server side is to allow the client-based graphing application to be automated and accessible on the server side. In some cases, it is desirable to produce graphs at the frontend as well as delivering automated reports with graphs at the backend. For the sake of consistency and development cost, we would like to produce the same style of graphs at both ends. Here are other scenarios where we may want to generate graphs on the server side:

- The application is required to run a scheduled task on the server side. It generates a regular summary report with graphs (for example Service Level Agreement report) and automatically e-mails the report to clients or users with a managerial role.

- The nature of the data requires a long time to compute for a graph. Instead, users send the parameters over to the server to generate a graph. Once it is finished, the chart setup is saved, then the users are notified to see a live Highcharts chart from the precomputed JSON setup.

- The application involves a vast amount of recurring data that is only kept for a certain period, such that from time to time data trend graphs are automatically produced and stored in image format for the records.

Highcharts on the server side

There are four techniques to run Highcharts on the server side. Please note that although GWT Highcharts by Moxie Group is mentioned on the Highcharts website, this is incorrect. It is a GWT solution that provides a framework for developers to implement web frontend in Java. All the server-side techniques have one thing in common — the chart is eventually exported to SVG format and converted into an image file. The first approach is to run both browser and web server on the server side. The second approach is using a Java implementation of a JavaScript engine on the server side. The third approach is to run a JavaScript webserver with a Highcharts module. The last approach, **PhantomJs**, a headless Webkit engine with JavaScript API, is the ultimate way to run server tasks in JavaScript. We explain each approach in the following sections and explore the approaches in more detail, from installation to producing a chart export on the server side. Throughout the chapter, we will use Ubuntu 12.04 as our server appliance for demonstrations.

Using Xvfb and web browsers (Unix solution)

This is one of the simplest methods to run JavaScript on the server side. Basically, we start with a very lightweight headless X Server, Xvfb. **Xvfb** is a standard tool that comes with Unix distribution. More information can be found at `http://en.wikipedia.org/wiki/Xvfb`. This runs a browser on the server. Before we start, let's make sure we have an HTML file that can produce a graph export.

Setting up a Highcharts export example on the client side

The example is pretty simple—create a chart and export it to SVG data. The sequence of operations is illustrated with the following diagram:

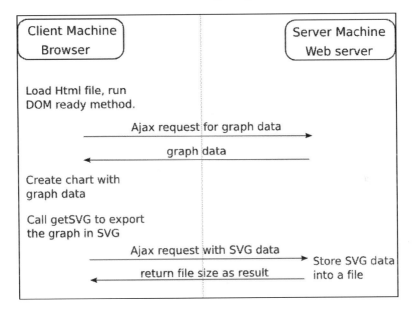

We first issue an Ajax query for the graph data and create a Highcharts graph once the graph data is returned. It is not mandatory to use an Ajax connection for the series data, as we can use embedding server-side language such as PHP or ASP.NET to resolve series data before the HTML page is served.

We use Formula 1 race lap times as the graph data and the following screenshot shows what the graph looks like:

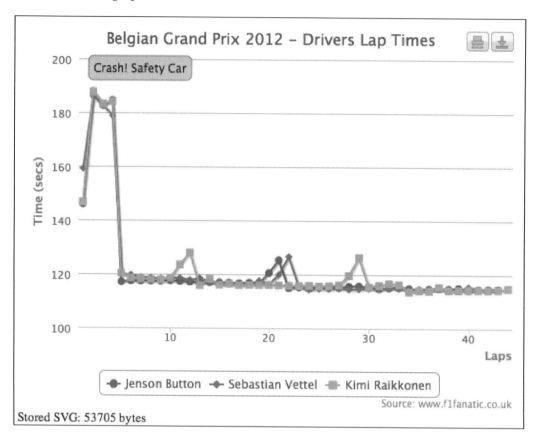

When we see the message **Stored SVG: ...** at the bottom left-hand side of the chart, it indicates that the SVG data has been sent to the server and saved into a file successfully.

If it is required to keep a backup copy of graph outputs, then it is preferable to store it in a raw SVG file in a compressed format. This is because we can reformat it to any image format, resize the image without losing quality, and most importantly, we can edit the source if we have to, such as removing the SVG group of legend box elements. As for converting SVG data into image files, there are always tools available. For our exercise, we use a utility from Imagick package convert, which can export SVG into different formats and includes many pre-processing features.

Let's see how we implement the whole solution; the following is the content of the HTML file, f1race.html:

```
<script>
<?php
  // Get the series data via file, db or remote host
  echo 'var seriesArray = ' . json_encode($series) .
    ";\n";
?>
$(document).ready(function() {

  // Create a Highcharts graph
  var gp_chart = new Highcharts.Chart({
    chart: {
      renderTo: 'container',
      animation: false
    },
    series: seriesArray,
    title: { ... },
    credits: { ... },
    ...
  }, function(chart) {

    // Create a label 'Crash! Safety Car' to the
    // graph data using Highcharts Renderer
    .....

    // Launch another Ajax query with the
    // graph SVG data
    $.ajax({
      url: './storeSVG.php',
      data: {
        svg: chart.getSVG()
      },
      type: 'POST',
      dataType: 'json',

      // Update the status of the SVG data
      // stored in the server
      success: function(data) {
        if (data.bytes) {
          $('#status').text("Stored SVG: "
          + data.bytes + " bytes");
        } else {
```

```
        $('#status').text("Unable to" +
        "store SVG export");
    }

    // At here, it means the SVG file is
    // generated and stored successfully
    // Close the browser itself
    var win = window.open("","_self");
    win.close();
    }
  });
  });
});
```

Basically, before the web server serves the previous HTML page to the client browser, the series data has been resolved and embedded inside the page. Then after the browser loads the page and renders the graph, it invokes the callback handler (second parameter in `Highcharts.Chart`). The handler exports the rendered graph into SVG content with the `chart.getSVG` method and issues an Ajax query with the content. The web server receives the SVG content and runs `storeSVG.php` to store the content into a file. Upon the return of an Ajax response, we close the current Firefox browser. The execution control resumes back to the caller that launches the Firefox browser with the HTML file. This process of sending the SVG data from browser to web server all within the server side is the core of this approach.

 In order to have the ability to quit the Firefox browser from within the JavaScript execution, the Firefox browser is required to be specially configured. In the location field, type `about:config` and a long list of browser settings is displayed on the screen. Set the option '**dom.allow_scripts_to_close_windows**' to **True**.

As the main purpose of this example is to get the SVG export, we set the `chart.animation` and `plotOptions.series.animation` options to `false` for both initial and update animation respectively. Next, we will see how to turn this HTML file into a server-side solution.

Installing Xvfb and a web browser

First of all we need to install Xvfb and a web browser (here Firefox) on our Ubuntu server. Also, make sure that fonts for X window and sound libraries Mesa are also installed.

```
sudo apt-get install xvfb firefox
```

Xvfb stands for X virtual frame buffer, which is a type of X window server that doesn't have any output to the screen. In other words, it's a fully functional X Server without the requirement of connecting to a physical screen. We use it as a tool to run X client programs like `firefox` in the background.

Starting up the Xvfb server

This approach can be depicted by the following diagram:

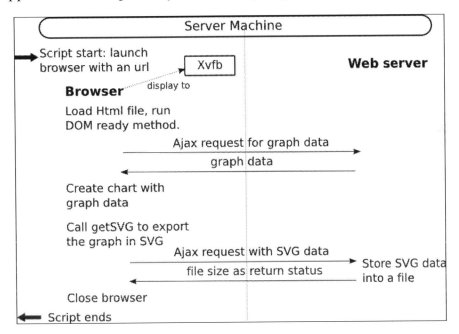

The vertical line in the previous diagram divides the browser client and web server processes, and both are running under the same physical machine, that is the server machine. The web browser process is running in the condition of connecting its display output to the Xvfb process. The whole export script process starts from launching the browser until it is terminated.

First, we start running Xvfb by giving a display ID of 1. The following command should be put in the machine run level `init` script or `/etc/rc.local`:

```
Xvfb :1 &
```

Once we need to export a chart to an image, we can launch a web browser to that display.

Applying server-side change

The next step is to create the web server script, `storeSVG.php`, which receives the SVG data and saves it into a file.

Alternatively, a slightly diverted approach that is suggested in the Highcharts forum is to use CutyCapt with Xvfb. **CutyCapt** is a tool built from Qt for rendering HTML page on the server side and takes the output directly into an image. We prefer to save the output into SVG and use Imagick `convert` for quality reasons.

```php
<?php
    // Save the SVG data into a file
    $result['bytes'] = file_put_contents("/tmp/chart.svg",
                        $_POST['svg']);
    // Return the size of output file as the
    // status of store process
    echo json_encode($result);
?>
```

Running the server task

Finally, we can kick start the whole process using a shell script to launch the web browser:

```sh
#!/bin/sh
# Do the cleanup first
rm /tmp/chart.svg
if [ $# -eq 2 ]; then
  param="?width=$1&height=$2"
fi

firefox --display :1 http://localhost/f1race.html$param
```

Firefox on the server side loads `f1race.html`, which eventually launches the Ajax request to `storesSVG.php`, then the JavaScript in `f1race.html` will close the Firefox browser, hence the Firefox process is terminated. The control is resumed again by the script caller. The approach is simple and clean, and can be run concurrently.

Rhino and Batik (Java solution)

Rhino is a Java implementation of the JavaScript console, which allows JavaScript to be run within the Java environment. One of the main uses of Rhino is to combine with Env.js (see `http://ejohn.org/blog/bringing-the-browser-to-the-server/` and `http://www.envjs.com/`), which is a simulated browser environment written in JavaScript. As a result, JavaScript source can be executed independently in `Rhino/Env.js` without relying on any real browsers. This creates an automated environment for running JavaScript code.

This approach has been developed into a solution, **Highcharts Server-side Export (HSE)**. The software provides an export engine that takes an object of the `ChartOptions` Java class, which is assembled by calling the framework (HSE) APIs. The structure of `ChartOptions` is based on the Highcharts options hierarchy. Inside the framework, the Rhino engine loads `Env.js` and Highcharts libraries including the exporting module. This `ChartOptions` object is then converted into a Highcharts configuration object. It then creates a chart and calls `getSVG` to return a SVG content string in the Rhino engine. Finally, the framework passes the SVG string to the Batik transcoder library (in Java) and formats it into an image. The approach is summarized with the following diagram; package and documentation can be found in github at `http://github.com/one2team/highcharts-serverside-export`.

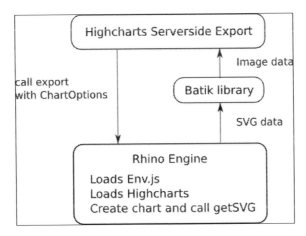

Node.js/Node and Node-Highcharts (JavaScript solution)

Node is one of the most exciting developments in JavaScript. It is not only a web server but also a platform for easily building fast, scalable network applications. It was created by Ryan Dahl and was built from Chrome's V8 JavaScript engine. The idea behind it is to provide a non-blocking I/O and event-driven network application. The idea of an event-driven web server is not new and there are several implementations available. The server can service requests in both efficiency and scalability. Node comprises of a large selection of APIs for server tasks and runs on Windows, Linux, and Mac OSX.

As the Node server tasks are implemented in JavaScript, it is possible to put Highcharts into server mode (this is also documented at `http://blog.davidpadbury.com/2010/10/03/using-nodejs-to-render-js-charts-on-server/`). In this section, we are going to set up only one server task and that is to create a Highcharts graph, export into SVG, and return an HTTP response.

Installing Node and modules

Let's start by installing the Node server onto an Ubuntu machine:

```
sudo apt-get install nodejs npm g++
```

The previous command installs the Node server and other required packages in one go. npm is a package manager tool for installing modules for Node. We need npm because there is another Node module required to run Highcharts, `node-highcharts` (see `http://github.com/davidpadbury/node-highcharts`). To install `node-highcharts`, we run npm as the following:

```
npm install node-highcharts -g
```

This step will download the package source and build it using a C++ compiler. This will also install the `jsdom` and `contextify` modules. The `-g` argument informs npm to install the packages globally, that is, in the default path of `node_modules`. Without the `-g` option, the module is installed locally to wherever npm is executed. We will then need to load the module with the full path:

```
var highcharts = require('/home/joe/node_modules/node-highcharts');
```

Or we need to load the module as the current directory as long as the Node server is started at the path `/home/joe/`.

```
var highcharts = require('./node-highcharts');
```

With the option to install globally, we can load the module with the following syntax with which it will search the non-core modules from the NODE_PATH environment:

```
var highcharts = require('node-highcharts');
```

Setting up the Node server

The next step is to set up the Node webserver running in listening mode and waiting for incoming HTTP requests. First, we need to create a script file exportSVG.js. Inside the script, we define how to process HTTP requests:

```
var http = require('http');
http.createServer(function (req, res) {
    ....
}).listen(5354, '127.0.0.1');
```

We load up the http module and call the createServer method to create an instance of the HTTP server. We call the listen method with a specific port and accept the incoming connection from the same host; hence the server is only available for internal use. Note that this does not interfere with the web server accepting external HTTP connections.

Once it starts and is listening for incoming HTTP connections, whenever an HTTP request arrives, the handler defined inside the createServer is called. The callback function has two arguments—one is to for incoming HTTP request – req and the other one is HTTP response – res. In this exercise, we only program one server task that exports a Highcharts graph to SVG.

Running the Node-Highcharts module

Inside the node-highcharts module, it relies on another module JsDom. JsDom is like Env.js, which is a DOM implementation in JavaScript but it is developed for Node. In a nutshell, the module internally creates a container <div> using the JsDom module and then creates a Highcharts graph with the chart.renderTo option pointing to the container. Note that the whole process is running on the server side while the HTTP request is being handled. Here is how we use the module:

```
var http = require('http');
var highcharts = require('node-highcharts');

http.createServer(function (req, res) {

    var reqComps = require('url').parse(req.url, true);
    var driver = reqComps.query.driver;
    var width = parseInt(reqComps.query.width, 10) || 350;
    var height = parseInt(reqComps.query.height, 10) || 300;
```

```
    // Get the series data either from file, db or
    // from another host
    var seriesArray = ....

    // Highcharts options
    var options = {
      chart: {
        width: width,
        height: height
      },
      exporting: { enabled: false },
      legend: {
        enabled: seriesArray.length ? true : false
      },
      series: seriesArray,
      ....
    };

    // Render the chart into PNG image data
    highcharts.render(options, function(err, data) {
      if (err) {
        var msg = 'Error: ' + err;
        console.log('Error: ' + err);
        res.statusCode = 500;
        res.write(msg);
      } else {
        require('fs').writeFile('/tmp/chart.png', data,
          function() {
            console.log('Written to chart.png');
          }
        );
        res.statusCode = 200;
        res.write("Output file to /tmp/chart.png");
      }
      res.end();
    });
}).listen(5354, '127.0.0.1');
console.log("Node server started & listening ...");
```

Basically, we start the HTTP request callback by loading up the `node-highcharts` module. We then construct the configuration object exactly the same way as we normally do in Highcharts. We finally pass the configuration to the module's `render` method, which creates a chart, calls the `getSVG` method, and converts the output to PNG data. At this point, we can either choose to store into a file or return the image data in the HTTP response. The following code illustrates how to return the image content in Node instead:

```
highcharts.render(options, function(err, data) {
  if (err) {
    // Write error
    ....
    res.end();
  } else {
    res.writeHead(200, {
      'Content-Type': 'image/png',
    });
    res.end(data, 'binary');
  }
});
```

Starting the Node server and issuing a URL query

To start the Node server with the server implementation and the module path, we run the following command at the Linux startup:

```
NODE_PATH=/usr/local/lib/ node /var/www/exportSVG.js &
```

Then, we can run the whole chart export method by issuing a URL query. In order to launch a query on the server side locally with a specific port (5354 set up previously in the `createServer` call), we can use the utility `curl`, as a part of the automation:

```
curl 'http://localhost:5354/f1race.html?driver=kimi+raikkonen&width=450&height=300'
```

PhantomJS (headless webkit)

Webkit is basically the backend engine that drives the browsers such as Safari and Google Chrome. It implements almost everything in HTML5 except the browser's user interface. PhantomJS (found at `http://phantomjs.org/`, created and maintained by Ariya Hidayat) is a headless webkit, which means that the webkit engine can be run as a standalone program. It is useful in a number of ways and one of them is server-side SVG rendering. This approach is by far the cleanest and the most direct way to export Highcharts graphs on the server side. PhantomJS is available on all the major platforms. On Ubuntu, we install it with the following command:

```
sudo apt-get install phantomjs
```

However, the Ubuntu distribution is packaged with PhantomJs 1.4 in which there have been lots of improvements since the version 1.4, especially that it doesn't rely on using Xvfb anymore. At the time of writing, the latest stable version is 1.7 and this is experimented with in this chapter.

Preparing the series data script

In order to export Highcharts graphs, we use PhantomJS in the following command line format:

```
phantomjs highchartsExport.js seriesData.js [ width ] [ height ]
```

The highchartsExport.js is the core export script executed by PhantomJS, which we will implement in the next section, whereas seriesData.js is the mandatory argument containing the raw series data:

```
var result = {
  "drivers":[{
      "name":"Jenson Button",
      "color":"#666699",
      "laps":[ 146.03, 187.77, 182.67, .... ]
    },{
      "name":"Sebastian Vettel",
      "color":"#5C85FF",
      "laps":[ 159.18, 185.94, 182.63, .... ]
    },{
      "name":"Kimi Raikkonen",
      "color":"#66C266",
      "laps":[ 146.73, 187.7, 183.13, .... ]
    }]
};
```

Preparing the PhantomJS script

In this section, we prepare the export script, highchartsExport.js, which is executed by PhantomJS. First of all, we need to import all the necessary modules and load the jQuery and Highcharts script files, by using the following code:

```
var system = require('system');
var page = require('webpage').create();
var fs = require('fs');
```

The previous code basically imports the PhantomJs webpage module that creates a page object. This object encapsulates a webpage that allows us to manipulate the page content, load JavaScript libraries into the page object space, and run the JavaScript code in the context of the page.

```
page.injectJs("../jquery-1.7.1.min.js");
page.injectJs("../highcharts/js/highcharts.js");
page.injectJs("../highcharts/js/modules/exporting.js");
```

We load the jQuery and Highcharts library files into the context of the created page object. The next part is to simply load up the series result file `seriesData.js`, provided from the command line, and build up a parameter object ready for the `WebPage.evaluate` method.

```
// Load the series result file
phantom.injectJs(system.args[1]);

var width = parseInt(system.args[2], 10) || 350;
var height = parseInt(system.args[3], 10) || 300;

// Build up result and chart size args for evaluate function
var evalArg = {
  result: result,
  width: width,
  height: height
};

// The page.evaluate method takes on a function and
// executes it in the context of page object.
var svg = page.evaluate(function(opt) {

  // Inject container, so Highcharts can render to
  $('body').append('<div id="container"></div>');

  // Build up the series array from the opt.result
  var seriesArray = [];
  $(opt.result.drivers, function(idx, driver) {
    seriesArray.push({
      name: driver.name,
      data: driver.laps,
      color: driver.color
    });
  });
```

```
     var chart = new Highcharts.Chart({
       chart: {
         renderTo: 'container',
         . . . . .
       },
       series: seriesArray,
       . . . . .
     });

     return chart.getSVG();

   }, evalArg);
```

Inside the function, we first insert a DOM container element into the body of the page using jQuery.append, so that Highcharts has an element that it can render to. Then we do the usual Highcharts implementation to create the chart, export into SVG, and return the SVG data. In order to access the series data within the function, we call the evaluate method with the evalArg variable.

Finally, the returned SVG content is assigned to an svg variable and we call the I/O methods from the fs module to save it into a file.

```
// Clean up data before we write the result
if (fs.isFile("/tmp/chart.svg")) {
   fs.remove("/tmp/chart.svg");
}

fs.write("/tmp/chart.svg", svg);
phantom.exit();
```

Note that instead of fiddling with SVG content, we can simply create the chart and finish with the evaluate call. Then we can use the page.render method to export the page content directly into an image file.

Comparison between the approaches

Among the first three approaches, the Unix solution is the simplest of all because as long as we have created a page that can export Highcharts graphs, we can apply it straight to the server side; there is no need to write new code. Another major advantage is that this approach is not restricted to any particular version of Highcharts; what works on the client side is mirrored on the server side. We can plug in the latest release of Highcharts and still it works perfectly fine. However, the only downside of this approach is that it's only available on Unix platforms.

Both Highcharts' server-side Export (HSE) and Node-Highcharts solutions embed with specific version of Highcharts, which may require the updating of the package as well. At the time of writing, Node-Highcharts is internally embedded with Highcharts 2.0.5, whereas HSE is embedded with version 2.1.4. Another slight disadvantage with these two techniques is that there is no direct access to the chart object. If we want to create additional SVG labels or shapes inside the graph through `chart.renderer` methods (such as the **Crash! Safety Car** label in our example), then it is not straightforward.

PhantomJS is a real solution for running server-side JavaScript and the good news is that Highcharts 3.0 will be fully supporting this scheme by the time this book hits the shelf. Check out `http://export.highcharts.com/demo.php` for the server-side demo.

Generating a server-side Highcharts image will be as simple as running the following command:

```
highcharts-convert.js -infile URL -outfile filename -scale 2.5 -width 300
-constr [Chart|StockChart] -callback callback.js
```

The code terms used in the preceding command are described, as follows:

- `infile` is the location of Highcharts configuration file
- `constr` is to instruct the export process to output a Highcharts or Highstock chart
- `callback` executes the JavaScript file once the server export process is finished

Summary

In this chapter, we described the purpose for running Highcharts on the server side and we surveyed four different techniques to do so—Unix solution with browser running in X virtual frame buffer, Java solution using Rhino and Batik, JavaScript solution by using `Node.js` webserver and Highcharts module, and by using the PhantomJS script.

We described each solution and demonstrated them right from installation to execution, for both Unix and JavaScript approaches. At the end, we compared the merits of each of the solutions.

So far we have accomplished and understood how easy it is to create dynamic and stylish HTML5 charts using Highcharts. The next major release is version 3.0 and this will have even more reasons to consider using Highcharts. There will be new series of charts, such as funnel, box plot, waterfall, bubble, and thresholding. By then, hopefully, I will have another opportunity to bring you a new edition. On that bombshell, thank you for reading and for your support.

Index

constr 331
contextify module 324
context menu, Highcharts extension
   displaying, on data point 309, 310
createChart method 262
createServer call 327
credits alignment 40
credits.position property 40
crosshairs configuration 68
Customer Data Attributes 250
CutyCapt tool 322

D

dashStyle option 68
data
   drilling, with point click event 273, 274
data field 61
dataIndex option 291
data labels
   adjusting 113-116
dataLabels.distance option 140
dataLabel settings 117
dataLabels.formatter option 133
data point, detail chart
   hovering, with mouseOut point
      event 228, 229
   hovering, with mouseOver point
      event 228, 229
data points, Highchart APIs
   selecting 191
   updating, with Point.update 203-206
data point, top-level chart
   selecting with point select 222, 223
   uselecting with unselect events 222, 223
datetime scale 148
datetime type 179
deliverChart method 188
detail chart
   about 226, 227
   chart click event, applying 229-234
   mouse cursor over plot lines, changing with
      mouseover event 235
   mouseOut, used for hovering over data
      point 228, 229
   mouseOver, used for hovering over data
      point 228, 229

series configuration, constructing 227
device properties
   detecting 260
dial option 156
directories, Highcharts
   adapters 23
   examples 22
   exporting-server 23
   graphics 22
   index.html 22
   is 23
   themes 23
donut chart
   preparing 139-141
donut charts, Highcharts extension
   plotting 299, 300
draw method 302
duration, animation jQuery 73
dynamic content dialog
   creating, with point click event 275-277

E

easing, animation jQuery 73
examples directory 22
exportChart method 186
exporting component 32
exporting-server directory 23
export modules 302
Ext.decode 288
extension
   URL, for downloading 282
Ext JS 4 Charts 16
Ext JS code
   implementing 283
   loading 283
Ext JS components
   about 283
   accessing 284, 285
   Ajax 288
   creating 284
   Ext JS code, implementing 283
   Ext JS code, loading 283
   JsonStore 289
   panel 286
   store 289
   viewport class 285

data point, selecting with point
  select 222, 223
data point, uselecting with unselect
  events 222, 223
selected area zooming, chart selection
  event used 223, 224
series configuration, constructing 220, 221
user interface, activating with chart
  redraw event 222
touch screen environments
  Highcharts in 258
twin dials chart
  Fiat 500 speedometer, plotting 148, 149

U

Unix solution 331
unselect event handler 223
unselect events
  used, for unselecting data point 222, 223
update animation 72
update button 268
update event
  used, for editing pie chart slice 246-248
Update Portfolio dialog box 247
user interface, top-level chart
  activating, with chart redraw event 222

V

verticalAlign property 39
verticalAlign property, chart label
  properties 37
vgchartz
  URL 132

W

web charts
  about 7
  Adobe Shockwave Flash (client side) 11
  HTML image map (server-side
    technology) 8

Java Applet (client side) and Servlet
  (server side) 9, 10
web fonts
  URL 158
window 288
window class 284

X

x axes, Highcharts extension
  numerical values 296
xAxis.categories array 27
X-axis category data, Highcharts
  extension 295
xAxis config 81
xAxis.labels.formatter property 48
xAxis property 26, 175
xAxis/yAxis component 32
xField option 293
x property, chart label properties 37
xtype option 284
Xvfb
  about 317
  installing 321
  server-side change, applying 322
  server, starting 321
X virtual frame buffer. *See* **Xvfb**

Y

y axes, Highcharts extension
  numerical values 296
Y-axis category data, Highcharts extension
  295
yAxis option 155
yAxis properties 175
y property, chart label properties 37
YUI 3 Charts 16

Thank you for buying
Learning Highcharts

About Packt Publishing

Packt, pronounced 'packed', published its first book "*Mastering phpMyAdmin for Effective MySQL Management*" in April 2004 and subsequently continued to specialize in publishing highly focused books on specific technologies and solutions.

Our books and publications share the experiences of your fellow IT professionals in adapting and customizing today's systems, applications, and frameworks. Our solution based books give you the knowledge and power to customize the software and technologies you're using to get the job done. Packt books are more specific and less general than the IT books you have seen in the past. Our unique business model allows us to bring you more focused information, giving you more of what you need to know, and less of what you don't.

Packt is a modern, yet unique publishing company, which focuses on producing quality, cutting-edge books for communities of developers, administrators, and newbies alike. For more information, please visit our website: www.packtpub.com.

About Packt Open Source

In 2010, Packt launched two new brands, Packt Open Source and Packt Enterprise, in order to continue its focus on specialization. This book is part of the Packt Open Source brand, home to books published on software built around Open Source licences, and offering information to anybody from advanced developers to budding web designers. The Open Source brand also runs Packt's Open Source Royalty Scheme, by which Packt gives a royalty to each Open Source project about whose software a book is sold.

Writing for Packt

We welcome all inquiries from people who are interested in authoring. Book proposals should be sent to author@packtpub.com. If your book idea is still at an early stage and you would like to discuss it first before writing a formal book proposal, contact us; one of our commissioning editors will get in touch with you.

We're not just looking for published authors; if you have strong technical skills but no writing experience, our experienced editors can help you develop a writing career, or simply get some additional reward for your expertise.

[PACKT] open source
PUBLISHING
community experience distilled

FusionCharts Beginner's Guide: The Official Guide for FusionCharts Suite

ISBN: 978-1-849691-76-5   Paperback: 252 pages

Create interactive charts in JavaScript (HTML5) and Flash for your web and enterprise applications

1. Go from nothing to delightful reports and dashboards in your web applications in super quick time

2. Create your first chart in 15 minutes and customize it both aesthetically and functionally

3. Create a powerful reporting experience with advanced capabilities like drill-down and JavaScript integration

gnuplot Cookbook

ISBN: 978-1-849517-24-9   Paperback: 220 pages

Over 80 recipes to visually explore the full range of features of the world's preeminent open source graphing system

1. See a picture of the graph you want to make and find a ready-to-run script to produce it

2. Working examples of using gnuplot in your own programming language... C, Python, and more

3. Find a problem-solution approach with practical examples enriched with good pictorial illustrations and code

Please check **www.PacktPub.com** for information on our titles

JasperReports 3.6
Development Cookbook

ISBN: 978-1-849510-76-9   Paperback: 396 pages

Over 50 recipes to create next-generation reports
using JasperReports

1. Create, size, and position the titles, headers,
    footers, and body of your report using
    JasperReports and iReport

2. Enhance the look and feel of your report using
    background images, watermarks, and other
    such features

3. Create multi-page and multi-column reports
    using multiple types of data in the same report

4. Generate reports from Java Swing applications
    or from your web application

iReport 3.7

ISBN: 978-1-847198-80-8   Paperback: 236 pages

Learn how to use iReport to create, design, format,
and export reports

1. A step-by-step, example-oriented tutorial
    with lots of screenshots to guide the reader
    seamlessly through the book

2. Generate enterprise-level reports using
    iReport 3.7

3. Give your reports a professional look with built
    in templates

4. Create master/detail reports easily with the
    sub-report feature

Please check **www.PacktPub.com** for information on our titles

Printed in Great Britain
by Amazon.co.uk, Ltd.,
Marston Gate.